W9-BTC-761

Aaron Burr
AND THE
American Literary Imagination

Recent Titles in
Contributions in American Studies
Series Editor: Robert H. Walker

The Indians and Their Captives
James Levernier and Hennig Cohen, editors and compilers

Concerned About the Planet: *The Reporter* Magazine and American
Liberalism, 1949–1968
Martin K. Doudna

New World Journeys: Contemporary Italian Writers and the Experience
of America
Angela M. Jeannet and Louise K. Barnett, editors and translators

Family, Drama, and American Dreams
Tom Scanlan

Hemispheric Perspectives on the United States: Papers from the New
World Conference
Joseph S. Tulchin, editor, with the assistance of María A. Leal

"Ezra Pound Speaking": Radio Speeches of World War II
Leonard W. Doob, editor

The Supreme Court: Myth and Reality
Arthur Selwyn Miller

Television Fraud: The History and Implications of the Quiz Show
Scandals
Kent Anderson

Menace in the West: The Rise of French Anti-Americanism in Modern
Times
David Strauss

Social Change and Fundamental Law: America's Evolving Constitution
Arthur Selwyn Miller

American Character and Culture in a Changing World: Some Twentieth-
Century Perspectives
John A. Hague, editor

Olmsted South: Old South Critic/New South Planner
Dana F. White and Victor A. Kramer, editors

In the Trough of the Sea: Selected American Sea-Deliverance Narratives,
1610–1766
Donald P. Wharton, editor

Aaron Burr
AND THE
American
Literary
Imagination

Charles J. Nolan Jr.

MIDDLEBURY COLLEGE LIBRARY

Contributions in American Studies, Number 45

GREENWOOD PRESS

WESTPORT, CONNECTICUT • LONDON, ENGLAND

PS
169
B85
N6

5/1981
am. Lit.

Library of Congress Cataloging in Publication Data

Nolan, Charles J
    Aaron Burr and the American literary imagination.

    (Contributions in American studies; no. 45
ISSN 0084–9227)
    Bibliography: p.
    Includes index.
    1. American literature—History and criticism.
2. Burr, Aaron, 1756–1836, in fiction, drama,
poetry, etc. I. Title.
PS169.B85N6   810'.8'0351   79–8291
ISBN 0–313–21256–2

Copyright © 1980 by Charles J. Nolan, Jr.

All rights reserved. No portion of this book may be
reproduced, by any process or technique, without the
express written consent of the publisher.

Library of Congress Catalog Card Number: 79–8291
ISBN: 0–313–21256–2
ISSN: 0084–9227

First published in 1980

Greenwood Press
A division of Congressional Information Service, Inc.
51 Riverside Avenue, Westport, Connecticut 06880

Printed in the United States of America

10 9 8 7 6 5 4 3 2 1

Acknowledgments

Columbia University Libraries, from Transcript of Alexander Hamilton to Elizabeth Hamilton, 10 July 1804, in John C. Hamilton Papers. Original manuscript owned by Columbia University Libraries and reprinted by their permission.

Charles A. Hallett, excerpts from *Aaron Burr*, Copyright © Charles A. Hallett 1964, 1969. Extensive revisions were made in 1974 to ready the manuscript for the stage.

Walter Flavius McCaleb, excerpts from *The Aaron Burr Conspiracy*, reprint edition published in 1966 by Argosy-Antiquarian, Ltd.; the selections reprinted here are used with the permission of Argosy-Antiquarian, Ltd.

Edgar Lee Masters, excerpts from "Aaron Burr and Madam Jumel," in *Dramatic Duologues: Four Short Plays in Verse*, by Edgar Lee Masters. Copyright ©, 1934, by Edgar Lee Masters; Copyright ©, 1962 (In Renewal), by Mrs. Edgar Lee Masters. Reprinted by permission of Samuel French, Inc.

The New-York Historical Society, excerpts from Aaron Burr to Alexander Hamilton, 18 June 1804; excerpts from Aaron Burr to Alexander Hamilton, 21 June 1804; excerpts from Nathaniel Pendleton's Earliest Description of Hamilton's Comments about Burr before Dr. Charles Cooper, 25 June 1804; excerpts from William P. Van Ness to Nathaniel Pendleton, 26 June 1804; excerpts from William P. Van Ness to Nathaniel Pendleton, 27 June 1804; excerpts from Alexander Hamilton's Discussion of His Anticipated Duel, 27 June—4 July 1804. Printed with the permission of The New-York Historical Society, New York, New York.

New York State Historical Association, excerpts from William P. Van Ness's Report of the Occurrences of 18 June 1804, in the Van Ness Duel Manuscript; excerpts from Alexander Hamilton to Aaron Burr, 20 June 1804; excerpts from Alexander Hamilton to Aaron Burr, 22 June 1804; excerpts from Aaron Burr's Notes to William P. Van Ness, 22 June 1804; excerpts from Aaron Burr to William P. Van Ness, 26 June 1804; excerpts from Nathaniel Pendleton to William P. Van Ness, 26 June 1804; excerpts from William P. Van Ness's Report of the Occurrences of 27–28 June 1804, in the Van Ness Duel Manuscript; excerpts from Van Ness and Pendleton's Press Statement, 11 July 1804; excerpts from William P. Van Ness's Amended Version of the Press Statement of 11 July 1804. Printed with the permission of the New York State Historical Association, Cooperstown, New York.

Hattie May Pavlo, excerpts from *Hamilton* by Hattie May Pavlo, Copyright © 1948 by Hattie May Pavlo. Copyright renewed 1975, by Hattie May Pavlo.

William T. Polk, excerpts from "Golden Eagle Ordinary" in *The Fallen Angel and Other Stories* by William T. Polk. Copyright © 1956 The University of North Carolina Press. Reprinted by permission of the publisher.

Princeton University Library, Coroner's Inquest on the Death of Alexander Hamilton, 2 August 1804, DS, formerly owned by Mr. C. P. G. Fuller, Fuller Collection of Aaron Burr (AM 15744), Box 2, III D1, page 3. Published with permission of Princeton University Library.

Edward Raiden, excerpts from *Mr. Jefferson's Burr*. Copyright © 1960, Edward Raiden. Published by Thunder Publishing Company. Reprinted by permission of Edward Raiden.

Chard Powers Smith, excerpts from *Hamilton: A Poetic Drama*. Copyright © 1930. Reprinted by permission of Eunice Clark Smith.

Anya Seton, *My Theodosia*. Copyright © renewed 1968 by Anya Seton Chase. Reprinted by permission of Houghton Mifflin Company.

James Thurber, excerpts from "A Friend to Alexander," Copr. © 1942 James Thurber. Copr. © 1970 Helen W. Thurber and Rosemary Thurber Sauers. From "A Friend to Alexander," in *My World—And Welcome to It*, published by Harcourt Brace Jovanovich, New York. Originally printed in *The New Yorker*.

Gore Vidal, excerpts from *Burr: A Novel*, Copyright © 1973, Gore Vidal. Reprinted by permission of Random House, Inc. and of Gore Vidal.

Eudora Welty, excerpts from "First Love" by Eudora Welty are reprinted by permission of Harcourt Brace Jovanovich, Inc. from her volume *The Wide Net and Other Stories*, Copyright © 1942, 1970 by Eudora Welty. World rights have been granted by Russell & Volkening, Inc.

Wesleyan University, excerpts from *Interview in Weehawken: The Burr-Hamilton Duel*, edited by Harold C. Syrett and Jean G. Cooke, with Introduction and Conclusion by Willard M. Wallace.

Winterthur Museum, excerpts from Aaron Burr to David Hosack, 12 July 1804, Courtesy, Henry Francis du Pont Winterthur Museum, Joseph Downs Manuscript Collection, Winterthur, Delaware.

Yale University Library, excerpts from Mrs. Theodosia Burr to Tapping Reeve and Sarah Burr Reeve, n.d., Park Family Papers, Yale University Library.

Every reasonable effort has been made to trace the owners of copyright materials in this book, but in some instances this has proven impossible. The publishers will be glad to receive information leading to more complete acknowledgments in subsequent printings of the book, and in the meantime extend their apologies for any omissions.

This, with love, for Pat

Contents

	Introduction	xiii
1	The Man Who Killed Hamilton	3
2	Catiline, Cain, Traitor, Predator, Victim	47
3	A Man For All Seasons	75
4	A Many-Sided, Aristocratic Jonathan	109
5	American Symbol—American Fears	157
	Selected Bibliography	187
	Index	201

ABOUT THE AUTHOR

CHARLES J. NOLAN, JR. is Assistant Professor of English at the United States Naval Academy in Annapolis, Maryland. He has contributed to *Resources for American Literary Study*, the *Chaucer Review*, *Seventeenth-Century News*, and other scholarly publications.

Introduction

In American society's calendar of villains, Aaron Burr stands out, for the majority of people at least, as one of the most detestable. The usual popular conception of him is that he is the cold-hearted murderer of Hamilton or the scheming conspirator who tried to wreck the Union for his own selfish ends. Largely created by early enemies and then later reinforced in the schools, such a view of Burr has acted over the years to distort reality and to confirm him in our imagination as an almost archetypal *bête noire*. But though he is linked to the darker side of American life, he has provoked considerable literary interest. He is, as might be expected, the subject of innumerable newspaper accounts, political pamphlets, scurrilous handbills, condemnatory sermons, popular poems, and dreadful election songs, but what comes as a surprise is that he also appears in thirty-three plays and forty-nine novels and stories.

The fact that such a large number of American writers treat Burr in their works points naturally to the question of why our authors find him so provocative. This study, which examines the literature in which he figures, seeks to provide an answer and to explore the reasons for it. Divided into five sections, the book suggests that Burr is connected with American culture in a way much more meaningful than might be suspected initially. Chapter 1 provides a sketch of the historical Aaron Burr, of the man as he really was, at least to the degree that doing so is possible for such a controversial character.

Chapter 2 tells a much different story. It treats the legendary Burr, the figure who emerges from the often vitriolic scribblings of the partisan press and from the writings of others who generally saw the Colonel in pejorative ways. Chapters 3 and 4, which deal with the Burr who appears in drama and in fiction, show how our imaginative authors, frequently influenced by legend, depicted the Colonel and how their view of him shifted over the years. Finally, chapter 5 offers a conclusion about what this changing treatment of Burr means—explains, that is, why the figure of Aaron Burr continues to haunt our national consciousness almost 150 years after his death. The answer provided there reveals as much about American society as it does about the man who killed Hamilton.

Aaron Burr
AND THE
American Literary Imagination

1. The Man Who Killed Hamilton

The sunny and warm weather that morning gave no indication that one of the more infamous events in our history was to occur; and the view from the Weehawken heights was such that, as Parton put it, "one glance . . . *ought* to have sent shame and horror to the duelist's heart."[1] Burr, meticulously attired in close-fitting pants, half boots, and a bombazine coat, and Van Ness, his second, arrived first; but because great events often partake of the mundane, the two spent the time before their opposites arrived ridding the area of underbrush. When Hamilton appeared around 7 A.M., the principals acknowledged each other formally, and the seconds began their preparations. They first stepped off the customary ten paces and then cast lots to decide who would select the positions and who would issue the command to begin firing. To Nathaniel Pendleton, Hamilton's second, fell both of these dubious honors. Next they primed the weapons in each other's presence, directing the duellists to take their places. The rules were clear: Pendleton was to ask each man if he were prepared, and, when both had indicated their readiness, he was to call out, "Present," after which the two were at liberty to fire. Hamilton looked out over the Hudson from where he stood, an undesirable position, really, because at that time of the morning the sun's angle caused a glare from the river; Burr, of course, stood opposite to him, the heights in the background. When Pendleton shouted the command, both men discharged their weapons; only Burr's shot, however, struck home.

Hamilton slumped to the same ground where, two years before, his son had also been mortally wounded. Impulsively, the vice president started to move toward his opponent, but Van Ness entreated his friend to leave before the surgeon and the bargemen, who had been summoned, could recognize him and therefore testify against him later. Burr complied but continually indicated a desire to go back to his wounded adversary. Wisely, Van Ness prevented his associate from returning and ordered their boat back to New York. It was too late to protect the vice president, however, because Hamilton's fall at Weehawken was the beginning of a tragic series of events that would include an indictment for murder, a trial for treason, a four-year, sometimes poverty-stricken exile, a prostrating loss of beloved grandson and daughter, a disastrous second marriage to a rich, former reprobate and child abandoner, and a lonely death in a rented hotel room.[2]

But, of course, there had been an earlier beginning.[3] Aaron Burr, born in Newark, on 6 February 1756, came from distinguished ancestors. His father, after whom he was named, was one of the founders of the College of New Jersey (now Princeton) and its second president; his maternal grandfather, Jonathan Edwards, was, of course, the most famous of the New England divines. Perhaps it was from the Reverend Aaron Burr that the boy inherited his decisiveness, because that illustrious clergyman took the twenty-one-year-old Esther Edwards as his bride only two weeks after renewing his friendship with the young woman whom he had last seen as a mere girl of fifteen. Perhaps, too, he derived his determination from a father who, though approaching exhaustion and suffering from a high fever that left him at times incoherent, worked dutifully on a funeral sermon for Governor Belcher and then journeyed forty miles to present it. Three weeks later he died. In any case, just after his second birthday, the young boy and his slightly elder sister, Sarah, became orphans, Esther Burr having died within six months of her husband's death.

Cared for first by the Shippen family of Philadelphia, the children soon became the wards of their uncle Timothy Edwards, a demanding taskmaster. Yet even harsh treatment could not break the will of the boy whose mother had earlier described as "very resolute . . . [requiring] a good Governor to bring him to terms";[4] twice before he was eleven, young Burr ran away from his new home. The second time, he came to New York and signed aboard a ship as cabin boy. When one day he saw his uncle approaching, obviously in pursuit, he climbed the masthead and refused to come down until he was assured of amnesty. "To the doctrine of unconditional submission," Davis remarks, "he never gave his assent" (Davis, *Memoirs*, 1: 26).

Such tenacity of purpose was reflected in his admittance as a sophomore to the College of New Jersey in 1769. When he had been denied admission two years earlier, primarily because of his youthful countenance, he had begun a course of study that he felt prepared him to be accepted as a junior; but second-year status was all the authorities would grant him. During his years at Princeton, when he often spent eighteen hours a day in study, he had occasion to write a now prophetic essay on the passions, the substance of which he might have remembered before anger drove him to challenge Hamilton. "Vicious desires," he wrote, "will produce vicious practices; and men, by permitting themselves to think of indulging irregular passions, corrupt the understanding, which is the source of all virtue and morality. The passions, then, if properly regulated, are the gentle gales which keep life from stagnating; but, if let loose, the tempests which tear every thing before them" (Parton, *Life*, 1: 371). He was able, however, to control his religious passions well enough to withstand the claims of a revival that swept through the college in 1771–72, though his curiosity did lead him to discuss the subject with the college president. At sixteen, he received his B.A., delivering a graduation address on the subject of "Building Castles in the Air," the ironical application of which he doubtless mused upon in later life. Then, after a year's advanced work at Princeton and an abortive twelve months in ministerial preparation, he finally turned to the law, studying under his brother-in-law and former tutor, Tapping Reeve.

When the Revolution began, however, Burr was eager to participate. He and his friend Matt Ogden took a letter to General Washington from Colonel Lewis Morgan, a delegate to the Continental Congress; the note asked the commander in chief to commission the two volunteers immediately. Washington, however, declined, pointing out that he had no power to promote anyone and that unassociated officers would be too expensive because no colony would be underwriting their expenses. Thus, perhaps, began the unpleasantness that was to mark Burr's relationship with the general and future president over the years. Their hopes disappointed, the young men eventually joined Colonel Benedict Arnold's march to Quebec. Dysentery, mud, snow, and limited rations made the journey a soldier's nightmare; and the siege of the city was raised soon after it began when Arnold discovered that his men had but five rounds of ammunition each. After General Montgomery brought reinforcements and supplies, however, the Americans again prepared to attack. On 31 December 1775, Montgomery with Burr in attendance led a contingent of three hundred men in single file against one side of the lower town, Arnold striking from the opposite end. As the general approached what appeared to be a private house, cannon and musket fire raked his troops. Montgomery fell dead in the snow; the soldiers panicked. Burr and some of his fellow officers urged the men forward, but Colonel Campbell, now in charge, ordered a retreat to save the men from their own chaos. Picking up his dead commander, Burr tried to bring the body back to the American lines, an event celebrated in Brackenridge's famous *The Death of General Montgomery at the Siege of Quebec*. But the road was narrow and snowpacked, the general big and unwieldy, and "little Burr" had to abandon the attempt. Praised by Arnold, Burr remained with the expedition for another five months before being appointed to Washington's staff at Richmond Hill, a mansion he was later to own.

Major Burr, finding his new duties dull and tiring, thought of resigning from the military, but John Hancock rescued him by arranging a transfer to General Putnam's staff. While he was with Putnam, he met, and tradition dubiously claims conquered, Margaret Moncrieffe, the thirteen-year-old daughter of a British major who had left her with American friends. Tradition is more accurate, however, in ascribing to Burr important service during the evacuation of New York. Near the end of the operation, Putnam ordered his aide, who had worked diligently all day at the boarding point, to collect dalliers. When Burr found a brigade under General Knox preparing to defend the vulnerable fort at Bunker's Hill, he advised Knox to take his men to Harlem Heights. The general refused; Burr then spoke directly to the troops, telling them that if they remained they would soon be dead or imprisoned, an argument they found persuasive. The major then led them back to the main army with only minor losses. A less successful event occurred during the winter. Summoned to Washington's headquarters, he and another officer were shown into the general's presence while he was busy writing. He indicated that they should be seated and then excused himself for a moment, leaving his papers on his desk. Foolishly, Burr began to read them, only to be surprised by Washington's return. It may have been this incident that led the general to block Burr's promotion on several subsequent occasions. Eventually, however, the major was appointed a lieutenant colonel and the virtual commander of Colonel William Malcolm's regiment, but not without a peevish complaint to Washington about the "late date" of his advancement.

During the disastrous winter of 1777, the Colonel, as he was thereafter called, was asked to handle a disciplinary problem for General McDougall. A capricious militia, guarding a pass eight miles from Valley Forge, thought it humorous to send false alerts to the sleeping soldiers at the main camp. Burr took charge of the group, instituting a rigid system of discipline for which the men hated him. Eventually, some of the troops planned to murder their new commander; but the Colonel, having been warned, secretly confiscated all ammunition and then ordered a moonlight formation. As he passed along the line, one of the mutineers stepped forward, aimed his musket, and shouted, "Now is your time, my boys." With his recently sharpened sword, Burr struck the soldier below the elbow, almost cutting the arm off, and ordered the man to return to his position; the next day the arm was amputated. Of this incident, Davis cryptically remarked, "No more was heard of the mutiny; nor were there afterwards, during Colonel Burr's command, any false alarms" (Davis, *Memoirs*, 1: 120–21). But during the Battle of Monmouth the Colonel contracted an illness, the result of exhaustion and sunstroke, that eventually forced him to resign his commission, though not before he restored order to the neutral ground between American and British forces on the Westchester lines by instituting public floggings for those found guilty of raiding homes in the area. On 3 April 1779, however, Washington finally agreed to allow Burr to resign, and the Colonel, now twenty-three and ruined in health, was once again a civilian. Even then the war would not let him rest, and he voluntarily took part in several dangerous operations for his country.

Though Burr recognized that patriotic lawyers would be able to make several fortunes after the war, his preparation for a legal career was delayed until he could regain his health. By the end of 1780, though, he was well enough to resume his studies, this time under Judge William Paterson of New Jersey, who started his pupil on the usual three-year course. Eager to establish himself, Burr quickly switched to the office of Thomas Smith, deciding that six months' work would be enough. At the end of that time, he petitioned the Supreme Court to grant him a waiver of the waiting period, citing his earlier training under Tapping Reeve and noting slyly that "no rule could be intended to have such retrospect as to injure one *whose only misfortune* [was] *having sacrificed his time, his constitution, and his fortune, to his country*" (Davis, *Memoirs*, 1: 231). Only after a personal appearance and a moving speech before the court, however, was he granted permission to take the law examination, which he easily passed. Thus, in April 1782, he was admitted to the bar. The following July he married the widowed Theodosia Prevost, ten years older than he, the couple and her two children moving first to Albany, where Burr had begun his practice, and then to New York. As a lawyer, he established himself quickly. With occasional sarcasm and studied persistence,[5] he won case after case, maintaining that the "best definition of law . . . [is] '*whatever is boldly asserted and plausibly maintained*' " (Davis, *Memoirs*, 2: 14). His good breeding and thorough grasp of details also contributed to his success,[6] as did his limiting his presentation before the court to a few important points.[7] By spring 1784, Burr was an assemblyman.

His one term in the state legislature was notable for his principled opposition to a bill calling for a corporation of the tradesmen and mechanics of the city of New York, the enactment of which would have given the group political strength detrimental to the common interest, and for his strong support of the anti-slavery movement. Neither won him friends. But from 1785 on, his political dealings were more successful. In 1789, he joined with Hamilton in supporting his good friend Judge Robert Yates for governor against the powerful incumbent, George Clinton. Although Clinton won, he recognized Burr's power and, preparing for the next election, appointed the Colonel state attorney general so that when the legislature chose new federal senators Burr would be elected. In this way, Clinton could secure the support of the powerful Livingston faction by appointing Morgan Lewis, Chancellor Livingston's brother-in-law, to fill Burr's vacated post. What seemed to be Burr's good fortune, however, was actually the beginning of a series of events that would end at Weehawken, because Burr's opponent in the 1791 senatorial race was Hamilton's father-in-law, General Philip Schuyler.

Burr's victory assured him of Hamilton's unrelenting political enmity. Thus, the next year, when the Colonel's friends worked to elect him governor, Hamilton checked his candidacy by supporting John Jay, whom he had persuaded to leave the Supreme Court to enter the race. And when Burr emerged that same year as a Republican vice presidential possibility along with Clinton and several others, Hamilton unleashed his hatred:

Mr. Clinton's success I should think very unfortunate. . . . But still, Mr. C. is a man of property, and in private life, as far as I know, of probity. I fear the other gentleman [Burr] is unprincipled, both as a public and a private man. When the Constitution was in deliberation, his conduct was equivocal; but its enemies, who, I believe, best understood him, considered him as with them. In fact, I take it, he is for or against nothing, but as it suits his interest or ambition. He is determined, as I conceive, to make his way to be the head of the popular party, and to climb *per fas aut nefas* to the highest honors of the State, and as much higher as circumstances may permit. Embarrassed, as I understand, in his circumstances, with an extravagant family, bold, enterprising, and intriguing, I am mistaken if it be not his object to play the game of confusion, and I feel it to be a religious duty to oppose his career.[8]

To another correspondent, he wrote even more forcefully: "Mr. Burr's integrity as an individual is not unimpeached. As a public man, he is one of the worst sort—a friend to nothing but as it suits his interest and ambition. . . . 'Tis evident that he aims at putting himself at the head of what he calls the 'popular party,' as affording the best tools for an ambitious man to work with—secretly turning liberty into ridicule, he knows as well as most men how to make use of the name. In a word, if we have an embryo Caesar in the United States, 'tis Burr" (Hamilton, *Works*, 5: 529). It was just this kind of language that led to Burr's challenge twelve years later.

After withdrawing in favor of Clinton, Burr devoted himself to other matters. He supported an anti-administration amendment to prevent those who held stock or offices in the Bank of the United States from being congressmen, defended Albert Gallatin against those who sought to unseat him, and opposed the appointment of John Jay as special envoy to England, preferring either Madison or Jefferson instead. Privately, he spent much of his time seeking medical advice for his increasingly ill wife. Periods of nausea and vomiting left her depleted, and separation from her husband, whose senatorial duties kept him in Philadelphia, contributed to her suffering. A desperate letter to the Reeves shortly before her death made clear her loneliness: "My dear friends where are you in all my distress. . . . come[,] I pray you[;] my sufferings are not to be committed to paper—Perhaps I may see you, perhaps not—I have wrote you many times, but I never heard from you[.] [D]o come, if Sally cannot. [C]ome Reeve[,] come I pray you; come I beg you, come . . . to your wretched friend & Sister."[9] Senator Burr, in Philadelphia tending his career, received news of his wife's death the day after she died.

At thirty-eight, Burr was left with his ambition and his treasured daughter, Theodosia, whose education he carefully oversaw. Having perceived a fine intelligence in his wife and having been excited by Mary Wollstonecraft's *Vindication of the Rights of Woman*, he wanted his daughter to develop a first-rate mind. Writing to his wife a year before her death, he indicated his plans for little Theodosia: "If I could foresee that Theo. would become a *mere* fashionable woman, with all the attendant frivolity and vacuity of mind, adorned with whatever grace and allurement, I would earnestly pray God to take her forthwith hence. But I yet hope, by her, to convince the world what neither sex appear[s] to believe—that women have souls!" (Davis, *Memoirs*, 1: 361–62). In addition to providing an army of tutors, who were to exercise the child in everything from Greek to the harpsichord, Burr used his letters and hers as pedagogical tools. In one, he corrected her spelling: "You write *acurate*," he told her, "for *accurate*; *laudnam* for *laudanum*; *intirely* for *entirely*; this last word, indeed is spelled both ways, but *entirely* is the most usual and the most proper" (Davis, *Memoirs*, 1: 370). And, in the same letter, after charging her to use all of the incorrect words again so that he could be assured she knew how to spell them, he set her another kind of task: "And tell me what is laudanum? Where and how made? And what are its effects?" (Davis, *Memoirs*, 1: 370). In another letter, he prescribed a journal: "Ten minutes every evening I demand; if you should choose to make it twenty, I shall be better pleased. You are to note the occurrences of the day as concisely as you can; and, at your pleasure, to add any short reflections or remarks that may arise. On the other leaf I give you a sample of the manner of your journal for one day" (Davis, *Memoirs*, 1: 366).

A demanding teacher, he was, however, quick to praise her for good work: "Io, triumphe! There is not a word mispelled [sic] either in your journal or letter, which cannot be said of a single page you ever before wrote" (Davis, *Memoirs*, 1: 375). But should she be careless or lazy, he was harsh: "Your last had no date; from the last date in the journal, and your writing about Christmas holydays as yet at some distance, I suppose you wrote about Sunday the 22d. Nine days ago! I beg you again to read over all my letters, and to let me see by your answers that you attend to them. I suspect your last journal was not written from day to day; but all on one, or at most two days, from memory. How is this? Ten or fifteen minutes every evening would not be an unreasonable sacrifice from *you* to *me*. If you took the Christmas holydays, I assent: if you did not, we cannot recall the time" (Davis, *Memoirs*, 1: 368). Sometimes, if he felt he had pushed his eleven-year-old too hard, he was apologetic: "I fear, my dear little girl, that my letter of the 13th imposed too much upon you; if so, dispense with what you may find troublesome. You perceive by this license the entire confidence which I place in your discretion" (Davis, *Memoirs*, 1: 374). And sometimes he was playful: "I beg, Miss Prissy, that you will be pleased to name a single *'unsuccessful effort'* which you have made to please me. As to the letters and journals which you *did* write, surely you have reason abundant to believe that they gave me pleasure; and how the duese [sic] I am to be pleased with those you *did not* write, and how an omission to write can be called an *'effort,'* remains for your ingenuity to disclose" (Davis, *Memoirs*, 1:371). Always, however, his letters were acts of love.

Though Theodosia's education progressed smoothly, the Colonel's political career did not. After an abortive candidacy for the governorship of New York in 1795, Burr was nominated by the Republicans to be Jefferson's running mate in the 1796 presidential campaign. But when the balloting was over, the Colonel had received a mere thirty electoral votes, compared to Adams's seventy-one, Jefferson's sixty-eight, and Pinckney's fifty-nine. Worse still, the Federalists now controlled the New York legislature and in March 1797 sent Philip

Schuyler to replace Burr in the Senate. A private citizen again, he turned to land speculation as a way of resolving his desperate financial situation. Investing heavily in Holland Land Company holdings—Burr borrowed enough for the initial payment on 100,000 acres—he was left in 1797 with no way to meet his next installment because the land market dropped precipitously after he had made his purchase. He also became involved in Canadian land schemes, whose French sponsorship seemed intended to establish French Directory control in Canada. In the midst of such dealings, however, Burr was reelected to the state legislature and began to use his power in support of his own political and financial interests. Working quietly and indirectly, he gained the support of Tammany but puzzled his opponents who wondered which party he favored when he first promoted Federalist preparations for war after the XYZ affair and then vigorously attacked the Alien and Sedition Acts, which were aimed at weakening Republic strength. Under the cover of civic interest, he also successfully passed a bill establishing the Manhattan Company, whose ostensible purpose was to provide a healthful water supply for New York—the recurring yellow fever epidemics were thought to result from putrid water—but whose actual objective was to found a Republican bank. Though the Bank of Manhattan became a reality, suspicion of Burr's motives led to his and his party's defeat in 1799. But 1800 was another year, and this time a president was to be chosen. Knowing that the Republicans could regain control of the legislature in the annual New York election and therefore would be able to deliver the state's twelve electoral votes, Burr went to Jefferson, who was to lead the national ticket, with promises of vigorous support. Then he returned to New York and set Tammany in motion. Thanks to several Federalist blunders, financial support from the Manhattan Company, and shrewd leadership from Burr, the Republicans won decisively. The Colonel himself was elected as assemblyman for Orange County. Shortly after, he received his party's endorsement as Jefferson's running mate.

Hamilton immediately began his attack. To Bayard of Delaware, he suggested that Burr was "as unprincipled and dangerous a man as any country [could] boast—as true a Catiline as ever met in midnight conclave.[10] The fact that some Federalists proposed voting for the Colonel as president so that the detested Jefferson could not rule inflamed him. Worse yet, from Hamilton's viewpoint, an electoral tie between the two Republicans became a possibility. The balloting in South Carolina would be significant and suggestive of what other states might do. At this time, Burr, believing that Jefferson had one more vote in South Carolina than he anyway, stated clearly to Smith of Maryland, a good friend, that he had taken no part in the Federalist plan to prevent Jefferson's election: "It is highly improbable that I shall have an equal number of votes with Mr. Jefferson; but, if such should be the result, every man who knows me ought to know that I would utterly disclaim all competition. Be assured that *the federal party can entertain no wish for such an exchange.* As to my friends, they would dishonour my views and insult my feelings by a suspicion that I would submit to be instrumental in counteracting the wishes and the expectations of the United States" (Davis, *Memoirs*, 2: 75). He then went on to give Smith his permission to make known his feelings should it become necessary. But South Carolina gave both candidates the same number of votes, and by late December a tie seemed assured. To Jefferson, he then wrote: "It is the unanimous determination of the republicans of every grade to support your administration with unremitted zeal. . . . As to myself, I will cheerfully abandon the office of V. P. if it shall be thought that I can be more useful in any active station."[11]

Burr, however, was not so innocent as he pretended. Though he had done nothing to encourage Federalist support, he had permitted it to continue by not immediately deferring to Jefferson once it was certain that the House would elect the next president. In Albany for Theodosia's marriage to Joseph Alston, the Colonel waited. Then in mid-February came Gallatin's startling suggestion: Burr could gain three crucial votes and thus the presidency if he would hurry to Washington to influence events. After consultation with Townsend and Swartwout, trusted advisers who urged him to go, he packed his bags—but, at the last minute, decided to remain in New York. To Gallatin he wrote that only if the Federalists should try to undermine the Constitution by using their votes to prevent either Republican from gaining the nine states required for election would he openly involve himself. To Jefferson, he stated: "I set down as calumny every tale calculated to disturb our harmony."[12] Thus, on the thirty-sixth ballot, Jefferson became the third president of the United States; Aaron Burr joined him at the inauguration.

The vice presidential years, however, led to political decline rather

than increased influence. The Clintons now controlled New York—
George in the statehouse and DeWitt, his nephew, in the legislature—
and they set out to neutralize Burr's appointment power. Through the
American Citizen, they attacked the Colonel's interference with John
Wood's scurrilous history of the Adams administration. The paper's
editor, James Cheetham, charged the vice president with preventing
the publication of Wood's book because it would offend the Federalists. Actually, through Van Ness, Burr bought all the printed copies of
the work, part of whose material he had supplied, because the *History* (1802) was so exaggerated that it would undoubtedly win sympathy for the Federalists. Then, several months later, Cheetham
wrote the more damaging *A View of the Political Conduct of Colonel
Burr* (1802), in which he charged Burr with attempting to steal the
recent election from Jefferson. This attack was followed in October
by a series of letters in the *American Citizen*, each of which reempha-
sized the original slander. Burr countered with two papers of his own,
the *Morning Chronicle* and the *Chronicle-Express*, but Cheetham's
accusations had been effective. Even Van Ness's *An Examination of
the Various Charges Exhibited Against Aaron Burr* (1803) could
not remove the suspicion with which the Republicans now viewed
their vice president. Jefferson, though apparently unmoved, was
secretly convinced of Burr's duplicity. Thus, by October 1803, the
Colonel's power within his own party had virtually disappeared. It
was, therefore, no surprise that the Republicans chose Clinton to run
with Jefferson in 1804. Burr did not receive a single vote at the Washington caucus.

The vice president had loyal friends, however, and they secured his
nomination as an independent candidate for the governorship of New
York. The "Burrites" felt that the Colonel might win because the
Federalists had decided not to run anyone and because John Lansing
was a weak Republican choice. But unexpectedly Lansing declined
the nomination; and, unfortunately for Burr, Morgan Lewis, chief justice of the New York Supreme Court, replaced him. Worse still,
Hamilton came out of retirement to oppose Burr, warning that the
Colonel wanted to lead the Northern states out of the Union. Had he
left it at that and had Burr not suffered a humiliating defeat—Lewis
won with the greatest majority that had ever been achieved in a New

York gubernatorial race—history might have been different. But Hamilton's intemperate language this time provoked a challenge. At a dinner party that Judge John Taylor held for his Federalist cronies shortly before the election, Hamilton had spoken harshly of Burr. Charles Cooper, Taylor's son-in-law, reporting the dinner conversation in a letter to Brown, noted that "Gen. Hamilton . . . [had] come out decidedly against Burr; indeed when he was here he spoke of him as a dangerous man, and [as one] who ought not to be trusted" (Syrett and Cooke, *Interview*, p. 45).[13] When this letter, instead of being delivered to Brown, found its way into *The Albany Register*, Dr. Cooper then wrote to Philip Schuyler that "the assertions therein contained are substantially true. . . . I assert, that Gen. HAMILTON and Judge KENT have declared, in substance, that they looked upon Mr. BURR to be a dangerous man, and one who ought not to be trusted with the reins of government" (Syrett and Cooke, *Interview*, p. 46). And, near the end of the letter, he included the now fateful remarks: "It is sufficient for me, on this occasion, to substantiate what I have asserted. I have made it an invariable rule of my life, to be circumspect in relating what I may have heard from others; and in this affair, I feel happy to think, that I have been unusually cautious—for really sir, I could detail to you a still more despicable opinion which General HAMILTON has expressed of Mr. BURR" (Syrett and Cooke, *Interview*, p. 48). This 23 April 1804 letter was also printed in the *Register*.

In mid-June, Burr told Van Ness that he had been aware of certain accusations Hamilton had reportedly made against him but that he had been unsure of their authenticity and had therefore taken no action. Now, however, someone had given him a newspaper containing Cooper's letter to Schuyler, and he had found in it "information, which he thought demanded immediate investigation" (Syrett and Cooke, *Interview*, p. 42). Accordingly, he wrote a note to Hamilton and asked Van Ness to deliver it. The letter directed Hamilton's attention to the clause in which Cooper had spoken of the "still more despicable opinion" Hamilton had allegedly expressed and asked the general for a "prompt and unqualified acknowledgment or denial of the use of any expressions which could warrant the assertions of Dr. Cooper" (Syrett and Cooke, *Interview*, p. 43). Hamilton asked for time. Two days later, on 20 June 1804, the general left a long letter for Burr, the bulk of which is best described as weaseling. He opened by saying that he "could not, without manifest impropriety, make the avowal or disavowal" which the Colonel demanded (Syrett and Cooke, *Interview*, p. 52) and then went on to justify his position. " 'Tis evident," he noted, "that the phrase 'still more despicable' admits of infinite shades, from very light to very dark. How am I to judge of the degree intended? Or how shall I annex any precise idea to language so indefinite?" (Syrett and Cooke, *Interview*, pp. 52–53). Then came a particularly Jesuitical paragraph:

Between Gentlemen, *despicable* and *more despicable* are not worth the pains of a distinction. When therefore you do not interrogate me, as to the opinion which is specifically ascribed to me [that Burr was "a dangerous man, and one who ought not to be trusted with the reins of government"], I must conclude, that you view it as within the limits, to which the animadversions of political opponents, upon each other, may justifiably extend; and consequently as not warranting the idea of it, which Doctor Cooper appears to entertain. If so, what precise inference could you draw as a guide for your future conduct, were I to acknowledge, that I had expressed an opinion of you, *still more despicable*, than the one which is particularized? How could you be sure, that even this opinion had exceeded the bounds which you would yourself deem admissible between political opponents? [Syrett and Cooke, *Interview*, p. 53]

Another two evasive paragraphs followed, after which Hamilton summarized his position: "I stand ready to avow or disavow promptly and explicitly any precise or definite opinion, which I may be charged with having declared of any Gentleman" (Syrett and Cooke, *Interview*, p. 54). He trusted, he said, that Burr would agree with him; but "If not," he declared ominously, "I can only regret the circumstance, and must abide the consequences" (Syrett and Cooke, *Interview*, p. 54).

Burr, a good lawyer himself, reacted strongly to such legalistic hairsplitting: "Political opposition," he wrote on 21 June, "can never absolve Gentlemen from the Necessity of a rigid adherence to the laws of honor and the rules of decorum" (Syrett and Cooke, *Interview*, p. 56). "The Common sense of Mankind," he continued, "affixes to the epithet adopted by Dr Cooper the idea of dishonor: it has been publicly applied to me under the sanction of your Name. The question is not whether he has understood the Meaning of the word or has used it according to syntax and with grammatical accuracy, but whether you have authorized their application either directly or by uttering expressions or opinions derogatory to my honor" (Syrett and Cooke, *Interview*, pp. 56–57). He concluded by noting that Hamilton's answer gave him "new reasons for requiring a definite reply" (Syrett and Cooke, *Interview*, p. 58). When Van Ness delivered this letter to the general on 22 June, Hamilton indicated that, since Burr had not complied with his request to point out any "precise or definite" expression, he could make no reply and that the Colonel would have to do whatever he thought proper. Then he sent for Pendleton, told him what had occurred so far, and, before leaving for his country home, gave him a note for Burr, dated 22 June, which accused the Colonel of "a style too peremptory" and which explained his position again (Syrett and Cooke, *Interview*, p. 63). Presuming that Hamilton's oral reply to Van Ness was final, Burr wrote a stinging letter, also dated 22 June, which his intermediary was to follow with the challenge itself. "[T]hese things must have an end" (Syrett and Cooke, *Interview*, p. 69), Burr declared. But neither was delivered because, when Van Ness saw Hamilton back in town on 25 June, the general mentioned that he had left with Pendleton an answer to Burr's second letter.

This information surprised Van Ness. He had met with Pendleton several times on the intervening days but had been given nothing from Hamilton. Instead, Pendleton had proposed that Burr write a letter "requesting to know in substance whether . . . any particular instance of dishonorable conduct was imputed to Col. Burr, or whether there was any impeachment of his private character" (Syrett and Cooke, *Interview*, p. 74). Hamilton would then reply that he could not remember "distinctly" his exact conversation but that "to the best of his recollection it consisted of comments on the political principles and views of Col. Burr, and the results that might be expected from them in the event of his Election as Governor, without referrence [sic] to any particular instance of past conduct, or to private character" (Syrett and Cooke, *Interview*, p. 75). Indicating to Hamilton that he would gladly receive the reply which the general made, Van Ness called on Pendleton, secured the letter, and discussed with Hamilton's friend what the general was prepared to state about the present difficulty. Later that day, the two intermediaries met again; this time Van Ness asked Pendleton to put into writing what Hamilton would say. When Burr read the document, he found that it was "a worse libel then even the letter of Dᴿ C" and felt that it showed "a disposition to evade," especially because Hamilton refused to give a general denial (Syrett and Cooke, *Interview*, pp. 87–88). Accordingly, Van Ness wrote to Pendleton on 26 June that the "denial of a specified conversation only, would leave strong implications that on other occasions improper language had been used. . . . No denial or declaration will be satisfactory unless it be general" (Syrett and Cooke, *Interview*, p. 91). Pendleton replied the same day that the general objected "to the very indefinite ground" which Burr had taken, seeing in it "nothing short of predetermined hostility" (Syrett and Cooke, *Interview*, p. 95), a phrase that various dramatists and novelists would use in their works. This letter triggered the challenge or, as Van Ness put it, "the simple Message which I shall now have the honor to deliver" (Syrett and Cooke, *Interview*, p. 98). Then on Thursday, 28 June, after the challenge had been issued and received, Pendleton called on Van Ness and attempted to deliver some additional written remarks that Hamilton had made. Van Ness indicated that, unless this new letter contained "a definite and specific proposition for an accomodation [sic]" (Syrett and Cooke, *Interview*, p. 103), he must refuse it because Burr viewed all correspondence as ended when the challenge was accepted. Since Hamilton's remarks were just a recapitulation of his refusal to make a general denial, they were declined. On 3 July, the two met again and established the morning of the eleventh as the time for the "fatal interview"; six days later they arranged the "particulars."

Both the principals then set about arranging their affairs. Hamilton had already written some remarks on the approaching duel, a document that contributed to his glorification after his death and that many authors were to use in their artistic rendering of the Weehawken event. In it the general enumerated, first of all, his reasons for desiring to avoid the interview: he was opposed to duelling on "religious and moral" grounds; he realized that his family needed him; he felt a sense of obligation to his creditors; he had no ill will toward Burr, "distinct from political opposition"; and he would "hazard much" and "gain nothing" from the event (Syrett and Cooke, *Interview*, pp. 99–100). But, he noted, there were "*intrinsick* difficulties" and "*artificial* embarrassments" which necessitated his presence at Weehawken. "Intrinsick—[,]" he admitted, "because it is not to be denied, that my animadversions on the political principles[,] character and views of Col Burr have been extremely severe, and on different occasions I, in common with many others, have made very unfavorable criticisms on particular instances of the private conduct of this Gentleman" (Syrett and Cooke, *Interview*, p. 100). The artificial embarrassments resulted from Burr's manner of proceeding in the affair. Still, he declared, "It is not my design, by what I have said[,] to affix any odium on the conduct of Col Burr, in this case" (Syrett and Cooke, *Interview*, p. 101). Then, near the end of the document, came a startling paragraph: "because it is possible that I may have injured Col Burr ... I have resolved, if our interview is conducted in the usual manner, and it pleases God to give me the opportunity, to *reserve* and *throw away* my first fire, and I *have thoughts* even of *reserving* my second fire— and thus giving a double opportunity to Col Burr to pause and to reflect" (Syrett and Cooke, *Interview*, pp. 101–02). He concluded by giving a further reason why he had to meet Burr. His "*relative* situation" demanded it, he believed; and "the ability to be in [the] future useful . . . would probably be inseparable from a conformity with public prejudice in this particular" (Syrett and Cooke, *Interview*, p. 102).

In addition to this and a number of legal documents, Hamilton also wrote two comforting letters to his wife, which were to be delivered only if he died. On 4 July, he told Elizabeth that he would have avoided the duel had he been able to do so but that "it was not possible, without sacrifices which would have rendered me unworthy of your esteem" (Syrett and Cooke, *Interview*, p. 111). "The consolations of Religion," he added, ". . . can alone support you; and these you have a right to enjoy. Fly to the bosom of your God and be comforted" (Syrett and Cooke, *Interview*, p. 111). In the second letter, written the night before he was shot, he declared that "The Scruples [*of a Christian have deter*]mined me to expose my own [*life to any*] extent rather than subject my[*self to the*] guilt of taking the life of [*another*]. This must increase my hazards & redoubles my pangs for you. But you had rather I should die innocent than live guilty. Heaven can [*preserve*] me [*and I humbly*] hope will, but in the contrary event, I charge you to remember that you are a Christian."[14]

Burr also prepared for possible death. He arranged his papers, made a will, and, on the night before the duel, wrote two revealing letters. The first, to his daughter, charged her to burn all of his papers that would injure anyone should they accidentally be published. "This is more particularly applicable to the letters of my female correspondents" (Syrett and Cooke, *Interview*, p. 134), he added. He then gave directions for the disposal of some of his own personal property—Frederick Prevost, for example, was to have his clothes and a sword or a pair of pistols; Peggy, one of his slaves, was to receive a small lot of land and "fifty dollars in cash as a reward for her fidelity" (Syrett and Cooke, *Interview*, p. 135)—and closed with an expression of love for his daughter. "I am indebted to you, my dearest Theodosia," he wrote, "for a very great portion of the happiness which I have enjoyed in this life. You have completely satisfied all that my heart and affections had hoped or even wished" (Syrett and Cooke, *Interview*, p. 136). Then, seemingly unable to avoid being the teacher one last time, he added: "With a little perseverence [sic], determination, and industry, you will obtain all that my ambition or vanity had fondly imagined. Let your son have occasion to be proud that he had a mother" (Syrett and Cooke, *Interview*, p. 136). To Alston, his son-in-law, he wrote a much less sentimental letter. He asked the future governor of South Carolina to assume his debts, discussed with him other financial matters, recommended friends and sons of friends, but only late in the note specified the reason for his remarks. "I have called out General Hamilton," he stated directly, "and we meet to-morrow morning. . . . The preceding has been written in contemplation of this event" (Davis, *Memoirs*, 2: 325). Then came more emotional lines: "If it should be my lot to fall . . . I shall live in you and your son. I commit to you all that is most dear to me—my reputation and my daughter" (Davis, *Memoirs*, 2: 325–26). He closed with a plea "to stimulate and aid Theodosia in the cultivation of her mind" (Davis, *Memoirs*, 2:326), indicating that Alston and his son would also profit from such an endeavor. Two postscripts were more jaunty. In the first, he discussed his stepson Frederick Prevost, whose shyness kept him from mingling in society. "The case seems almost remediless," Burr joked, "for alas! *he is married!*" (Davis, *Memoirs*, 2: 326). In the second, he revealed his fondness for one of his many conquests: "If you can pardon and indulge a folly," he told Alston, "I would suggest that Madame Sansay, too well known under the name of Leonora, has claims on my recollection. She is now with her husband at St. Jago of Cuba" (Davis, *Memoirs*, 2: 326). Having thus fulfilled his obligations, Burr went to bed and slept soundly till morning.

What exactly happened after Pendleton gave the word to begin firing will probably remain unknown. In their joint statement for the press later that day, the seconds admitted that two crucial matters were in dispute—who had fired first and what the length of time was between the shots. They did agree, though, that "the conduct of the parties . . . was perfectly proper as suited the occasion" (Syrett and Cooke, *Interview*, p. 142). Eight days later, however, Pendleton published an amended version of the joint account. In it, he listed his reasons for believing "that General Hamilton did not fire first—and that he did not fire at all *at Col. Burr*" (Syrett and Cooke, *Interview*, p. 150). He noted that at least ten days before the duel Hamilton had raised the possibility of not returning Burr's first shot and that on the evening before the event he had declared his intention "*not to fire at Col. Burr the first time, but to receive his fire, and fire in the air*" (Syrett and Cooke, *Interview*, p. 151). Next, Pendleton pointed to Hamilton's last words before he was wounded. After receiving his weapon, the general was asked if he wanted the hair spring set, and he had replied, "*Not this time*" (Syrett and Cooke, *Interview*, p. 152). Then too, said Pendleton, there was Hamilton's first statement after being laid in the boat: "*Pendleton knows I did not mean to fire at Col. Burr the first time*" (Syrett and Cooke, *Interview*, p. 152). Later, seeing one of the boatmen pick up his pistol to put it away, Hamilton, according to his second, had also warned: "*Take care of that pistol— it is cocked. It may go off and do mischief*" (Syrett and Cooke, *Interview*, p. 152), a statement showing that he was unaware of having fired at all. Finally, Pendleton said, he and a friend had gone back to Weehawken to see if they could determine the trajectory of Hamilton's shot and had found that the ball had passed through a tree limb twelve and a half feet above the ground and four feet wide of the line between the adversaries.

Van Ness told a different story. In his amended version, he stated that, after the seconds had handed the pistols to the duellists, "Gen Hamilton elevated his, as if to try the light, & lowering it said I beg pardon for delaying you but the direction of the line renders it necessary, at the same time feeling his pockets with his left hand, & drawing forth his spectacles[,] put them on" (Syrett and Cooke, *Interview*, p. 154). Then, Pendleton having given the command "*present*," "the pistol of General Hamilton was first discharged and Col Burr fired immediately after, only five or six seconds of time intervening" (Syrett and Cooke, *Interview*, p. 154). Van Ness was certain, he said, that his account was accurate because he had heard Hamilton's shot and then had looked at Burr to see if he had been hit, observing at that time the Colonel's fire. Noting Burr's "slight motion" after Hamilton's gun had discharged, he thought the vice president might have been wounded. But when he discussed this point with his principal on their way back to the city, Burr "ascribed that circumstance to a small stone under his foot, & observed that the smoke of G Hs pistol obscured him for a moment previous to his firing" (Syrett and Cooke, *Interview*, p. 155).

Recently, Merrill Lindsay has lent some credence to Van Ness's report. Writing in the *Smithsonian*, he pointed out that the duellists had used pistols belonging to John B. Church, Hamilton's brother-in-law, and that these weapons had hidden hair triggers. Hamilton, he maintained, could have secretly set his gun to go off when he applied only a slight half-pound squeeze on the trigger. Unaware of such a mechanism in the pistols, Burr would have had to use the usual ten- or twelve-pound pull. Thus Hamilton had a theoretical advantage but one that turned out to be an actual detriment; the general, Lindsay believes, may have booby-trapped himself. In the tense situation of the duel, Hamilton may have held his weapon too tightly and hence accidentally fired high and wide.[15]

Provocative reasoning this, but probably specious, at least in part. Two pieces of evidence make Lindsay's speculation questionable. First, in his amended version of the events at Weehawken, Pendleton had cited, as one of his reasons for believing that the general did not intend to fire, Hamilton's negative response to a query about setting the "hair spring" (Syrett and Cooke, *Interview*, p. 152). Had Burr been unaware of the adjustable trigger and had he believed that Hamilton had unfairly gained an advantage, Van Ness would surely have seized upon Pendleton's comment and would probably have mentioned the matter in his amended account, which was published after Pendleton's.[16] Second, Burr was familiar with the pistols. He had used them once before when he had challenged Church in 1799 for accusing him of accepting a bribe from the Holland Land Company. After one round, however, Church had apologized, and the parties had retired.

Though the details of the duel remain uncertain, its result, unfortunately, was clear. Struck in the chest—the ball fractured the second or third rib, passed through the liver and diaphragm, and came to rest in the first or second lumbar vertebra—Hamilton fell to the ground, declaring to the surgeon, "This is a mortal wound, Doctor" (Syrett and Cooke, *Interview*, p. 160). On the trip back to the city, he had revived enough, however, to give thoughtful directions to his friends: "Let Mrs. Hamilton be immediately sent for—let the event be gradually broken to her; but give her hopes" (Syrett and Cooke, *Interview*, p. 162). For the rest of the day, though surrounded by his family, he suffered intensely. To Bishop Moore, who questioned him about his moral state preparatory to administering communion, he declared: "I have no ill will against Col. Burr. I met him with a fixed resolution to do him no harm—I forgive all that happened" (Syrett and Cooke, *Interview*, p. 146). Attempting to calm his "half distracted wife," he charged her repeatedly: "*Remember, my Eliza, you are a Christian*" (Syrett and Cooke, *Interview*, p. 164). Then, after a fitful night, his pain seemed to diminish somewhat. But his condition gradually grew worse, and by 2 P.M. the next afternoon he was dead. Dr. Hosack sent a bill for $87.50 (Syrett and Cooke, *Interview*, p. 166).

In the interim, Burr had returned to Richmond Hill, where he breakfasted with a cousin who had unexpectedly appeared. So great was the Colonel's composure that the young man refused to believe an acquaintance who rushed up to him later in the day with the news that "Colonel Burr [had] killed General Hamilton in a duel [that] morning" (Parton, *Life*, 2: 13). On Thursday, 12 July, the vice president sent a note to Dr. Hosack, requesting the surgeon "to inform him of the present state of Gen[l]. H. and of the hopes which are entertained of his recovery" and wanting to know "at what hours of the [day] the D[r]. may most probably be found at home, that he may repeat his inquiries" (Syrett and Cooke, *Interview*, p. 143). Of course, after Hamilton died, the vice president remained secluded, writing to Alston on 13 July that "The malignant Federalists or Tories, and the embittered Clintonians, unite in endeavoring to excite public sympathy in his [Hamilton's] favor, and indignation against his antagonist" (Parton, *Life*, 2: 14). By the following week, the situation was worse. He told his son-in-law that "Every sort of persecution is to be exercised against me. A coroner's jury will sit this evening, being the *fourth* time. The object of this unexampled measure is to obtain an inquest of murder. Upon this a warrant will be issued to apprehend me, and, if I should be taken, no bail would probably be allowed" (Parton, *Life*, 2: 15). Recognizing that safety demanded he leave New York, he journeyed to Philadelphia, stopping on the way to visit his old friend Commodore Truxtun. He was with Charles Biddle in Pennsylvania, however, when a coroner's jury declared on 2 August that he, Van Ness, and Pendleton "feloniously[,] wilfully and of their Malice aforethought did kill and murder, against the peace of the People of the State of New York and their Dignity" (Syrett and Cooke, *Interview*, p. 158).

Burr found that the South viewed matters differently. Discussing the duel correspondence, for example, Virginia's John Randolph declared: "how visible is his [Burr's] ascendancy over him [Hamilton], and how sensible does the latter appear of it! . . . On one side, there is labored obscurity, much equivocation, and many attempts at evasion, not unmixed with a little blustering; on the other an unshaken adherence to his object, and an undeviating pursuit of it not to be eluded or baffled. It remined me of a sinking fox, pressed by a vigorous old hound, where no shift is permitted to avail him."[17] Wherever the vice president traveled, it seemed, he was feted. In Petersburgh, Virginia, for example, he noted: "I came here on the morning of the 29th, intending to stay two hours. The hospitalities of the place have detained me three days. . . . An invitation from the republican citizens, communicated through the mayor, to a public dinner, was made in terms and in a manner which could not be declined" (Davis, *Memoirs*, 2: 347). In Savannah, he was even serenaded from beneath his window.

But Burr's duties as president of the Senate called him to Washington, where he arrived on 4 November. Public hostility had somewhat abated, but a New Jersey Federalist judge had indicted him for murder, and some members of the Senate were embarrassed that he would preside over them. Senator Plumer wrote: "What a humiliating circumstance that a man Who for months has fled from justice—& who by the legal authorities is now accused of murder, should preside over the first branch of the National Legislature!"[18] But Jefferson courted him. The president, hostile to the judiciary, wanted Samuel Chase, an associate justice of the Supreme Court, impeached; and Burr would act as judge at the trial in the Senate. Chase had angered Jefferson by condemning the nullification of a number of circuit judgeships in Maryland and by excoriating the state's adoption of a bill that guaranteed all citizens the right to vote.

With his keen sense of drama, the Colonel ordered the carpenters to turn the Senate chamber into a magnificent courtroom. Then he conducted the trial with what one newspaper called "the dignity and impartiality of an angel, but with the rigour of a devil" (Davis, *Memoirs*, 2: 360). Randolph prosecuted, though he was no match for Chase's attorney, the brilliant if alcoholic Luther Martin, who two years later would defend Burr at his trial. When the Congress failed to provide the necessary two-thirds majority on any of the eight articles, Chase was acquitted, and Burr, cheered. The next day, his timing seemingly perfect, the vice president gave his farewell address to the Senate. Speaking extemporaneously, he made several recommendations for changes in the rules, commented upon his methods in conducting the Senate, and then eloquently pointed to the importance of that body. "This house," he noted, "is a sanctuary; a citadel of law, of order, and of liberty; and it is here—it is here, in this exalted refuge—here, if anywhere, [that] . . . resistance [will] be made to the storms of political phrensy and the silent arts of corruption; and if the Constitution be destined ever to perish by the sacrilegious hands of the demagogue or the usurper, which God avert, its expiring agonies will be witnessed on this floor."[19] Then, after a discussion of his feelings about leaving the Senate, he retired. Many in the audience had shed tears as he spoke, and it was half an hour before business could again be conducted. It had been Burr's finest hour.

The next two years of the Colonel's life, 1805–07, feature what came to be called the Burr conspiracy.[20] For us, the tangled events in the West seem much less engaging than the duel, but American authors devote a great deal of attention to the alleged treason. A private citizen once more, Burr now pursued more actively the western schemes that he had begun in the spring of 1804. In May of that year, his friend from Revolutionary days, General James Wilkinson, had visited the vice president, probably with suggestions for driving Spain from the West; and that summer the Colonel had made shocking proposals of his own to the British minister, Anthony Merry, through an intermediary. Merry's letter to his superiors revealed his amazement: "I have just received an offer from Mr. Burr, the actual Vice-President of the United States (which situation he is about to resign), to lend his assistance to his Majesty's government in any manner in which they may think fit to employ him, particularly in endeavoring to effect a separation of the western part of the United States from that which lies between the Atlantic and the mountains, in its whole extent."[21] The suggestion was probably designed to get money from England for Burr's claimed objective, the conquest of Mexico for the United States if war with Spain broke out, but historians still debate the Colonel's intentions.[22]

In any case, the ex-vice president left Washington in March 1805 for a tour of the West, stopping first in Philadelphia, where he continued negotiations with Merry. Then he rode to Pittsburgh to meet General Wilkinson, who had recently been appointed military governor of the northern portion of the Louisiana Territory. The general had been delayed, however, and Burr set off down the Ohio River in a specially built ark, replete with kitchen, dining room, and two bedrooms. Along the way, he stopped out of curiosity at Blennerhassett's Island, near Marietta, where Mrs. Harman Blennerhassett, her husband unfortunately away, received him warmly. She and Harman, who, it later turned out, was also her uncle, had left Ireland because of family pressure and because of fear that the children would discover the illicit nature of their parents' marriage. A wealthy man, Blennerhassett took his family to the United States in 1796, where he bought Backus Isle and squandered most of his fortune in creating a paradise in the wilderness. Scholar, scientist, violinist, the unworldly Irishman was looking for a way to regain his wealth and hence willingly joined Burr later, even when matters looked bleakest. At Cincinnati, the Colonel discussed plans for an Indiana canal project with Senator Smith of Ohio and Senator Dayton of New Jersey and then floated to Lousiville, from which he rode to Frankfort, Lexington, and Nashville. There, at a public dinner in his honor, he renewed his acquaintance with Andrew Jackson and was soon a house guest at Jackson's home, the Hermitage. Like many in the West, Jackson detested the Spaniards; and so, with a Spanish war seemingly assured, the Tennesseean listened eagerly to Burr's plans and to his insinuations that he was in secret communication with the secretary of war. From Nashville, the Colonel proceeded to Fort Massac, where he at last met Wilkinson. The two spent five days discussing their plans, after which Burr left for Natchez and, finally, New Orleans. When he reached New Orleans, he quickly sought out such dissatisfied groups as the Mexican Association, whose purpose was to liberate or conquer Mexico. A meeting with the bishop of New Orleans brought him the cooperation of the Catholics, who were worried about Spanish oppression in Mexico. Then, having added substantially to his support, he set out for Wilkinson's headquarters in St. Louis, stopping again at many of the places he had visited on his trip down the river.

But now the press began to speculate on Burr's activities. The *United States' Gazette* in Philadelphia wondered:

How long will it be before we shall hear of Colonel Burr being at the head of a revolutionary party on the Western waters? Is it a fact that Colonel Burr has formed a plan to engage the adventurous and enterprising young men from the Atlantic States to Louisiana? Is it one of the inducements that an immediate convention will be called from the States bordering on the Ohio and Mississippi to form a separate government? Is it another that all the public lands are to be seized and partitioned among these States, except what is reserved for the warlike friends and followers of Burr in the revolution? Is it part of the plan for the new States to grant the new lands in bounties to entice inhabitants from the Atlantic States? How soon will the forts and magazines and all the military posts at New Orleans and on the Mississippi be in the hands of Colonel Burr's revolutionary party? How soon will Colonel Burr engage in the reduction of Mexico by granting liberty to its inhabitants, and seizing on its treasures, aided by British ships and forces? What difficulty can there be in completing a revolution in one summer, among the Western States, when they will gain the Congress' lands, will throw off the public debt, will seize their own revenues, and enjoy the plunder of Spain? [McCaleb, *Burr Conspiracy*, p. 38]

Widely circulated, such supposition reads like a guidebook for the ways many American authors would treat Burr's schemes in their imaginative works.

The collaborators' plans for conquering Mexico were now unfortunately public, and Wilkinson began the foot-shuffling that would eventually lead him to the Richmond courtroom as the government's chief witness against Burr. A pensioner of Spain as well as an officer of the United States, the duplicitous general feared that the newspaper reports would compromise his position with both governments. Thus, although he received Burr cordially in St. Louis, he also sent a note of warning about the Colonel to the secretary of the navy. Burr then left for Washington, stopping first at Vincennes with a letter for William Henry Harrison and later at Theodosia's home in South Carolina for a visit with his ailing daughter. When he arrived in Washington, he hurried to see the British minister. He described to Merry the readiness of the West for independence, stressing that New Orleans, not the Ohio Valley, was the key to his plans. With naval support and £110,000 from England, he could begin the revolution by late April or early May. Once Louisiana and the western country became independent, he told Merry, the eastern states would separate from the southern, and U.S. power would thus be substantially diminished (Adams, *History*, 3: 230–32). Then, while he waited to hear from the British government, he called on Jefferson, only to learn the disastrous news that now there would be no war with Spain. For a price, the president told him, Napoleon would force the Spaniards to relinquish Florida.

Discouraged both by England's ominous silence and by U.S. policy, the versatile Burr then turned to Spain for financing. He sent Dayton to the Spanish minister, Casa Yrujo, with a wild story of seizing Jefferson and other top officials, taking the federal arsenal, looting the Bank of the United States, and establishing himself as ruler. If the scheme failed, he would burn all but two or three Navy Yard ships, which he would use to sail to New Orleans with his followers and his appropriated money. There he would announce the independence of Louisiana and the West (Abernethy, *Conspiracy*, pp. 39–40). Somehow believing this fantasy,[23] Yrujo gave Dayton $1,500 and later another $1,000, primarily, however, for revealing the plans of Francesco de Miranda, who was preparing an expedition to free his native Venezuela. Later, the wiser Spanish home government refused Burr any further aid. The only good news by the end of 1805 was that Blennerhassett had decided to join the Colonel in his Mexican endeavors.

Seeking other supporters, Burr in January contacted "General" William Eaton, former U.S. consul at Tunis, who was disgruntled because the Jefferson administration had denied his reimbursement claims for money he had advanced while consul and for expenses he had incurred in the war with Tripoli. According to Eaton's later testi-

mony at Burr's trial, the Colonel divulged "his project of revolution-
izing the territory west of the Allegany; establishing an independent
empire there; New Orleans to be the capital, and he himself to be the
chief; organizing a military force on the waters of the Mississippi, and
carrying conquest to Mexico."[24] Eaton also maintained that Burr had
indicated he would drive Congress out, have the president done away
with, and establish himself at the head of the new government, if he
could get the necessary marine corps and naval support (Adams,
History, 3: 240). To his friend Truxtun, Burr also made proposals, but
the commodore refused to join any group not specifically sanctioned
by Jefferson. For the next seven months, the Colonel traveled the East
Coast, attempting to strengthen his support and gain financial
backing. Then, with Alston's funds, in July 1806 he was able to buy
the 400,000-acre Bastrop lands on the Washita River in Orleans
Territory. He maintained ever after that these lands were to be a
staging area for the conquest of Mexico, *if* the United States declared
war with Spain; if not, the men gathered there would become settlers.

The preliminaries now accomplished, Burr was ready to move. He
told Blennerhassett to expect him at the island by 20 August and
ordered to New Orleans another recruit, Dr. Erich Bollman, famous
for his attempt to free Lafayette from an Austrian prison. Then to Wilkinson, Burr wrote the crucial cipher letter, dated 29 July 1806, which
was to be so important at the trial. It said in part:

Your letter, postmarked thirteenth May, is received. At length I have obtained funds, and have actually commenced. The Eastern detachments, from
different points and under different pretences, will rendezvous on the Ohio
first of November. Everything internal and external favors our views. Naval
protection of England is secured. Truxtun is going to Jamaica to arrange with
the admiral on that station. It [naval support] will meet us at the Mississippi.
England, a navy of the United States, are ready to join, and final orders are
given to my friends and followers. It will be a host of choice spirits. Wilkinson
shall be second to Burr only; Wilkinson shall dictate the rank and promotion
of his officers. Burr will proceed westward first August, never to return. . . .
Already are orders given to the contractor to forward six months' provisions
to points Wilkinson may name; this shall not be used until the last moment,
and then under proper injunctions. Our object, my dear friend, is brought to a
point so long desired. Burr guarantees the result with his life and honor, with
the lives and honor and the fortunes of hundreds, the best blood of our coun-

try. Burr's plan of operation is to move down rapidly from the Falls, on the fifteenth of November, with the first five hundred or a thousand men, in light boats now constructing for that purpose; to be at Natchez between the fifth and fifteenth of December, there to meet you; there to determine whether it will be expedient in the first instance to seize on or pass by Baton Rouge. . . . The people of the country to which we are going are prepared to receive us; their agents, now with Burr, say that if we will protect their religion, and will not subject them to a foreign Power, that in three weeks all will be settled. The gods invite us to glory and fortune; it remains to be seen whether we deserve the boon. [McCaleb, *Burr Conspiracy*, pp. 68–69]

Two things are clear from this letter. First, Burr would tell anyone whatever best suited his purposes at the moment. The promise of naval support from England and from the United States, for example, was a lie. Second, the Colonel's actual intentions cannot be determined from the letter. Indeed, historians have used it either to prove that his intended goal was Mexico or to show that he was a traitor with designs on New Orleans. Coolly, Burr reserved his options.

During the first week in August 1806, the Colonel left Philadelphia as planned. By the twenty-first, he was in Pittsburgh, where all the forces were to meet, overseeing enlistments and calling on prominent people. During dinner at the farm of Colonel George Morgan, the founder of New Madrid, Burr declared that within five years the West would leave the Union and made other remarks that upset his host. Later, Morgan sent an account of this meeting to Jefferson. Other places the Colonel now visited were Marietta, Frankfort, Lexington, and, of course, Nashville, where he continued to play on Jackson's hatred of the Spanish. Meanwhile, Comfort Tyler, Burr's commissary officer, increased the expedition's stores. Best of all, however, war with Spain again seemed likely, and Wilkinson had been ordered to take care of the crisis on the Sabine. When the Spanish had refused to yield a small bit of land between the river and the Arroyo Hondo, the general had been told to drive them from it. Everything in the West seemed propitious.

But then came trouble. In Washington, the president heard from Gideon Granger of Burr's overtures to Eaton and promptly called a cabinet meeting on 22 October to discuss the western problem. During the meeting, the administration decided to alert the governors of Ohio, Indiana, Mississippi, and Orleans and to instruct the district attorneys of Kentucky, Tennessee, and Louisiana to watch Burr closely. If he were to commit any overt act, they were to try him for treason or for misdemeanor. The cabinet met again two days later and still another time on the twenty-fifth, when they decided to send the marines to New Orleans and to replace Wilkinson as governor of Louisiana (but not as military chief) with John Graham. Jefferson's spy, as several dramatists were to label him, had the power to arrest Burr, should events warrant such action, and could easily alert the other governors, should trouble arise. At this critical point, Wilkinson betrayed the Colonel. Having finally received Burr's famous cipher letter on 8 October, he knew that he had to commit himself. Hence, on 20 October, he wrote to Jefferson, outlining a plot he had discovered to attack Mexico but withholding names because, he sanctimoniously proclaimed, he did not want "to injure anyone undeservedly" (McCaleb, *Burr Conspiracy*, pp. 122–23). The next day, Wilkinson sent the president a sickening letter designed to protect himself. In it, he expressed his fears that newspaper reports, linking him with Burr's secessionist schemes, might have shaken Jefferson's confidence in him but that he knew that his honorable service under three presidents would be recognized as sufficient guarantee of his loyalty. Still, he declared, he was upset: "Pardon, I beseech you, the honest pride which impels me to bare my bosom to you.—My ultimate views are limited to the acquisition of an honorable fame.—I have ever contemned the sordid interests of the world, and estimate property by its immediate utility only—and it is the highest ambition of my soul on a proper occasion, to spend my last breath in the cause of my country.... To you I owe more than I will express, lest I should be suspected of adulation, which I detest" (McCaleb, *Burr Conspiracy*, p. 126). Determined now to play the savior of his country, he made peace with Spain and rushed to New Orleans to capture Burr. Both his paymasters, he felt, would reward him.

There were others, however, who wanted the Colonel arrested, notably Joseph Daveiss, the district attorney of Kentucky. A year before, he had warned Jefferson about both Wilkinson and Burr; now, in early November 1806, he brought the ex-vice president to trial in Frankfort for plotting to attack Mexico. About this time, too, Andrew Jackson learned that the Colonel might be contemplating a division of the Union and promptly warned Governor Claiborne of New Orleans. Jackson's loss to the expedition was discouraging, but crippling was the president's proclamation of 27 November, announcing an unauthorized military attack against Spanish territory and warning anyone who had joined to withdraw immediately.[25] All claims to legitimacy had now disappeared. Even so, the Kentucky trial ended well. On 5 December, a friendly grand jury acquitted the Colonel, whose lawyer, Henry Clay, had likened Daveiss to a Spanish inquisitor. That night there was a ball in Burr's honor.

Meanwhile, Tyler led the first contingent of the Colonel's men down the Ohio River to Blennerhassett's Island, arriving on 8 December. But four days later the group left hastily in the early morning hours because the Wood County Militia was rumored to be on the way. When the militia did arrive, only Mrs. Blennerhassett greeted the troops, some of whom then spent the night drinking and pillaging. At Jeffersonville, the flotilla met Davis Floyd and his boats and proceeded down river; Burr was to join them at the mouth of the Cumberland. In New Orleans, however, Wilkinson was fortifying the city as if he expected a major attack. He was also attempting to enrich himself by notifying the Spanish governor of Florida that he would protect Spain's interest against those Americans with designs on Baton Rouge and Mexico. Illegally, he then arrested three of the Colonel's chief lieutenants—Bollman, Ogden, and Swartwout—denied them counsel, and shipped them off to Washington. By this time, Burr had joined the flotilla, which soon reached the Mississippi, landing first at New Madrid to recruit more men and then journeying to Bayou Pierre in the Mississippi Territory. There, on 10 January 1807, the Colonel learned of Jefferson's proclamation and saw his own cipher letter to Wilkinson printed in the Natchez *Messenger*. He must have known then that he was finished.

Meeting with the territorial governor, Cowles Mead, Burr agreed to place himself under the control of civilian authorities and to allow his boats to be searched for military equipment. When the inspectors arrived, however, they found nothing but rifles; forty muskets complete with bayonets had been cleverly lowered beneath the water line. In New Orleans, Wilkinson kept busy. He arrested John Adair and shipped him to Baltimore, furnished Jefferson with the latest news from the West, and sent a party to arrest Burr and bring him to New Orleans after his trial in Mississippi. In Washington, the president sent a report to Congress on 27 January, detailing the history of the conspiracy and naming the ex-vice president as the "prime mover" in the affair (Richardson, *Compilation*, p. 412). Although he admitted that the material he had received from various people contained "such a mixture of rumors, conjectures, and suspicions as [rendered] it difficult to sift out the real facts," he evidently had no trouble naming Burr "as the principal actor, whose guilt is placed beyond question" (Richardson, *Compilation*, p. 412). John Adams, discussing this condemnation, declared that even if the Colonel's guilt were absolutely certain, the president should not proclaim Burr a traitor before the case had gone to court.[26] But Jefferson's remarks had little effect on the Mississippi grand jury, which not only acquitted Burr but also condemned the authorities for arresting him.

After the verdict, the Colonel joined the flotilla to tell his men that he would flee instead of returning to the court's jurisdiction as required. Without him, then, the expedition proceeded to Natchez, where it was seized. Once again, no military equipment was found, and the men were told that they might do whatever they wished with their boats and stores but that their leaders were to be held. Fearing that Wilkinson might hang him if he came within the general's control, Burr then decided to seek safety in Spanish territory. Disguised as a boatman, he got as far as Wakefield, Alabama, where Lieutenant Edmund Gaines arrested him. Then, from Fort Stoddart on 5 March 1807, he began the one-thousand-mile trip to Richmond to be tried again for treason. When the party reached South Carolina, however, the Colonel made an attempt to escape. As the group passed a crowd in one of the towns along the way, he jumped from his horse, declaring: "I am Aaron Burr, under military arrest, and claim the protection of the civil authorities." Perkins, the commander of the mission, also sprang to the ground and, with both his pistols pointed at the prisoner, demanded that he remount. The Colonel shouted defiantly, "*I will not!*" Unwilling to shoot, Perkins grabbed "little Burr" around the waist and placed him in the saddle, after which the guards rushed him away from the stunned villagers. When the party stopped to collect itself a few miles from town, Perkins found the ex-vice president "in a flood of tears" and observed that the man who led the Colonel's horse, "touched by the spectacle of fallen greatness, was also crying" (Parton, *Life*, 2: 100–01).

Defending Burr in Richmond against charges of high misdemeanor and treason were Luther Martin, famous for his defense of Justice Chase, Edmund Randolph, former secretary of state, and John Wickham, an outstanding Virginia lawyer. George Hay was to prosecute, assisted by District Attorney Caesar Rodney, Lieutenant Governor Gordon MacRae, and young but skillful William Wirt. Throughout the trial their silent partner was the president of the United States, who gave instruction and advice to offset what he saw as Chief Justice John Marshall's political opposition. Finding an impartial grand jury to determine if there were sufficient cause for an indictment was impossible, but after much discussion and many challenges the jurors, with John Randolph as foreman, were finally sworn in. Without Wilkinson, who was en route, the government was forced to offer such witnesses as Peter Taylor, Blennerhassett's illiterate gardener, and foreign-born Jacob Allbright, a sometime laborer at the island. Burr electrified the court by asking that Jefferson and certain relevant papers be subpoenaed—a constitutional crisis which Marshall carefully avoided. He ruled that the president might send the requested documents without coming himself, should he find his governmental obligations more pressing. Another explosive scene came when Bollman, offered a pardon in open court, refused to accept it. But Wilkinson's arrival caused the greatest excitement.

Appearing before the jury on 15 June, Wilkinson was at last forced to confront the friend he had betrayed. Washington Irving, who in this case was decidedly pro-Burr, described the encounter in a letter to James K. Paulding:

Burr was seated with his back to the entrance, facing the judge, and conversing with one of his counsel. Wilkinson strutted into Court, and took his stand in a parallel line with Burr on his right hand. Here he stood for a moment swelling like a turkey-cock, and bracing himself up for the encounter of Burr's eye. The latter did not take any notice of him until the judge directed the clerk to swear General Wilkinson; at the mention of the name Burr turned his head, looked him full in the face with one of his piercing regards, swept his eye over his whole person from head to foot, as if to scan its dimensions, and then coolly resumed his former position, and went on conversing with his counsel as tranquilly as ever. The whole look was over in an instant; but it was an admirable one. There was no appearance of study or constraint in it; no affectation of disdain or defiance; a slight expression of contempt played over his countenance, such as you would show on regarding any person to whom you were indifferent, but whom you considered mean and contemptible.[27]

Although Burr's lawyers attacked Wilkinson's credibility, the jury evidently believed him because on 24 June they indicted the Colonel and Harman Blennerhassett for treason (planning the separation of the western states) and high misdemeanor (plotting to attack Spanish territories). Burr's trial date was set for 3 August 1807.

In the meantime, the Colonel was housed in a spacious, third-floor apartment in the state prison. To Theodosia, he noted that his "friends and acquaintance of both sexes [were] permitted to visit [him] without interruption, without inquiring their business, and without the *presence of a spy*" and offered her "a bedroom and parlour" on the same floor as his if she would come for the trial (Davis, *Memoirs*, 2: 410). Fortunately, she and her husband were with him on 17 August, when, after fourteen days of trying without success to find an impartial jury, he heard the indictment read. It stated in part that he, "not having the fear of God before his eyes . . . but being moved and seduced by the instigation of the devil . . . did compass, imagine and intend to raise and levy war, insurrection and rebellion against the said United States" (Robertson, *Reports*, 1: 430). The penalty for such a crime was death.

Burr and his lawyers showed definitively that the Colonel had been in Kentucky and not on Blennerhassett's Island at the time charged in the indictment and maintained that, before he could be called to answer for his actions, Blennerhassett would have to be proven guilty first. But the prosecution held that Burr, not the Irishman, was "the *Alpha* and *Omega* of this treasonable scheme" (Robertson, *Reports*, 2: 39). In a speech that may have given a number of American authors the idea of portraying the Colonel as Satan, William Wirt declaimed: "Who is this Blannerhassett [sic]? A native of Ireland, a man of letters, who fled from the storms of his own country to find quiet in ours. . . . But he carried with him taste and science and wealth; and lo, the desert smiled! Possessing himself of a beautiful island in the Ohio, he rears upon it a palace and decorates it with every romantic embellishment of fancy. . . . In the midst of all this peace, this innocent simplicity and this tranquillity, this feast of the mind, this pure banquet of the heart, the destroyer comes; he comes to change this paradise into a hell" (Robertson, *Reports*, 2: 96–97). But the crux of the trial was the definition of treason itself. In an extraordinarily long opinion, in which he cited a number of legal authorities, Marshall made clear that neither in fact nor by construction could Burr be said to have been present at the assembly on the Ohio.[28] The Colonel had not taken part in an overt act of war witnessed by two people; intention was not sufficient grounds for conviction on such a serious charge.

The next day, 1 September 1807, the jury reached a decision on the charge of treason: "We of the jury say that Aaron Burr is not proved to be guilty under this indictment by any evidence submitted to us. We therefore find him not guilty" (Robertson, *Reports*, 2: 446). There was no doubt that this was a verdict of acquittal rather than of innocence, and Burr immediately objected to its wording. It was "unusual, informal and irregular" (Robertson, *Reports*, 2: 446), he maintained, and asked Marshall to send the jury back to alter the decision or to change it himself. The chief justice, however, allowed the verdict to stand, though he did order the record to read "not guilty" (Robertson, *Report*, 2: 447). Hay then declared that he would pursue the indictment for misdemeanor (plotting an attack against Spanish dominions) and that he would also ask the court to commit Burr to Kentucky where the treasonable, overt act of war had allegedly occurred. For seven weeks, the misdemeanor trial and the commitment hearings proceeded tediously with only one bright moment; the Colonel was able to expose enough of Wilkinson's questionable activities to keep him under suspicion for another five years. By late October, it was clear that because of Marshall's rulings Burr could not be convicted anywhere of treason, though he was ordered to stand trial in Ohio for misdemeanor. When Hay indicated, however, that the government would not pursue the case, the Colonel was essentially if not legally free—but ruined.

Though so dejected after the trial that one of his friends feared he might commit suicide,[29] Burr was recovered enough by 6 June 1808 to sail for England under an assumed name with hopes of finding European sponsors for his plan to free Mexico.[30] But with characteristic bad fortune, the Colonel reached Britain on the very day that Joseph Bonaparte arrived in Madrid. Hence, neither France, which now wished to preserve the Spanish empire, nor England, which supported the exiled Spanish king, were interested in Burr's revolutionary schemes. For the next four years, he wandered through Europe and the Scandinavian countries, visiting such notables as Jeremy Bentham and Walter Scott. Sometimes feted, sometimes spurned, he continued to pursue his plans until he finally realized their hopelessness and decided to return to the United States. But through the machinations of the American chargé d'affaires in Paris, Jonathan Russell, and the American consul, Gordon MacRae, his passport was held up because technically he had fled from prosecution in Ohio. In a letter to Burr, Russell disdainfully noted that the "fugitive from justice, during his voluntary exile, has a claim to no other passport than one which shall enable him to surrender himself for trial for the offences with which he stands charged" (Davis, *Memoirs*, 2: 423). Shunned by American citizens in Paris, Burr spent a poverty-stricken year during which he was forced to sell many of the books and other gifts he had bought for Theodosia and her family in order to buy food. Eventually, however, the passport was granted, and, on 8 June 1812, he reached New York, "just four years since we parted at this very place" (Burr, *Private Journal*, 2: 477).

Apparently rising from the ashes of a blasted career, the Colonel made $2,000 during the first twelve business days after he reopened his law office in a lady friend's home. He had borrowed Troup's library, put a notice in the paper announcing the resumption of his practice, and nailed up "a very small tin sign, bearing only his name" (Parton, *Life*, 2: 245). The result was, of course, cheering; but Burr's good fortune was not to last. Within six weeks, he received a despairing letter from Theodosia that his beloved grandson, Aaron Burr Alston, was dead: "There is no more joy for me; the world is blank. I have lost my boy" (Parton, *Life*, 2: 246). The Colonel had taken great interest in the child, fondly reporting his achievements to friends and carefully selecting gifts for him during the years in Europe, so the boy's death was a severe blow. This loss, however, was only the prelude to a greater disaster. While sailing to New York aboard the *Patriot* to visit her father, Theodosia was lost at sea during a storm. Because no wreckage or survivors were ever found, there were rumors that pirates had captured the *Patriot*, murdered the crew, and carried Theodosia off—a melodramatic story that some American authors were to pick up. But it was the weather, not pirates, that had taken Theodosia.

Burr found his daughter's loss crushing. To Alston, he wrote that he felt "severed from the human race" (Parton, *Life*, 2: 248). She had occupied his thoughts since he had taken charge of her education and had been his emotional support during his exile in Europe. Indeed, at one of the most discouraging times in his sojourn, she had written movingly:

I witness your extraordinary fortitude with new wonder at every new misfortune. Often, after reflecting on this subject, you appear to me so superior, so elevated above all other men; I contemplate you with such a strange mixture of humility, admiration, reverence, love and pride, that very little superstition would be necessary to make me worship you as a superior being, such enthusiasm does your character excite in me. When I afterwards revert to myself, how insignificant do my best qualities appear. My vanity would be greater if I had not been placed so near you; and yet my pride is our relationship. I had rather not live than not be the daughter of such a man. (Wandell and Minnigerode, *Burr*, 2: 251)

So great was his pain that, for a time, Burr put away anything that would remind him of her.

The Colonel's last twenty years, though less dramatic than those that embraced the shooting of Hamilton and the trial for treason, were certainly not commonplace. His tumultuous life, for example, had made him sympathetic to friends in adversity and generous to anyone in need. Thus, when he found Luther Martin, his former defense attorney, sick and destitute, he took him into his home and cared for him until his death. There were, in fact, innumerable cases of Burr's unusual charity. In the middle of his law office, he kept a book-laden table, the center of which served as the repository for all his money. When visitors would come begging a loan, he would reach into this well and give the supplicant whatever was required. Ironically, too, in 1816, General José Alvarez de Toledo, acting on behalf of his countrymen, offered the Colonel direction of the Mexican revolution. He declined, however, perhaps recognizing then what he had not seen in 1806—that the times were not right. Later, when Texas gained its independence, he pointed to his unfortunate, earlier misjudgment but noted the essential correctness of his position: "*There*! [Y]ou see? I was right! I was only thirty years too soon! What was treason in me thirty years ago, is patriotism now!" (Parton, *Life*, 2: 319).

In later life he also continued his altogether uncommonplace relationship with women. He was a sexual predator from the start, and even his friend and biographer, Matthew Davis, spoke harshly of this aspect of his character:

> In his intercourse with females he was an unprincipled flatterer, ever pre-pared to take advantage of their weakness, their credulity, or their confi-dence. . . . His intrigues were without number. His conduct most licentious. The sacred bonds of friendship were unhesitatingly violated when they oper-ated as barriers to the indulgence of his passions. For a long period of time he seemed to be gathering, and carefully preserving, every line written to him by any female, whether with or without reputation; and, when obtained, they were cast into one common receptacle,—the profligate and corrupt, by the side of the thoughtless and betrayed victim. All were held as trophies of victory,—all esteemed alike valuable.
>
> .   .   .   .
>
> In this particular [his sexual predation], Burr appears to have been unfeeling and heartless. And yet, by a fascinating power almost peculiar to himself, he so managed as to retain the affection, in some instances, the devotion, of his deluded victims. (Davis, *Memoirs*, 1: 91-92)

Even as a ministerial student of eighteen, Burr had developed a re-putation as a gallant, writing to his sister of his embarrassment at being teased about dallying with the Litchfield girls.[31] But it was, of course, in his maturity that his greatest sexual activity occurred. Be-sides Clara, Julia, Leonora, and Celeste, he had relationships with an Indian girl during the campaign for Quebec (this affair is of doubtful authenticity), a New York lady of middle years, and innumerable women of all stations who wrote him compromising letters, which in his will he directed Davis to burn. (He did!) In his journal that he kept for Theodosia during his European exile, Burr recorded frequent "*rencontres*" with prostitutes, sometimes even noting the amount of satisfaction they provided. Thus, on 25 October 1809, he wrote: "In the evening walked out, intending to go to the park again, but the gate was locked, though only 8 o'clock. In walking, however, a *renc. [ontre]*; 2 r.[ix] d.[ollars]; *passab[le]*" (Burr, *Private Journal*, 1: 253). Or, a year later, he noted more cryptically: "*Renc.* and 6 francs. *Assez bien*; another, 2 francs" (Burr, *Private Journal*, 2: 21). Once, at least, he was badly disappointed: "Walked ½ hour. *Fol.[ie]*; pros.

only; 5 francs 10 sous. Dwarf. Bah!" (Burr, *Private Journal*, 2: 212).
He took love wherever he found it. One day to his surprise, he indicated, "the maid at the usual hour brought tea but in a very unusual
style. A splendid tea service of silver and two cups. I asked why she
brought two cups (I being alone). She said with perfect simplicity and
without any smile or queer looks that she supposed *Madame* would
have staid to tea" (Burr, *Private Journal*, 1: 253). Sometimes, his
needs were so intense that he required a series of liaisons to satisfy
himself, as his entry of 2 November 1810 made clear: "Gave a pair of
gloves to Cath'e which with the *chose*, 3 francs 5 sous. We (Crede and
I) parted at 8. *Renct. inspect.*, 2 francs; another, my gloves and 10
sous; another resembling exceedingly S. Reeve. We went to a *M'e de
Vin* and took supper, 3 francs 10 sous; very cheap, costing 25 sous.
(*La Cordonniere.*) *Voila, au folie*, 10 francs 10 sous and my
glo.[ves]!" (Burr, *Private Journal*, 2: 32).

From such frequent and various activity, children occasionally
resulted, though how many no one was ever to know with any certainty. Women often pointed to him as the father of their illegitimate new-
born, and the Colonel never disputed their accusations, even when
they were obviously untrue. Asked about his patience, he replied:
"Sir, when a lady does me the honor to name me the father of her
child, I trust I shall always be too gallant to show myself ungrateful for
the favor!" (Parton, *Life*, 2: 302). Three, however, were definitely his:
a silversmith, Aaron Columbus Burr, who had been born in France
and was later educated in America by his father; and two youngsters,
Elizabeth and Frances Ann, who were listed in the Colonel's will as
his principal heirs.[32] Charles Burdett, a law clerk in Burr's office and
later a novelist who provided a memorial of sorts for the Colonel in his
writing,[33] was a probable fourth;[34] and it was at least possible that
Martin Van Buren was another of Burr's natural children. Contemporaneous gossip pointed to such a relationship, and a remark in John
Quincy Adams' *Memoirs* suggested its truth. Adams had noted that
in 1827 Van Buren was working in much the same way as Burr had in
1799-1800 and that there were many similarities, including physical
appearance, between the two political figures.[35]

Now, in later life, the Colonel was still sexually vigorous. In 1815,
he began an eight-year affair with Rebecca Blodgett, a widow whose
property litigation he undertook at her request. He and the former deb-

utante had been friendly in the past; but, after he accepted her case, the relationship evidently became intense—at least on her part. Later, for a four-year period beginning in 1828, he became entangled with "a lovely and voluptuous looking woman" in her early twenties, who clearly used her charms to get money from him.[36] Burr was seventy-two when this dalliance began. Then, in his seventy-seventh year, came Madame Jumel. She was a rich widow when he wooed her in 1833, but she had started poor. As Eliza Bowen, the uneducated daughter of a sailor had led a dissolute life in Providence, where she had given birth to and quickly abandoned her illegitimate child, George Washington Bowen. In New York, rumor indicated that her beauty had attracted many of the great names of society, including Hamilton and maybe Burr. Gossip, in fact, linked her to the Weehawken duel, a suggestion at least one American author was to follow. Her charms eventually captivated Stephen Jumel, a wealthy merchant, who took her to live with him, as our ancestors used to say, without the benefit of clergy. By feigning a mortal illness, she soon became his wife, and he bought and refurbished the Roger Morris house in Harlem for her. Nothing, however, could restore her reputation, and so, after five years of being snubbed, the couple sailed for France, where as Betsy Bowen she had once been brought and bought by a willing ship captain and where now as Madame Jumel she was a smash. Eventually, she returned to the United States with control of her husband's money and, when he died in a fall from a wagon in 1832, became eligible for marriage.

The reasons for Burr's suit may have been mixed. At fifty-seven, Elizabeth Jumel was still an attractive woman, but her wealth may have been even more attractive. In any case, after twice being refused, the Colonel married her on 1 July 1833, when he appeared at her mansion with a minister. Soon, however, the fighting started. Without his wife's knowledge, Burr made a disastrous investment with her money in a settlement of Germans in Texas—the colonists balked, and the property title was not clear. When she discovered the loss and questioned him about it, he reminded her that he was her husband and that he would manage her affairs as he saw fit. A series of separations and reunions followed, but the end was clear when on 12 July 1834 Eliza B. Burr filed for divorce, charging the Colonel with infidelity "at divers times with divers females" but particularly with Jane McManus of Jersey City (Wandell and Minnigerode, *Burr*, 2: 327). Initially, he contested the suit, threatening to prove her an adulteress and declaring that he had left her because of her "violent and ferocious temper" and because of "her abusive and insulting conduct toward him" (Wandell and Minnigerode, *Burr*, 2: 328), but eventually he withdrew his complaint and allowed her suit to proceed.

Burr's final days were comfortable enough but without the consolation of those whom he had loved most, Theodosia and her little boy. In 1835, after he had suffered a second, devastating stroke, Mrs. Joshua Webb, a friend from former times, looked after him at her boardinghouse. Though her neighbors whispered that she had taken him in because she was either his natural child or his mistress, she remained disdainful of the gossip and treated him with graciousness until her house was closed before being torn down. Just prior to his removal from Mrs. Webb's, his health grew worse, and it appeared that death was close. Hence, during what he thought might be a final visit and with a view toward history, Matthew Davis asked the Colonel if in fact he had intended to divide the Union. Impatiently, Burr replied: "No; I would as soon have thought of taking possession of the moon, and informing my friends that I intended to divide it among them!" (Davis, *Memoirs*, 2: 379n). Earlier, in a conversation one day with Mrs. Webb about his fondness for the sentiment in *Tristram Shandy*, he had also spoken of Hamilton: "If I had read Sterne more," he had maintained, "and Voltaire less, I should have known that the world was wide enough for Hamilton and me" (Parton, *Life*, 2: 322).

Burr recovered, however, and so new quarters were necessary. Judge Ogden Edwards, wanting his cousin near him (although perhaps fearful of public opinion, not so near as his own home), lodged the ailing man in a rented room at Winant's Hotel on Staten Island. There the Reverend P. J. Van Pelt visited him during his last days at Edwards' request. Although the Colonel was polite, thanking the clergyman each time for his attentions, he never asked for communion. And although Van Pelt believed—and so recorded—that it always gave the sick man great pleasure to see him, such a view may at least be questioned, given the minister's behavior during Burr's last moments. Noticing that the Colonel's pulse was erratic, the clergyman had felt it his duty to inform Burr that the end was near. Then, in what must surely be the longest and most involved question ever put to someone about to die, he had asked: "In this solemn hour of your apparent dissolution, believing, as you do, in the sacred Scriptures, [and in] your accountability to God, let me ask you how you feel in view of approaching eternity; whether you have good hope, through grace, that all your sins will be pardoned, and God will, in mercy, pardon you, for the sake of the merits and righteousness of his beloved Son, our Lord Jesus Christ, who in love suffered and died for us the agonizing, bitter death of the cross, by whom alone we can have the only sure hope of salvation?" As if to puncture such pomposity and impertinence, the Colonel had replied: "On that subject I am coy" (Parton, *Life*, 2: 330). But within the hour, the man whose political life had ended thirty-two years before at Weehawken was dead at eighty. That same day, 14 September 1836, Madame Jumel's divorce, specifying that she might remarry whenever she pleased but that her former husband was denied that privilege until her death, was finally granted. Her lawyer's name was Alexander Hamilton.[37]

Notes

1. James Parton, *The Life and Times of Aaron Burr*, enlarged ed., 2 vols. (Boston: Ticknor and Fields, 1867), 1: 354, hereafter referred to in the text and in the notes as *Life*. Besides Parton, the indispensable biographical and historical works dealing with Burr are Thomas Perkins Abernethy, *The Burr Conspiracy* (New York: Oxford University Press, 1954), hereafter cited as *Conspiracy*; Aaron Burr, *The Private Journal of Aaron Burr*, ed. William K. Bixby, 2 vols. (Rochester: The Genesee Press, 1903), hereafter referred to as *Private Journal*; I[saac] J[oslin] C[ox], "Burr, Aaron," in *Dictionary of American Biography*, ed. Dumas Malone (New York: Charles Scribner's Sons, 1929); Matthew L. Davis, *Memoirs of Aaron Burr*, 2 vols. (New York: Harper & Brothers, 1836–37), hereafter cited as *Memoirs*; Walter Flavius McCaleb, *The Aaron Burr Conspiracy*, expanded ed. (1936; rpt. New York: Argosy-Antiquarian, 1966), hereafter cited as *Burr Conspiracy*; Walter Flavius McCaleb, *A New Light on Aaron Burr* (1963; rpt. New York: Argosy-Antiquarian, 1966), hereafter cited as *New Light*; Herbert S. Parmet and Marie B. Hecht, *Aaron Burr: Portrait of an Ambitious Man* (New York: Macmillan, 1967), hereafter cited as *Portrait*; Harold C. Syrett and Jean G. Cooke, eds., *Interview in Weehawken: The Burr-Hamilton Duel as told in the Original Documents* (Middletown, Conn.: Wesleyan University Press, 1960), hereafter cited as *Interview*; and Samuel H. Wandell and Meade

Minnigerode, *Aaron Burr*, 2 vols. (New York: G. P. Putnam's Sons, 1925), hereafter cited as *Burr*. Though I have drawn from all of these and from other works in writing this sketch, I have used Parmet and Hecht, *Portrait*, as my basic guide and major source. It has provided me with a wealth of factual information and a clear direction in presenting it; the book, of course, has also led me to the primary and secondary material dealing with Burr. For all of these reasons, my debt to the authors of this important Burr biography is enormous and is, therefore, gratefully acknowledged.

2. In the following sketch, I have tried to present the facts as neutrally as possible in order to set the record straight. But because American authors make repeated use in their imaginative works of certain aspects of the Colonel's career, I have given disproportionate stress to such matters as the 1800 election, the duel, and the conspiracy.

3. In my discussion of Burr's life up to the time of the duel, I generally follow Parmet and Hecht, *Portrait*.

4. Josephine Fisher, "The Journal of Esther Burr," *New England Quarterly* 3 (1930): 315.

5. William Kent, *Memoirs and Letters of James Kent, LL.D.* (Boston: Little, Brown, and Company, 1898), p. 31.

6. C. H. Truax, "Judicial Organization and Legal Administration from 1776 to the Constitution of 1846," *History of the Bench and Bar of New York*, ed. David McAdam et al., vol. 1 (New York: New York History Company, 1897), p. 274.

7. William A. Duer, *Reminiscences of an Old Yorker* (New York: W. L. Andrews, 1867), p. 24.

8. John C. Hamilton, ed., *The Works of Alexander Hamilton*, vol. 5 (New York: J. F. Trow, 1851), p. 527, hereafter cited as *Works*.

9. Mrs. Theodosia Burr to Tapping Reeve and Sarah Burr Reeve, n.d., Park Family Papers, Yale University Library.

10. Henry Cabot Lodge, ed., *The Works of Alexander Hamilton*, 12 vols. (New York: G. P. Putnam's Sons, 1904), 10: 387.

11. Burr to Jefferson, 23 December 1800, Jefferson Papers, Library of Congress.

12. Burr to Jefferson, 12 February 1801, Jefferson Papers, Library of Congress.

13. I primarily follow Syrett and Cooke, *Interview*, in my treatment of the duel. For the discussion of events after this affair, I generally rely upon Parmet and Hecht, *Portrait*.

14. Syrett and Cooke, *Interview*, p. 133. I have printed the letter exactly as Syrett and Cooke give it. The italicized, bracketed material they have taken from a transcript in the John C. Hamilton Transcripts, owned by the Columbia University Libraries and reprinted here by permission.

15. Merrill Lindsay, "Pistols Shed Light on Famed Duel," *Smithsonian* 7, no. 8 (1976): 94–98.

16. Burr does, however, write his son-in-law on 20 July, "Several circumstances not very favorable to the deceased are suppressed [from Van Ness's amended account]; I presume, from holy reverence for the dead" (Parton, *Life*, 2: 15).

17. William Cabell Bruce, *John Randolph of Roanoke, 1773–1833*, 2nd ed., rev., 2 vols. in one (New York: G. P. Putnam's Sons, 1922), 1: 298.

18. William Plumer, *William Plumer's Memorandum of Proceedings in the United States Senate, 1803–1807*, ed. Everett Sommerville Brown (New York: Macmillan, 1923), p. 185.

19. Aaron Burr, ["Burr's Farewell Address to the Senate"], *Washington Federalist*, 13 March 1805, cited in Davis, *Memoirs*, 2: 362.

20. In my discussion of the conspiracy and of the treason trial, I generally follow Parmet and Hecht, *Portrait*.

21. Henry Adams, *History of the United States of America*, vol. 2 (New York: Charles Scribner's Sons, 1891), p. 395. This important work is hereafter referred to as *History*.

22. McCaleb in *Burr Conspiracy* and *New Light*, for example, argues that the Colonel's motives were pure; but Adams, *History*, and others take a more doubtful view.

23. McCaleb, *Burr Conspiracy*, pp. 57–58.

24. David Robertson, *Reports of the Trials of Colonel Aaron Burr*, 2 vols. (Philadelphia: Hopkins and Earle, 1808), 1: 475, hereafter referred to as *Reports*.

25. James D. Richardson, ed., *A Compilation of the Messages and Papers of the Presidents, 1789–1897*, vol. 1 (Washington, D.C.: Government Printing Office, 1896), pp. 404–05, hereafter referred to as *Compilation*.

26. Albert J. Beveridge, *The Life of John Marshall*, vol. 3 (Boston: Houghton Mifflin, 1919), p. 338, n. 2.

27. Pierre M. Irving, ed., *The Life and Letters of Washington Irving*, vol. 1 (London: Richard Bentley, 1862), pp. 158–59.

28. See Robertson, *Reports*, 2: 401–45, for the full opinion.

29. Charles Biddle, *Autobiography of Charles Biddle* (Philadelphia: E. Claxton and Company, 1883), pp. 322–23.

30. In Section 4, I generally follow Parmet and Hecht, *Portrait*; however, I also rely upon Wandell and Minnigerode, *Burr*, in my treatment of Burr's women, bastard children, and divorce, and upon Parton, *Life*, in my discussion of the Colonel's final days.

31. See Parton, *Life*, 1: 365–69. In this journal, he also wrote rather frank observations on the sexual conduct of some of the "Bucks & Bells" of the

Connecticut neighborhood (see p. 368), anticipating his later journal entries to Theodosia, written while he was in exile in Europe.

32. Wandell and Minnigerode, *Burr*, 2: 322.

33. See Charles Burdett, *The Beautiful Spy* (Philadelphia: John E. Potter and Company, 1865) and "Reminiscences," newspaper clipping, New York Public Library, reprinted in part in Samuel H. Wandell, *Aaron Burr in Literature* (1936; rpt. Port Washington, N.Y.: Kennikat Press, 1972), pp. 44–47.

34. See Parmet and Hecht, *Portrait*, pp. 333–34, for details of Burdett's parentage and history.

35. Charles Francis Adams, ed., *Memoirs of John Quincy Adams*, vol. 7 (Philadelphia: J. B. Lippincott & Co., 1875), p. 272.

36. Burdett, "Reminiscences," in Wandell, *Aaron Burr in Literature*, pp. 44–47.

37. This astonishing fact is recorded in Parmet and Hecht, *Portrait*, p. 339.

2. Catiline, Cain, Traitor, Predator, Victim _____

The Aaron Burr who emerges during and soon after each of the major historical events in which he is involved is not a complex human being but a kind of stock figure created for political purposes by the partisan press and popular poets. Thus the major image of Burr that arises after the Revolution is that of a political opportunist, a Catiline, as he moves from New York assemblyman to vice president to gubernatorial candidate. Immediately after Hamilton's death, however, the Colonel is seen primarily as a murderer, a Cain, although his Catilinian qualities still are stressed occasionally. Once he becomes enmeshed in his Western schemes, he is portrayed most often as traitor, as a villain whom ambition and desperation drive to despicable deeds. Now and then, Burr is also depicted as a sexual predator, a favorite charge of his political enemies, and, during the treason trial and after his death, occasionally as a victim of a vengeful government or of slanderous foes. The needs of the moment, then, account for the many one-dimensional, contemporaneous faces of Aaron Burr—portraits that American dramatists and writers of fiction later use or modify for their own artistic purposes.

Somewhat surprising is the fact that the Colonel's heroic efforts to carry Montgomery's body back to American lines during the siege of Quebec were not celebrated immediately and widely in the press. Instead, the newspapers concentrate upon the plan of battle, the twin attacks on the city from opposite ends by Arnold and Montgomery, and the illustrious general's death. Burr, when he is mentioned at all, is given only brief coverage. For example, an entry published in the

Pennsylvania Evening Post three weeks after the storming of the city notes: "The former [the attack upon the lower town at St. Rocks] was conducted under the immediate command of the General himself [Montgomery]; but here a most unfortunate event early took place, viz. the fall of that gallant and able commander, which no doubt damped the ardor of his troops, and was the occasion of a repulse, though not till they had passed the first barrier, and were preparing to attempt the second. . . . The officers distinguished themselves by their good conduct, and Lieut. Col. Green, Majors Bigelow and Meiggs, and Captains Oswald and Burr, are particularly mentioned as having done themselves great honor."[1] Perhaps the details of Burr's deeds had not yet reached Philadelphia—news from Canada was slow in coming in 1776—or perhaps his actions were not thought to be so remarkable as to justify extended discussion; in any case, the Colonel's heroism was not immediately championed.[2]

A different kind of wartime exploit, however, is celebrated in Edmund Clarence Stedman's "Aaron Burr's Wooing" (1887), a poem dealing with one of the Colonel's more pleasurable activities during his military service, his courtship of Theodosia Prevost.[3] Although the portrait Stedman presented is not contemporaneous, it nonetheless deserves mention because of its Revolutionary background and because of its content: the Burr depicted in the piece is a sexual predator. Early in the poem Burr's amatory habits and the current object of his attentions are made clear:

> Through the camp runs a jest, "There's no moon,
>   'twill be dark—
> 'Tis odds little Aaron will go on a spark,"—
> And the toast of the troopers is, "Pickets, lie low,
> And good luck to the Colonel and Widow Prevost!"

And, in the final stanza, Burr's sexual prowess is fully highlighted: "Where's the widow or maid with a mouth to be kist, / When Burr comes a-wooing, that long would resist?" Not surprisingly, such a portrait appears occasionally throughout the Colonel's career, usually in darker tints, and becomes a principal preoccupation of nineteenth-century imaginative writers.

An earlier poem, however, presents a more frequently used image of the Colonel—that of political opportunist. In his *Democratiad* (1795), Lemuel Hopkins satirically attacks those Democratic senators, Burr among them, who in 1795 opposed Jay's treaty with England.[4] In the manner if not with the skill of Pope, Hopkins depicts the Colonel as an ambitious, unprincipled man of intrigue, devoted solely to his own interests:

> Next in the train, the courtly Burr is seen,
> With piercing look, and ever varying mien;
> Tho' small his stature, yet his well known name,
> Shines with full splendor on the rolls of fame;
> Go search the records of intrigue, and find,
> To what debasement sinks the human mind,
> How far 'tis possible for man to go,
> Where interest sways and passions urge the blow;
> While pride and pleasures, haughtiness and scorn,
> And mad ambition in his bosom burn.
>
> [Hopkins, *The Democratiad*, ll. 153-62]

It is this view of Burr that predominates during the years just after the presidential election of 1800, when Cheetham, who would later become notorious for his political perfidy and for his virulent attack upon Paine, viciously assails the Colonel. Editor of the *American Citizen* and then Jefferson's chief popular proponent, Cheetham excoriates Burr in his paper and in a series of pamphlets. The first of these longer pieces to have wide effect is his *Narrative of the Suppression by Col. Burr, of the History of the Administration of John Adams, Late President of the United States* (1802).[5] In it, Cheetham gives several slanderous reasons for the vice president's attempt to prevent the publication of Wood's *History*:

To what then shall we ascribe the suppression? On the one hand, to a desire to conciliate the affections of most of the federalists who acted prominent parts in the late administration, and whose conduct was severely censured by Mr. Wood; and on the other, to represent in a novel but unfavourable light, in the *new history*, of which he was to furnish the materials, the character of Mr. Jefferson and that of several of his most distinguished friends. If it should be asked what end these machinations were to answer? The response is at hand. To prepare the way for that *union* with the *federalists* which there is reason to believe is now *half completed*; to sully the lustre and to tarnish the reputation of the executive. [Cheetham, *Narrative*, p. 38]

With such a purpose, it comes as no surprise that Cheetham attacks Burr's character throughout the pamphlet. Early in the piece, for example, he condemns the Colonel as wily: "There is about his actions [in suppressing Wood's work] a *cunning*, a sort of *legerdemain*, which, while it defies conclusive proof, eludes the most acute research" (Cheetham, *Narrative*, p. 9). A few pages later, he portrays the vice president as a malignant, secret, and duplicitous force that corrupts as it operates: "Versed in the art of hocus-pocus, while sitting in his state room waiting the entrance of his political tools into the anti-chamber, his mandates fly through the union and extend to its extremities. Hence his invisible spirit insinuates itself into every circle, and with its deleterious qualities corrupts whatever it touches" (Cheetham, *Narrative*, p. 11). In his call for action, Cheetham compares Burr to Catiline—a comparison to which he will return in later pieces: "It is time for 'a union of all honest' *Republicans* to take place. A few individuals, desperate in fortune, devoid of good principle, of great enterprize, and unbounded ambition, however insignificant in their origin, may, by national indifference, grow to a size which, like the memorable conspiracy of *Catiline* of old, will menace the overthrow of the empire. By timely attention and spirited exertion[,] that ruin may be averted with which the Union is in some sort now threatened" (Cheetham, *Narrative*, p. 39). Finally, in a kind of summary designed to suggest the frightful results to the nation should Burr ever become president, the editor of the *American Citizen* depicts the Colonel as the worst kind of political opportunist: "It cannot be concealed that he is a man of *desperate fortune*; bold, enterprizing, ambitious, and intriguing; thirsting for military glory and *Bonapartian* fame. A man of no fixed principle, no consistency of character, of contracted views as a politician, of boundless vanity, and listless of the public good; one who is pursuing with an 'appetite keen as death, and a hand steady as time,' projects disreputable to himself and injurious to the country" (Cheetham, *Narrative*, pp. 39-40).

Had Cheetham stopped with this pamphlet, Burr might have overcome the damage done to his reputation, but the ex-hatter continues his abuse with *A View of the Political Conduct of Aaron Burr, Esq.*,

Vice-President of the United States (1802).[6] While tracing the Colonel's career from wartime service to 1802, Cheetham depicts the vice president primarily as a Catiline, replete with the flaws that that infamous Roman possessed. Lest there be any confusion about the way in which Burr is to be portrayed, the pamphleteer makes the analogy between the Colonel and the conspirator in his introduction. Because Burr had not answered the editor's various charges, Cheetham notes that "Catiline [had] treated with disdain the denunciations of Cicero, until every avenue of retreat was cut off. I hope *America* is not destined to furnish an example of this *treasonable* pertinacity!" (Cheetham, *View*, p. 4). Cheetham then goes on to portray the faults that led him to such a harsh comparison. Burr, he believes, is corrupt, having none of the "steadiness and rectitude of principle" that public officers should possess (Cheetham, *View*, p. 6). "Cupidity," he notes as well, ". . . appears to have been an attribute of Mr. BURR from his youth upwards" (Cheetham, *View*, p. 9). And the vice president is without principle, he suggests, because he switched parties merely to satisfy his ambitions: "It was soon discovered that Mr. Burr viewed with envy the superior estimation in which the federal party held his rival General Hamilton. The same ardently aspiring spirit which governs him now, swayed him then. Like Caesar, he could not brook a superior. They were jealous rivals at the bar; but in the view of the federal party, Burr, in comparison of Hamilton, was truly a secondary character. This mortifying consideration, together with the ascendency of the Republican party . . . and the appointment of Hamilton to the office of Secretary of the Treasury in preference to himself, have always been considered as the cause of Mr. Burr's uniting himself to the Republicans" (Cheetham, *View*, p. 14). Duplicitous and self-seeking, Cheetham claims, he "always appeared intent upon playing the part of a *wily*, rather than that of an *honest*, comprehensive, and profound statesman. With the eyes of a lynx, he was more on the watch to convert incidental circumstances to his private advantage, to the furtherance of his immeasurably ambitious views, than to seize and appropriate them to the public weal" (Cheetham, *View*, p. 25). Like a snake, then, the editor notes, Burr—in his career to 1800—manifested "a convenient versatility; a species of *refined cunning*, which savours more of scholastic disingenuity, than of guileless innocence." "We perceive," he continues, "his eye steadily fixed upon the grand object òf his ambition, and his body and mind moving, as a *serpent*, heedless of the means by which he might attain it" (Cheetham, *View*, p. 34).

The Colonel's most salient fault that leads Cheetham to link the vice president with the Roman traitor, however, is his having conspired with the Federalists during the voting in the House of Representatives to place himself rather than Jefferson in the presidential chair. The fact that he did so, Cheetham declares, makes him not only a Catiline but a Benedict Arnold as well: "To obtain the chief magistracy, he *crouched*, and *fawned*, and *surrendered* himself to that party who had viewed him as a *miscreant*. He threw himself at their feet; he was heedless of the means; he was willing to do any thing, however abject, however dishonorable, however grating to the feelings of a magnanimous soul, to obtain the presidency. The following *indubitable* fact [that, while he was in New York, Burr negotiated with the heads of the Federalist party in Washington] justifies these assertions, and is sufficient of itself to induce every *honest* man, of whatever party, to frown upon and avoid him as an Arnold!" (Cheetham, *View*, p. 57). "Surely," Cheetham adds to reinforce the image, "the dissimulations of *Cataline* [sic] were never more profound, never more atrocious!" (Cheetham, *View*, p. 59). Although the editor continues with a discussion of Burr's abuses while he was vice president, the one-dimensional portrait is essentially complete at this point in the scurrilous pamphlet.

Intent upon destroying any chances Burr might have in the next presidential election, Cheetham continues his attack in a series of open letters addressed to the Colonel, which he prints in the *American Citizen* and publishes in a collected edition entitled *Nine Letters on the Subject of Aaron Burr's Political Defection, with an Appendix* (1803).[7] He makes clear his purpose and plan of development in the first letter: "That you are guilty of those acts which we have laid to your charge [conspiring with the Federalists to steal the presidency from Jefferson], we shall, in the course of these letters, notwithstanding your denial, endeavour to prove by the testimony of men respectable for their years, [for] their approved good standing in society, and for their talents. It, however, best comports with our views first to give a general historic sketch of your political conduct, and then to offer proof in contradiction to your denial" (Cheetham, *Nine Letters*,

p. 9). Restating many of the arguments he had used in his *View*, Cheetham portrays the Colonel in ways similar to those he had used before. Burr, he declares in the second letter, is a man without principle: "The first function of the Republic tempted your ambition, and, pursuing the Jusuitical [sic] maxim that the end will justify the means, you grasped at the prize before it had been awarded to you by your country (Cheetham, *Nine Letters*, p. 10). In the third letter, he accuses the vice president of utter self-interest: "Every step of your political life has been marked more by *cunning* than by *wisdom*. Instead of attaching yourself with zeal and sincerity to that party from whose bounteous hand you had received in advance the distinguished honor you enjoyed, you were wrapped in *selfishness*, and looked forward only to the accomplishment of unwarrantable designs" (Cheetham, *Nine Letters*, p. 17). And, in the fifth letter, he depicts Burr as disgustingly duplicitous: "In every step we have advanced [in tracing the Colonel's career], we have beholden you, like Proteus, transforming yourself with facility into shapes adapted to your various passions and projects" (Cheetham, *Nine Letters*, p. 24). But the major portrait is that of an unscrupulously ambitious man:

AMBITION, as we have seen, has been the spring to every political act of your life, and you have pursued it with the constancy of time and a zeal that no adversity could mitigate. In pursuit of this haunting spectre of your mind, you have not been scrupulous about the means you have used to attain the supreme object of your heart, the chief magistracy of the union. Ambition, regulated by legitimate desires, is not only laudable, but conducive to public freedom and national magnanimity. But that ambition, Sir, that seeks by art and corruption, to set at nought the *combined suffrages of the commonwealth*, to sap the foundations of the state, is more destructive than a pestilence. Of this nature is *your* AMBITION. [Cheetham, *Nine Letters*, pp. 24-25]

Burr, of course, had his defenders, notably William Peter Van Ness, who, under the pseudonym of Aristides, attempted to clear his friend from Cheetham's accusations. In *An Examination of the Various Charges Exhibited Against Aaron Burr, Esq.* (1803), Van Ness answers each of the libels, portraying the Colonel throughout as an innocent man unjustly accused by the Clintonian faction for political gain.[8] In addition, in order to reveal to the public the kind of men behind Cheetham's attacks, he digresses from his principal purpose to detail the corruption of Burr's chief opponents. Thus of DeWitt Clinton, he says: "He may justly be ranked among those, who, though destitute of sound understanding, are still rendered dangerous to society by an intrinsic baseness of character, that engenders hatred to everything good and valuable in the world; who with barbarous malignity view the prevalence of moral principles, and the extension of benevolent designs; who, foes to virtue, seek the subversion of every valuable institution, and meditate the introduction of wild and furious disorders among the supporters of public virtue" (Van Ness, *Examination*, p. 51). Such eye-for-an-eye viciousness did little to change the general opinion of the vice president, however, nor was Peter Irving's Burrite *Morning Chronicle* any more successful in removing public suspicion.

Before Cheetham's attacks, popular sentiment had been more favorable to the Colonel. During the balloting to break the tie between him and Jefferson, for example, Augustus Brevoort Woodward, the noted Epaminondas, had called for Burr's election in his address *To the Federal Members of the House of Representatives of the United States* (1801).[9] Afraid that the detestable Jefferson might become president, Woodward had offered to his fellow Federalists a patriotic Burr, a man capable of putting the public interest before partisan politics: "To minds at once enlightened and impartial; to the few who are accustomed to see consequences in their causes, and to trace the remote relations of things, the conduct of Mr. Burr, so far from appearing to proceed from party principles, may, on the contrary, be found to have resulted from a no less vigorous, and a more enlightened zeal, for his Country's welfare, than can be justly claimed by some of the uniform approvers of the measures of government" (Woodward, *Federal Members*, p. 14). And a poet calling himself Democraticus had published *The Jeffersoniad* (1801) on Inauguration Day.[10] Celebrating the triumph of Republicanism, the poem was rich in praise for both Jefferson and Burr, though the focus of the piece, as the title suggests, was upon the president. The Colonel, however, was depicted as a man of superior qualities, whom the people had chosen to run with their champion:

> But yet another chief the people want,
> And Heaven, propitious to their wishes, grant

> A man superior and of firmest mind,
> Who to the people's cause had long inclin'd:
> Him, second in the van, they quickly place,
> And then prepare to try th' important race;
> 'Twas BURR, long destin'd in the ranks to shine,
> To close the column and to form the line;
> He in the camp had num'rous toils endur'd,
> 'Till Independence was to us secur'd.
> [Democraticus, *Jeffersoniad*, ll. 181-90]

But by 1803 *The Jeffersoniad* had long been forgotten, and Epaminondas's effect had been dissipated by time and by Cheetham's accusation that Woodward wrote his essays "in Mr. Burr's *library*" (Cheetham, *View*, p. 66). Unfortunately, the image of the Colonel as political opportunist—as Catiline—now predominated.

Such a portrayal of Burr is reinforced and darkened during the New York gubernatorial election of 1804. Again the editor of the *American Citizen* leads the attack. Commenting upon a pro-Burr handbill which fallaciously suggested that the Republican members of the legislature had nominated the Colonel for governor at a recent gathering, Cheetham, on 20 March 1804, once more condemns Burr as duplicitous: "The meeting mentioned, is the one which nominated Morgan Lewis and John Broome. Aaron Burr, however, and his friends have, with an admirable dexterity, converted it into the Burrite meeting, which consisted of *sixteen persons* and who, lest they should be *discovered*, assembled slily in a *small bedroom*! . . . This meeting, which the Burrites are endeavouring by the most flagrant of falsehoods to palm upon the different counties as the one which in fact nominated Mr. Lewis and Mr. Broome, was entirely composed of the *strolling players*, who, having *secretly* nominated Mr. Burr at Albany, travelled with their machinery to Troy and other villages in the state!"[11] A few days later, on 24 March, Cheetham publishes a letter to the editor, signed "Puss in the corner," which portrays the Colonel as a Catiline: "It is well known that Mr. Burr, Vice-President of the United States, is now in this city, and daily holding caucuses to promote his own election for Governor of this state.—Every artifice is resorted to which cunning can invent, and no promises are considered too gross to be made, if only a tool can be secured."[12] And, on 26 March, he falsely depicts

Burr as a swindler who deprived Albrecht Behrens's heir of $20,000 by withholding his inheritance:

The Chronicle [the Burrite *Morning Chronicle*] intimated that Mr. Burr, or his friends, would justify the manner in which the would-be *federal* Governor pocketted the *small* sum of *twenty thousand dollars* which the German [Behrens] left at his death. No justification has yet appeared. . . . Silence on the part of Mr. Burr on this subject shall avail him nothing. *The man who cannot be trusted as the guardian of twenty thousand dollars of a person deceased, and who obtained it, if not in the teeth of the law, certainly in a manner dishonorable even to himself, is unfit to be the Governor of this highly respectable state.* He who cannot be trusted as a guardian ought not to be trusted as a Governor.[13]

As the campaign proceeds, the attacks on Burr intensify. In a letter to the editor of the *American Citizen* on 29 March, for example, an anonymous writer portrays him as derelict in his duty:

The conduct of Mr. Burr as Vice-President is alone sufficient to convince every dispassionate person of his unworthiness to fill any office. The principal duty of [the] Vice-President is to preside in the Senate of the United States, for which he gets an annual compensation of 5,000 dollars. . . . If Congress adjourn on the 27th of March as was expected, then the time of their sitting from March 1803, to March 1804, will be about five and a half months, nearly half a year: during which time Mr. Burr was not more than six weeks at his post. The residual of the time was employed in circulating scurrilous publications, intriguing for the Vice-Presidency, or electioneering for the government of this state. Here has been compensation without service with a witness.[14]

On 3 April, Cheetham yet again depicts the Colonel as a base man without principle: "He is a man of cunning, of licentious habits, of infinite vanity, of vast profusion, and of unbounded ambition. His *pecuniary* circumstances are known, and to know them is enough! His morals are lax in the extreme. His prodigality is such and his minions are so many, that he may with facility distribute among them a million of dollars a year. And yet those who know him, know he is not rich. Are the well-disposed part of society willing to see SUCH A MAN at the head of our government? Can they confide in his integrity?"[15]

Popular poets and songwriters also lend their meager talents to the attack. One anonymous rhymester, for example, playing upon the story in Exodus of the Jews' worship of the golden calf, depicts Burr on 20 March as the traitorously ambitious, biblical Aaron, who led God's chosen people into idolatry while Moses (i.e., Jefferson) was on the mountain:

Aaron appear'd, proud to be rear'd
To such a lofty station [second to Moses];
Great feats at first, did from him b[urst,]
Which pleas'd the mighty nation.

At last grown proud, he vaunted loud,
And brim full of ambition;
Oh! horrid thought! this Aaron [sought]
To sow around sedition.

Moses away, in Mount did pray,
While Aaron left behind,
To gain applause, forgot his laws,
And shew'd a treach'rous mind.[16]

And an election songwriter adds a new detail to the usual portrait of the Colonel by depicting him as a man rejected by his own party.[17]

By far the most scurrilous charge focuses upon Burr's sexuality. For instance, in one of Cheetham's most imaginative and most slanderous pieces—the Burrite Creed (30 March 1804)—the Republican editor depicts the Colonel as a thoroughly despicable creature whose sexual depravity, among other faults, is infamous. Thus a true follower of Aaron Burr believes, the creed proclaims, "that fornication and adultery are not crimes; and that any unmarried man or widower, before or after he is governor of the state, has a right to keep a seraglio, or make appointments at the Manhattan Bath, or be a Solomon with three hundred wives and concubines, if he pleases."[18] Even more vicious, however, is a campaign poster that portrays Burr as so depraved that he did not protect the dying Theodosia from the insults of a notable whore.[19] But it is the image of Burr as sexual plunderer, a portrait Cheetham reinforces by reprinting a scandalous handbill the Federalists had used in the previous presidential election, that had perhaps the most potent effect. Entitled simply "AARON BURR!," the handbill boldly proclaimed:

His ABANDONED PROFLIGACY, and the NUMEROUS UNHAPPY WRETCHES who have fallen VICTIMS to this accomplished and but too successful DEBAUCHEE, have indeed long been known to those whom similar habits of vice, or the amiable offices of humanity have led to the wretched haunts of female prostitution—but it is time to draw aside the curtain in which he has thus far been permitted to conceal himself by the forbearance of his enemies, by the anxious interference of his friends, and much more by his own crafty contrivances and unbounded prodigality.

· ·

I do not mean to tell you of the late celebrated courtezan N—, nor U—, nor S—, nor of half a dozen more of whom first his INTRIGUES have RUINED, and his SATIATED BRUTALITY has afterwards thrown on the town, the prey of disease, of infamy, and wretchedness—It is to a more recent act, that I call your attention, and I hope it will create in every heart, the same abhorrence with which mine is filled.

When Mr. Burr last went to the city of Washington about two months [ago] to take the oath of office, and his seat in the august Senate of the United States, he SEDUCED the daughter of a respectable tradesman there, and had the cruelty to persuade her to forsake her native town, her friends and family, and to follow him to New-York. She did so—and she is now IN KEEPING in Partition-street.[20]

Burr's minions, of course, again support him. One of them, for example, writes an election song in which he presents the Colonel as a patriotic and virtuous man.[21] Another composes a handbill, published on 12 March, which lists the various reasons why the electorate should vote for the Colonel. Here, of course, Burr is depicted as a noble man—a portrait made especially apparent in the tenth item: he is "Gallant and intrepid in war, amiable in private life, affable in his deportment, tempered with dignity, wisdom and an habitual prudence; persuasive in argument without insulting the understanding of his adversary; singularly active and adroit in the dispatch of business; sagacious in the choice of talents for the execution of office; freed from the bias of narrow party distinctions, destructive of public benefit.[22] And, as always, the *Morning Chronicle* supports Burr and attempts to vindicate him from charges of a hostile press. Though such efforts did help him to carry the city by a slim one hundred votes, the forces of Cheetham and Clinton gave Lewis an eight-thousand-vote victory overall. Of course, there had also been Hamilton.

Immediately after the duel, though the Catilinian elements of the portrait are still occasionally emphasized, the primary image is that of Burr as a cold-hearted murderer, who with cool deliberation brings Hamilton down, a Cain, who kills his brother and is sent, guilt-plagued, into exile. Perhaps those who make the connection between the Colonel and the biblical slayer see Burr and Hamilton as brothers because of the similarity of their careers: both distinguish themselves in the Revolutionary War, both become dominant forces in New York politics, and both rise to high national office. Or perhaps they hope to enhance the horror of Burr's crime by linking him with the proto-typical murderer. Whatever the case, the *American Citizen*, for example, is quick to picture the monster: "Wrap[ped] up in himself—to appease his resentment, to gratify his ambition, he is capable of wading through the blood of his fellow citizens and of laughing at the lamentations of widows and orphans."[23] The newspapers' favorite charge, however, is that the Colonel is guilty of "predetermined hostility," a phrase that echoes through the editorials for a month after Hamilton's death. "That Col. Burr's conduct was the result of *predetermined hostility*[,]" Cheetham delares on 30 July 1804, "of a system projected by his adherents and approved by himself, is to me as clear as the light of heaven."[24] Usually this accusation is made as the various editors review the duel correspondence. Again the *American Citizen* is typical: "If additional facts were necessary to evince that GENERAL HAMILTON'S fall is the inevitable effect of *predetermined hostility*, of combinations unprecedented in their form and for purposes unequalled in the annals of individual calamity, we are abundantly furnished with them in the gross yet seemingly subtle letters of him whose cruel hand has infested sorrow into every heart and cast an awful gloom over the dawning hopes of a hapless family."[25]

A variation on this portrait of cold-bloodedness comes in the accusation that Burr gives sanction to a society of duellists, whose purpose is to murder the Colonel's political enemies:

Besides, GENERAL HAMILTON, although, perhaps, the most formidable opponent, was not the only one whose *death* was meditated by Mr. Burr and those with whom he confidentially associated. They avowed their intention to accomplish, if possible, by acts of desperation, by spilling the blood of their fellow citizens, those, in their opinion, desirable objects which by other means they could not attain. For some time previous to the late election, from twelve to fifteen of these bloody villains assembled together in the night, and, under injunctions of secrecy and pledges of mutual support, planned the diabolical work and selected for destruction those who were viewed as the most formidable obstacles in the way of Mr. Burr's designs. In one word, it was their determination to fight their way through an host of opposition which could not, in their opinion, be subdued without *blood*! . . . The twelve or fifteen mentioned were the *duellists* systematically organized into a company with the approbation, if not under the eye of Mr. Burr. GENERAL HAMILTON, however, was to be the first victim.[26]

And the various papers add to this slanderous depiction by publishing reports that Burr had practiced his marksmanship for three months before the duel, that he and Van Ness had expressed "mutual congratulations" when they returned to the shore after the affair, and that the Colonel had apologized to his second for not hitting Hamilton in the heart.

The principal portrait in the papers, however, is that of Burr as murderer, as Cain. In an open letter to the Colonel on 26 July, for instance, an anonymous "CITIZEN," forecasting what the next few months will bring, makes the link between the biblical fratricide and Hamilton's slayer: "You may indeed continue to be Vice-President till next March, when your political career will terminate, and a new scene begin. Till that time you may carry a tolerable countenance, unless the Lord should put a mark on you, as he did upon one of old, which you have great reason to fear."[27] Later in the letter, the writer also points to Burr's fate as a Cain-like exile: "Peace has taken an eternal farewell of your breast. You will (if God spares your life) hereafter wander from place to place to get rid of your distress . . . yet you will find it to be a constant companion wherever you go" (*American Citizen*, p. 2). And, finally, with the story of brotherly enmity clearly in mind, he asks: "[Were] it possible for them [Burr's ancestors] to look down from the realms of bliss and behold their son, what would they say? O? Aaron, Aaron, where art thou, and what hast thou done? Hast thou shed thy brother[']s blood?" (*American Citizen*, p. 2). William Coleman, editor of the Federalist *New York Evening Post*, also makes this same connection between Burr and Cain on 3 August in the last article of his series devoted to the duel. However, in a summary of sorts, he first depicts all of the Catilinian elements in the Colonel's portrait:

[B]ehold his [Hamilton's] adversary—without a wife, without children, with scarcely a tie of kindred, with a few adherents indeed, but men feeling themselves bound to him by far other sentiments than those which constituted the alliance between a Hamilton and those who loved him—this isolated being, whose heart never palpitated with any passion but what springs from systematic selfishness; dead to all pleasure and all enjoyment but what is connected with the wish of personal aggrandizement; a man whose bosom was never moved by pity, at the cries of distress, nor enlivened by participating in the pleasures of the innocently happy; whose affections are all concentrated in an unprincipled ambition; whose exquisite hypocrisy can assume all forms and affect every virtue; whose glossy duplicity can impose equally on the unsuspecting and on the incredulous; who has long since, as it were, substituted an *artificial* man, in place of that which nature made; so that neither compassion nor remorse should ever be permitted to usurp even a momentary sway in his breast to turn him from his settled purposes.[28]

Then, near the end of the editorial, comes the condemnation and the biblical comparison: "We therefore do not scruple to pronounce that ALEXANDER HAMILTON *was willfully and maliciously* MURDERED *by the hand of* AARON BURR, *Vice President of the United States.* He is now an exile from the State; but wheresoever he flies, unless he can escape from himself, the *voice of a brother's blood will cry aloud to the Almighty from the ground*" (Coleman, *New York Evening Post*, p. 2).

Similar images emerge from the pamphlets and sermons occasioned by the duel. In *A Letter to Aaron Burr* (1804), for example, which provides "an investigation of the origin, a definition of the nature, and a review of the history of duels" in order to condemn the barbaric practice, William Ladd, calling himself Philanthropos, makes perhaps the most complete linking of Burr and his biblical archetype.[29] Addressing the vice president directly, Ladd notes: "The history of the murder of Abel by his unnatural, inhuman, cruel brother Cain, you doubtless, have read. Monstrous crime! Heavy the doom of the perpetrator! Hear it from the mouth of the dread judge—*The voice of thy brother's blood cryeth unto me from the ground. And now art thou cursed from the earth, which hath opened her mouth to receive thy brother's blood from thy hand. When thou tillest the ground, it shall not henceforth yield unto thee her strength. A fugitive and a vagabond shalt thou be in the earth*" (Ladd, *A Letter*, pp. 16-17). And, in his celebrated *Discourse Delivered in the North Dutch Church* (1804), a sermon attacking the practice of duelling and glorifying Hamilton in the process, Eliphalet Nott, soon to be president of Union College, depicts Burr by implication as a murderer.[30] Detailing the exact nature of the duellist's and therefore the Colonel's deed, the moralistic Nott, whose homilies on character formation and lectures on the dangers of intemperance would later become famous, here declares: "I am sensible that in a licentious age, and when laws are made to yield to the vices of those who move in the *higher circles*, this crime is called by I know not what mild and accommodating name. But before these altars; in this house of GOD, what is it? It is MURDER—*deliberate, aggravated* MURDER" (Nott, *A Discourse*, pp. 10-11).

In *The Danger of Ambition Considered* (1804), another sermon prompted by Hamilton's death, Hezekiah N. Woodruff points to the vice president's ambitious and cold-blooded nature.[31] Calling his listeners to sorrow, the prelate portrays by indirection a now familiar Burr: "Here [in the manner of Hamilton's death] we may lament the sad effects of growing ambition. To what a fatal and alarming height has it risen! What security have we for life, with all our boasted civil and religious liberty, when, with impunity, men cooly [sic] may revenge their own imaginary wrongs?" (Woodruff, *Danger of Ambition*, p. 18). And, in explaining why the challenger in a duel frequently survives, Woodruff suggests again the Colonel's cold-hearted deliberateness: "Trace the history of the single combat, and you will generally find the challenger successful.—You will say this is an evidence of his innocence. I tell you NO: It is an evidence that his heart is steeled with murderous intentions—With a premeditated plan, and with a fixed design, he becomes cool and deliberate. With a heart grown hard in murderous designs, with steady hand he dexterously aims the fatal blow" (Woodruff, *Danger of Ambition*, p. 19). But perhaps the most effective address in prejudicing the people against Burr is J. M. Mason's *Oration* (1804).[32] Primarily a hymn of praise for Hamilton, the address does, however, depict Burr as an ambitious, vengeful murderer. In a series of rhetorical questions, calling for an end to the horrible practice of duelling, Mason indirectly creates the damning portrait:

Ah! what avails it to a distracted nation that HAMILTON was murdered for a punctilio of honour? My flesh shivers! Is this, indeed, our state of society? Are transcendent worth and talent to be a capital indictment before the tribunal of ambition? Is the Angel of Death to record, for sanguinary retribution, every word which the collision of political opinion may extort from a political man? Are integrity and candour to be at the mercy of the assassin? And systematic crime to trample under foot, or smite into the grave, all that is yet venerable in our humbled land? My countrymen, the land is defiled with blood unrighteously shed. [Mason, *Oration*, p. 28]

Like the pamphleteers and sermonizers, the popular poets frequently portray a despicable Burr. Americanus, for instance, just two days after the great Federalist's death, presents a familiar image of the Colonel. Hamilton, he notes, was "Slain by a hand who ne'er took honest aim, / Stung by disappointment, rage and shame."[33] He continues: "A Cat'line sheds an upright Patriot's blood, / Who always acted for his country's good. / Columbia mourns, while faction may rejoice, / That virtue's fallen by the hand of vice." A "Young Lady of Baltimore," in a longer poem condemning the practice of duelling, detailing the events following Hamilton's death, and praising the great leader by tracing his glorious deeds from the Revolution to the present, pauses to depict and to curse the furious, vengeful fiend who killed "the glory of the age": "May dark oblivion blast the monster's name / To rank or fortune, whatso'er his claim, / Whose keen revenge, or whose relentless rage, / The sword must glut, and human blood assuage."[34] In his rather heavily footnoted *Hamiltoniad* (1804), a poem revealing the effects of the discord Hamilton's death unleashed, Joseph R. Hopkins portrays a base, raging, and ungrateful Burr:

> AND *Thou*! contemner of thy country's laws,
> *Pretended Patriot* in fair Freedom's cause;
> Thou furious Mortal, whose unhallow'd ball,
> Caus'd this *Great Man* with Honor's [sic] crown'd to fall.
> Basely indeed hast thou repaid that *Vote*!
> Which made thee eminent, and gave thee note.
>
> .   .   .   .

Ungrateful man! thy country's sore disgrace,
Doth not confusion beam upon thy face?
. . . .

See, see thy shame takes wing and upward flies,
Tainting the aether of yon azure skies.[35]

The poem's notes, which are an important part of the *Hamilton-iad*, also depict an unfavorable image of Burr. For example, the reference to the phrase "furious Mortal," just cited, pictures the vice president as a fury-torn miscreant:

There is one circumstance . . . which I have purposely omitted in the poem, and which occasioned the above expression, that in justice to myself I shall mention—It is this—That B-rr after having mortally wounded his supposed antagonist, (for I cannot believe that either Mr. B-rr, or the seconds on either side, knew of his determination not to fire) walked towards him, while on the ground weltering in his blood, and with a countenance in which anger was depicted, asked Hamilton, if he was satisfied? the latter replying that he was mortally wounded, he [Burr] turned upon his heel and left the ground, apparently unappeased—I shall make no comments—reader 'tis thine to think and likewise to reflect. (Hopkins, *Hamiltoniad*, p. 27)

Such a portrait, of course, suggests the Federalist bias pervading the piece.

But the most frequent image of Burr in popular verse is that of heartless killer. One of the anonymous poets, for example, wondering why God did not punish the Colonel immediately, condemns him on 18 July as an unfeeling murderer, whose act springs from disappointment and envy:

For what wise purpose did the Almighty stay
His avenging rod on that eventful day?
Why struck he not the m - - - - - - r to the ground,
Who could with coolness aim so deep a wound?
Who could with sullen disappointment's gloom
Plot for his country so reverse a doom,
And with malignant envy's direful hand
Deluge in tears Columbia's happy land.[36]

Reflecting her feelings in "On the Death of General Hamilton" (1804), a "Lady" also portrays the vice president as a man of cold deliberateness:

> But ruthless B—r the fatal deed was thine!
> Could nothing but his blood appease thy rage?
> His blood proclaim thee, therefore, to the age.
> Unmask the safe, black monument of state,
> Unprecedently deliberate.[37]

Patrioticus, expressing every upright citizen's anger at Burr's crime in "To the Memory of Gen. Hamilton" (1804), presents a similar image: "'Vengeance lights each *honest* feature, / 'Gainst the dark, malignant hand, / Who *coldly* shot a fellow creature, / A man belov'd by all our land.'"[38] And, with heavy use of the apostrophe, the anonymous "On the Murder of Hamilton: A Scotch Ballad" (1804) also depicts a cold-hearted slayer:

> Oh! wo betide ye, Aaron Burr!
>   May mickle curse upo' ye fa'!
> Ye've kill'd as brave a gentleman
>   As e'er liv'd in America.
>
> Wi' bloody mind ye ca'd him out,
>   Wi' practic'd e'e on him did draw,
> And wi' deliberate, murderous aim,
>   Ye kill'd the flower of America.[39]

The *Morning Chronicle*, of course, again supports Burr. Five days after the duel, Peter Irving assures his readers that the vice president was justified in the action he took: "While we consider these details [of the duel] imperiously demanded by the numerous and injurious reports naturally consequent to an event of this nature; and while we deeply regret the melancholy termination of this unfortunate contest; we have also the most satisfactory assurances, that when a fair and candid statement is laid before the public, the conduct of Col. Burr will be justified by every disinterested and unprejudiced man, who considers the honor of a gentleman under the protection of his own arm."[40] Though the promised defense comes in a series of articles written by a supporter calling himself Vindex, its effect is minimal. The image of Burr as Cain sticks.

During and immediately after the indictment hearings and the Richmond trial, the primary portrait of the Colonel is, of course, that of traitor. His guilt is so widely assumed that he and his treason become the subject of a popular toast: "Aaron Burr, the man who once received the confidence of a free people—May his treachery to his country exalt him to the scaffold, and hemp be his escort to the republick of dust and ashes."[41] Even before the grand jury finishes its deliberations to determine whether a trial is necessary, the newspapers prejudge him. The *Aurora General Advertiser*, for example, notes in mid-June 1807: "With such a mass of evidence as is before them, the public cannot view Burr as innocent—the oaths, of as good men as there are in the union, have been published in the news-papers of all parties, and until Burr shall be declared guiltless by the due course of law, the suspicions of the people cannot and will not be removed."[42] Later that same month, Duane, the *Aurora*'s editor, gives another reason for believing the Colonel a traitor: "Burr and his counsel exhibit the very best evidence of their inability to make a good defence—their objections and their remarks are not those of conscious innocence: guilt alone would shelter itself under the cover of petty forms and precedents, neither applicable nor just. . . . All the equivocation and subterfuge, we notice, is that of a consciously guilty individual—the boldness of innocence is no where to be remarked, every syllable breathes suspicion and fear."[43] About this same time, Burr's nemesis, James Cheetham, also depicts the Colonel as guilty: "Delicacy has hitherto restrained me from expressing my opinion on the proceedings of the court, but I cannot help saying that to me the *propositions* of Mr. Burr appear unparalleled for assurance:— . . . The propositions portray guilt, but of what nature or degree the criminal's country must decide."[44]

During the treason trial itself, there is no improvement in the way Burr is seen. If anything, the portrait is darkened when, for example, the newspapers seize upon a melodramatic incident to provide further proof that Burr is a traitor. Thus, when the servant of one of the prosecution's witnesses tries to poison his master (a Mr. Duncan) on the promise that, if he is successful, he will receive his freedom and seven hundred dollars, the press speculates that Burr's guilt prompted him to order the attempted murder. The *American Citizen*, for instance, has only the slightest hesitancy on 25 September 1807 in suggesting Burr as the evil force behind the plot: "Having no testimony in relation to the 'poisoning scene' . . . we cannot at this distance determine by whom the slave of Mr. Duncan was instigated to take away the life of his master, but if Burr deemed it essential to the saving of his own neck that the bowl should be administered, on whom in the judgment of the reader would the direction of the poisoning hand fall?"[45] Shortly after the trial is concluded, a "PORTRAIT OF AARON BURR" appearing in the *Richmond Enquirer* makes clear that, though the Colonel was technically acquitted, the popular mind still pictures him a traitor:

A. Burr must have had three objects in view:
   To separate the Western from the eastern states.
   To invade Mexico, or
   To effect a temporary settlement on the Ouachita [Washita].
   The first was the foremost in his hopes and first in the period of its attempted accomplishment. The second was but to turn into a new course the very same means which he had collected, and the very passions which he should have excited for the attainment of the first. And the last, was to have been at once the asylum of his despairing ambition, and the germ of new schemes, where it[,] "hush'd in grim repose[,] expects its evening's prey."
   Take the principal points of the evidence as they have been disclosed during this examination, and see how they bear us out in these conclusions.[46]

Burr, of course, does have some backing during the affair. A political oddity of sorts occurs when several Federalist sheets, which after Hamilton's death had called for blood, take up his cause. For them, the Colonel becomes a convenient weapon to use against a tyrannical Republican administration. Hence, the *United States' Gazette*, for example, depicts Burr on 19 August as a victim of injustice:

Nothing can show in a stronger light the improper and flagitious conduct of the government, and the government prints, in the condemnation of col. Burr, previous to the trial, than the proceedings of the court which we are now detailing [in another part of the paper]. Last winter Mr. Jefferson, in an official document which has gone upon record, and must be handed down to posterity as a solemn act of the government, pronounced that the guilt of colonel Burr *was placed* BEYOND A DOUBT. This declaration was repeated, amplified and illustrated time after time in all Mr. Jefferson's Intelligencers, Auroras, Chronicles, Citizens *et id genus omne*. After hunting the man down in this manner for several months this same government order[s] him to be put upon his trial that it may be ascertained whether his guilt can be *placed beyond a doubt*.[47]

But such an image pales beside the darker portrait of Burr as traitor, which becomes inextricably associated with his name.

Twenty-nine years after his trial for treason, when Burr dies, there is again a rekindling of interest in him in the press. Some papers, of course, are still condemnatory. The *New York Evening Post*, for example, holding to its earlier view, depicts Burr on 19 September 1836 as an evil man:

When we read of "admiration for his greatness," "respect for his memory," and "condolence for his loss," we are tempted to ask ourselves if the community have ceased to discriminate between the good and the bad actions of men. The truth is, nobody is to be condoled with for his loss, no respect is entertained for the memory of one so profligate in private and publick life, and though Colonel Burr was a man of acute and active mind, he did not rise to the measure of intellectual greatness, as he certainly was at a deplorable distance from moral greatness.[48]

And the *United States' Gazette*, reversing itself, agrees, though with a note of sadness: "Few men have occupied more of public attention than Mr. Burr—few men of his rank and talents, have so bitterly drunk of the chalice which their own wickedness poisoned."[49]

But others are willing to look for the good. The *New York Star* notes on 14 September: "Colonel Burr occupied a large span in the history of this country. He was a man of extraordinary talents, of undoubted courage, and his services during the war of the Revolution were great and varied."[50] And the *New York Courier and Enquirer* is also celebratory:

He was burried [sic] in the college burying place [at Princeton], near the tombs of his ancestors, in his native state, under the superintendence of the fathers of that seat of learning, where the budding of his mighty mind first displayed itself—where it was matured and cultivated, and where the foundation was laid for those intellectual endowments, which he afterwards exhibited on the great theatre of life. He has shed a halo of literary glory around Nassau Hall. . . . In this—her last act of respect for his memory—she has repaid those kind feelings in which he indulged during a long life; and heartless must be the friend of the deceased who remembers not with gratitude this testimonial of regard for the giant mind of him who must fill a large space in the history of his country. Peace to his manes.[51]

Unlike the newspaper accounts, which are plentiful, little of the verse occasioned by Burr's death remains, if in fact there was much to begin with. One poem that is extant, however, has special relevance. Written by Mrs. Joshua Webb, who took care of Burr during his last year, "To One Whom the World Reviled" (1836) depicts the Colonel as a generous man, unjustly maligned:

> To thee no widow told her woes
>   And found them unredressed;
> To thee no shivering orphan came
>   But found a home and rest:
> And many—would they truth reveal—
>   Have on thy bounty fed,
> Who, when thine hour of sorrow came,
>   The van of slander led.[52]

Not surprisingly, perhaps, the sympathy Mrs. Webb expresses becomes a standard element in later poems. Frank Lee Benedict's "Aaron Burr," for example, calls in 1860 for a new treatment of the Colonel: "Give his faults to the Past—leave his soul to his God."[53] Though the poet recognizes Burr's guilt, he nonetheless pities the Colonel for the desolation and opprobrium that followed him even beyond the grave. Thus, Benedict depicts Burr in part as a kind of victim:

> The world's bitter scorn hath so heavily lain,
>   And cast down its night on his desolate tomb—
> At least let the broad-visioned Present refrain,
>   Nor scatter the ashes that lie in the gloom.
>
> The spirit of vengeance hath followed the dead,
>   And deepened the shadows that slander hath cast;
> Ah! sweep back the mists which have shrouded his bed;
>   That the starlight may fall on his bosom at last.

In the early years of the twentieth century, sympathy contributes to an exoneration of Burr. Thus, in his "Colonel Aaron Burr" (1903),

Marion Laird Law portrays his subject as an innocent and noble man, victimized by jealousy and slander:

> And in the pursuit of his trusted ways
>   No taint of sin had made his record dim.
>
> Till in the shadow of publicity
>   A traitor's whisper found an echo there—
> And those who for his place had jealousy
>   Helped swell the echo till it filled the air.
>   · · · · · · · · · · · · · · · ·
> And time shall prove that Colonel Aaron Burr
>   Was guiltless of the treachery they claim—
> That courage, truth and valor were
>   The attributes concentred in his name.[54]

That same year, John H. Farrell calls for a restoration of Burr's reputation in "A Plea."[55] Seeing the Colonel as an innocent victim, he asks: "O, men of conscience, men of state, / Why stand aloof, or hesitate? / A wrong was done, continued in, / Do you condemn or praise the sin?" Then, vigorously, he declares: " 'Tis not your mercy, I ask more, / In justice do his name restore." But the poems of Benedict, Law, and Farrell are later pieces; perhaps Mrs. Webb's is more typical of the immediate response to Burr's death.

In any case, her sympathetic portrait of the Colonel is little more accurate than the harsher delineations that precede it; from the moment Burr enters public life, he is depicted in ways that distort reality. The primary images associated with him—Catiline, Cain, Traitor, Predator, Victim—oversimplify the aspects of his character and life that give rise to them, although there is enough truth in the representations to explain in part why they continue to haunt his name. Repeated again and again, these distortions soon harden into legend and then act to modify our historical perception of important events and men. Of course, our dramatists and writers of fiction pick up these images, and their use of them gives the depictions an added imaginative power that serves to solidify further the hold they have upon our popular conceptions. But there are other elements at work, elements involving our deepest societal fears and, therefore, because of the way our psyches work, not immediately apparent. These emerge from a discussion of the plays, novels, and stories examined in succeeding chapters.

Notes

1. Benjamin Towne, ["The Siege of Quebec"], *Pennsylvania 'Evening Post*, 23 January 1776, p. 3. Wherever it is likely, I have assumed that the editors or, in some cases, the publishers of the various newspapers cited throughout wrote the editorials from which I quote. Since these pieces are unsigned, however, absolute certainty is impossible. In addition, though the title of the same paper may vary somewhat over the years, I have used a standard title throughout.

2. Possibly such broadsides as "Two Songs on the Brave General Montgomery, and Others, Who Fell within the Walls of Quebec, Dec. 31, 1775" (n.p.: Danvers 1776), depict Burr as a hero, but I have been unable to secure copies of them. Brackenridge, of course, was to celebrate the Colonel a year later in his famous play. See Chap. 3 for a discussion of that work.

3. Edmund Clarence Stedman, "Aaron Burr's Wooing," *Harper's New Monthly Magazine* 75 (1887): 666–67.

4. Lemuel Hopkins, *The Democratiad: A Poem in Retaliation for the* Philadelphia Jockey Club (Philadelphia: Thomas Bradford, 1795).

5. James Cheetham, *Narrative of the Suppression by Col. Burr, of the History of the Administration of John Adams, Late President of the United States*, 2nd ed., rev. and corrected (New York: Denniston & Cheetham, 1802).

6. James Cheetham, *A View of the Political Conduct of Aaron Burr, Esq., Vice-President of the United States* (New York: Denniston & Cheetham, 1802).

7. James Cheetham, *Nine Letters on the Subject of Aaron Burr's Political Defection, with an Appendix* (New York: Denniston & Cheetham, 1803).

8. Aristides [William Peter Van Ness], *An Examination of the Various Charges Exhibited Against Aaron Burr, Esq. Vice-President of the United States; and a Development of the Characters and Views of His Political Opponents* (New York: Ward and Gould, 1803).

9. Epaminondas [Augustus Brevoort Woodward], *To the Federal Members of the House of Representatives of the United States* (New York: Hopkins for Lang, 1801).

10. *The Jeffersoniad; or, An Echo to the Groans of an Expiring Faction* (Fredericktown, Md.: Bartgis, 1801).

11. James Cheetham, "A Good Joke," *American Citizen*, 20 March 1804, p. 2.

12. "Correspondence," *American Citizen*, 24 March 1804, p. 2.

13. James Cheetham, ["Conduct of Aaron Burr"], *American Citizen*, 26 March 1804, p. 2.

14. "Communication," *American Citizen*, 29 March 1804, p. 2.

15. James Cheetham, ["Man without Principle"], *American Citizen*, 3 April 1804, p. 2.

16. "A Fragment," *American Citizen*, 20 March 1804, p. 2.

17. "Republicans Won't Let Him Rule O'er the Nation," *New York Evening Post*, 3 April 1804, p. 2.

18. James Cheetham, "The Creed," *American Citizen*, 30 March 1804, p. 2.

19. Campaign poster, Burr-Lewis, 1804, New York Public Library.

20. "Aaron Burr!," *American Citizen*, 28 April 1804, p. 2.

21. "Rise! Rise Columbians, Make Your Stand," Broadside, New York Public Library.

22. "Hand-Bill," *American Citizen*, 12 March 1804, p. 2.

23. James Cheetham, "General Hamilton's Death," *American Citizen*, 21 July 1804, p. 2.

24. James Cheetham, "*Same subject continued* [General Hamilton's Death]," *American Citizen*, 30 July 1804, p. 2.

25. James Cheetham, "General Hamilton's Death," *American Citizen*, 27 July 1804, p. 2.

26. James Cheetham, "General Hamilton's Death," *American Citizen*, 21 July 1804, p. 2.

27. "To Aaron Burr, Vice-President of the United States," *American Citizen*, 26 July 1804, p. 2.

28. William Coleman, ["Burr's Conspiracy to Kill Hamilton"], *New York Evening Post*, 3 August 1804, p. 2.

29. Philanthropos [William Ladd], *A Letter to Aaron Burr* (New York: John Low, William Barlas, and John Reid, 1804), p. 4.

30. Eliphalet Nott, *A Discourse Delivered in the North Dutch Church* (Albany: Charles R. and George Webster, 1804).

31. Hezekiah N. Woodruff, *The Danger of Ambition Considered, in a Sermon, Preached at Scipio, N.Y.* (Albany: Charles R. and George Webster, 1804).

32. J[ohn] M[itchell] Mason, *An Oration, Commemorative of the Late Major-General Alexander Hamilton* (New York: Hopkins and Seymour, 1804). Samuel H. Wandell, *Aaron Burr in Literature* (1936; rpt. Port

Washington, N.Y.: Kennikat Press, 1972), p. 162, notes the wide effect of this address.

33. "Communication ['Hamilton's Death']," *American Citizen*, 14 July 1804, p. 3.

34. *A Poem on the Death of Genl. Alexander Hamilton* (Baltimore, Md.: Wane & Murphy, n.d.), pp. 5–6.

35. Joseph R. Hopkins, *Hamiltoniad: or, The Effects of Discord* (Philadelphia: D. Hogan, 1804), pp. 27–28.

36. ["The Death of Hamilton"], *American Citizen*, 18 July 1804, p. 2.

37. "On the Death of General Hamilton," *American Citizen*, 4 August 1804, p. 3.

38. "To the Memory of Gen. Hamilton," *American Citizen*, 8 August 1804, p. 3.

39. "On the Murder of Hamilton: A Scotch Ballad," from *The Western Telegraph*, reprinted in Wandell, *Aaron Burr in Literature*, p. 120.

40. Peter Irving, ["Burr Justified"], *Morning Chronicle*, 16 July 1804, reprinted in the *New York Evening Post*, 17 July 1804, p. 3.

41. See Luther Martin's letter of 23 July 1807 published in the *Baltimore Federal Gazette* and reprinted in the *United States' Gazette*, 31 July 1807, pp. 2–3.

42. William Duane, ["The Persecution of Burr"], *Aurora General Advertiser*, 12 June 1807, p. 2.

43. William Duane, ["Proceedings of Burr's Case"], *Aurora General Advertiser*, 23 June 1807, p. 2.

44. James Cheetham, "Mr. Burr's Trial," *American Citizen*, 20 June 1807, p. 2.

45. James Cheetham, "Burr and Wilkinson," *American Citizen*, 25 September 1807, p. 2.

46. "Portrait of Aaron Burr," *Richmond Enquirer*, reprinted in the *National Intelligencer & Washington Advertiser*, 4 November 1807, p. 2. The author of this piece misquotes a line of Thomas Gray's "The Bard": "That, hush'd in grim repose, expects his evening-prey" (l.76).

47. Enos Bronson, ["Burr Victimized"], *United States' Gazette*, 19 August 1807, p. 3.

48. William Cullen Bryant, "Funeral of Aaron Burr," *New York Evening Post*, 19 September 1836, p. 2.

49. Joseph R. Chandler, "Aaron Burr," *United States' Gazette*, 16 September 1836, p. 2.

50. ["Burr's Death"], *New York Star*, 14 September 1836, reprinted in the *Richmond Enquirer*, 20 September 1836, p. 2.

51. "Funeral of Col. Burr," *New York Courier and Enquirer*, reprinted in the *United States' Gazette*, 20 September 1836, p. 2.

52. Mrs. Joshua Webb, "To One Whom the World Reviled," reprinted in *The Life and Times of Aaron Burr*, by James Parton, enlarged ed., vol. 2 (Boston: Ticknor and Fields, 1867), p. 333.

53. Frank Lee Benedict, "Aaron Burr," in *The Rivals: A Tale of the Times of Aaron Burr and Alexander Hamilton*, by Jeremiah Clemens (Philadelphia: J. B. Lippincott & Co., 1860), p. xi.

54. Marion Laird Law, "Colonel Aaron Burr," in *The Aaron Burr Memorial*, ed. Grand Camp of the Aaron Burr Legion (Boston: Mount Vernon Book & Music Co., 1903), p. 1.

55. John H. Farrell, "A Plea," in *The Aaron Burr Memorial*, ed. Grand Camp of the Aaron Burr Legion, p. 21.

3. A Man For All Seasons _____

Although Burr's life seems in essence a subject for classical tragedy—a man of noble ancestry becomes a hero in a war that establishes his country's independence, rises to the second highest office in the land, then through his own deeds brings himself to grief—American dramatists often choose the less rule-bound form of historical drama. Some try to follow events accurately, even going so far as to weave Burr's recorded remarks into their works; others shape history according to their personal biases or dramatic needs. Sometimes in verse but more often in prose, American playwrights tend to focus on several major aspects of the Colonel's life: the Revolutionary War years, the Burr-Hamilton relationship, especially its culmination in the duel, and the conspiracy. Some, however, take a broader view and recount Burr's life from early to late. Whatever the approach, the Colonel's story is a good one, seemingly made for the theater. Yet most of the works that treat it are undistinguished, and a number remain unpublished. Perhaps their lack of appeal results in part from the one-dimensional figure who often appears in them; perhaps it springs from their authors' conspicuous inabilities. In any case, spanning, as they do, the three centuries of our national existence and ranging from jingoistic Revolutionary drama to contemporary revisionism in stage dress, these plays depict Aaron Burr in a variety of ways. He becomes in the American theater a fascinating preoccupation.[1]

The first to portray Burr in drama is Hugh Henry Brackenridge, whose black verse tragedy *The Death of General Montgomery at the Siege of Quebec* (1777) was written during the War for Independence.[2] Designed to engender patriotic fervor, the play was "intended for the private entertainment of Gentlemen of taste, and martial enterprize, but by no means for the exhibition of the stage" (Brackenridge, *Death of Montgomery*, p. [iii]). In it, Brackenridge recounts the unsuccessful assault upon Quebec in which Burr became a hero. Typical of most dramas treating the Colonel's wartime service, this work presents a positive image of Burr throughout. His first appearance, for example, marks him as a noble soldier, eager for battle. When Macpherson, another of Montgomery's aides, asks him for his thoughts about the impending battle, he replies: " 'Tis full of peril, but it gives me joy, / And, wakes the bosom, with Ideas warm'd, / Of high invention, and bold thought in war" (II.2.19).[3] Later, after Montgomery has fallen, Burr is presented as grief-stricken over the loss of his leader. Embracing the fallen general, he makes evident his noble soul:

> O father, father, groaning, fainting, dead!
> Let me embrace thee to my grief-sick heart,
> And pour my warm soul in thy bleeding veins,
> Wet with the crimson of thy noble blood,
> Unchang'd, I'll wear these sprinkled garments home,
> And shew my countrymen each ruddy drop,
> Each ruddy drop, and with my words wake up,
> In every breast, susceptible of rage,
> The sullen anger of an injured soul.
>
> > [IV.2.36–37]

But most famous, of course, is his heroic attempt to carry the slain Montgomery back to American lines amidst enemy fire. He cries: "O, no, the vultures shall not have thy corpse, / If I can bear it from the blood-stain'd field, / On these poor shoulders" (IV.2.37). As it turns out, he cannot, and the general is left to the mercy of the wicked British commander, Carleton.

It is doubtful, however, whether even this heroic Burr saves Brackenridge's "school piece" from pedestrianism. Of the play's merit, the author admits, "I know myself to be capable of producing something much better, had I leisure for that purpose" (Brackenridge, *Death of Montgomery*, p. [iii]). The reader is quick to agree; the work is so obviously slanted for nationalistic purposes that Brackenridge's emerging talent is almost buried. Typical of Revolutionary drama, the play swiftly reveals that God is on our side and that the British are inhuman tyrants. To make this last point, the author gives us a General Carleton who roasts an ox, tells the Indians that it is the carcass of a Bostonian, and invites them to drink the warm blood that flows from the sizzling meat. It is no surprise, then, that, after the Americans have surrendered, the British general is portrayed as eager to turn his prisoners over to the savages; he is restrained from doing so only because he fears that, if he gives in to his desires now, he might receive similar treatment later should he fall into American hands. Brackenridge never issued the promised "Second Edition, more *correct* and *finished*" (Brackenridge, *Death of Montgomery*, p. [iv]).

Another play that treats Burr's experiences in the war is Jerome Dowd's *Burr and Hamilton: A New York Tragedy* (1884).[4] As the title suggests, however, the drama focuses upon the relationship between the two men. Tracing their rivalry from Revolutionary days to the Weehawken "interview," Dowd portrays Burr favorably throughout and in so doing helps to establish a number of directions that later playwrights were to take or modify.[5] Here is Brackenridge's eager soldier again, one devoted to his country's goals: "I have always longed for glorious war. Now as it has come I give it my strength and mind. And though my slender frame may not give assurance of distinction, yet so long as blood warms my veins I shall devote every energy to the cause in which I am enlisted" (I.1.3–4). But here, too, is the Aaron Burr whom women find irresistible. Dowd is thus one of the earlier dramatists to deal with the Colonel's sexual attractiveness but, unlike many others, in a way that is not damaging to his titular character. Although Burr is described as having "great powers of fascination" (I.1.7), he is presented as always honorable in his relationship with women. He will not, for example, publicly clear himself of the charge that he seduced and betrayed Dora Morgan, the daughter of a friend, because, as he says, "To question, to discuss, even to defend a woman's character before the world is to blast it" (I.1.9). And he breaks off his affair with Margaret Moncrieffe, though he truly loves her, because he recognizes the impossibility of their ever marrying, given the fact that her father is a British major. Dowd is also one of the earlier playwrights to present a Burr who may put his own ambition first, though such a suggestion is carefully subordinated to the image of a man possessing independent judgment. Thus, in a discussion with his friend Ogden about the task of individual soldiers, the Colonel (then a captain) declares: "For my part, I shall fight independently and to the purport of my own mind. And whenever I can gain a point on my own or my country's enemy, I will gain it regardless of orders and even of discipline" (I.1.4–5).

Dowd also is one of the first to use Hamilton as a contrasting figure. Here Burr's antagonist is presented as jealous and revengeful. He whispers slanderous rumors in Washington's ear during the Revolution so that he can supplant Burr as the general's aide, and he does whatever he can to check his rival's political career after the war. In a soliloquy late in the play, Hamilton makes clear his motivation:

The foul name of Burr haunts my breast and awakens discontent. Many times I have wished such a rival had not been born. I have devoted a life, almost, to suppressing his fame; but at every turn I have met defeat. . . . I believe Burr to be as low and cunning as the devil. To-morrow I will end the strife. If the setting sun does not crown me with victory [in ruining Burr's gubernatorial chances in the 1804 election] I will bid farewell to revenge, and seek repose in my quiet and charming home. But how much greater will be my joy if we succeed in giving the infernal regions a repulse. Oh, how sweet will be revenge! [IV.1.23]

Dowd also foreshadows the way in which many twentieth-century dramatists will treat the Colonel by presenting him as victim. When Hamilton's treachery has finally been made known to him, Burr himself points to this role: "My enemies have ruined me. Their teeth are like spears and their tongues like two-edged swords. Day and night· they prowl and engender violence and strife. Their breath smells of hell's vilest odors. Every day of life they mark my words and dog my steps. They seize upon me in the dark and like cowards steal away in silence" (IV.3.27).

Though no character, especially the hero, should be made to talk in such a way, Dowd seems unaware of that fact and a few lines later reaches perhaps the ultimate in stilted language. Attempting to turn Burr into an Elizabethan tragic figure—an image later playwrights also were to invoke occasionally—Dowd has the Colonel exclaim: "Farewell, Hamilton! Arise, thou clumsy sluggard of revenge! O hell, fume with all thy invective fire! Roll and convulse with thy scorching pestilence! Belch up from thy bottomless pit the stings and torments of conscience! Pour into Hamilton's soul all thy discontent! O, roast him! censure him! damn him!" (IV.3.27). Even Dowd's favorable treatment of the Colonel as a tragic figure—his justly killing Hamilton ruins him—cannot redeem such prose.

Another playwright to deal with the Burr-Hamilton relationship is Charles Felton Pidgin. In the dramatic prologue to his *Blennerhassett; or, The Decrees of Fate* (1901), which deals primarily with the conspiracy and its tragic results, he focuses on the duel.[6] Taking the details of his scene from Parton, Pidgin presents Burr in this introductory stage piece—essentially a play in small—as a good man with a just grievance. In fact, Hamilton is also portrayed favorably, the duel being depicted as the inevitable result of the refusal by two men to yield their positions. Burr emerges in the prologue as a chivalrous gentleman. When the milkmaid, Kate Embleton, angers and loses her lover by defending the Colonel, Burr, whom she does not know and therefore does not recognize, gallantly tells her: "I know this Col. Burr; in fact, I am an intimate acquaintance. He is not such a bad man as they say he is—in my opinion—but he would be the last person to wish any lady to defend him, if by so doing she lost the love of an honest man. He would say, as I do, make up your quarrel; whether Col. Burr is a villain or a saint should not trouble a happy home in Jersey" (Prologue, p. 7).

Burr's character—monster or angel—troubles three dramatists who take Hamilton as their main character in treating the relationship between the two men. In his *Hamilton: A Poetic Drama* (1930), Chard Powers Smith sets up a contrast between Hamilton as idea incarnate and Burr as fallible human being.[7] Smith points to his intention for the great Federalist when he notes in his foreword that the "one quality we may be assured that he [Hamilton] possessed was a passionate political idealism . . . [that took] its fatal effect upon his private life, consuming first the hope of happiness of all who loved him—friend, mistress, daughter, wife and son—and finally the life of his own body" (Foreword, p. [1]). Thus, in tracing Hamilton's career from 1788 to 1804, Smith depicts his titular character as a visionary political idealist, as one willing to sacrifice his family and his reputation for his country, and as a private friend but public enemy of Burr. The Colonel's image emerges as a contrast to this abstract and inhuman figure. Smith portrays Burr first, for example, as a generous spendthrift. Hence, early in the work, when Hamilton speaks of his new position in Washington's cabinet, he tells the Colonel: "When I'm Secretary of the Treasury, I shall consider you a factor in the annual redistribution of national wealth. You make enough to keep ten other lawyers; but your generosity must pour wine into all of the unshaven mouths in Battery Park, and keep you running along the brink of credit" (I.1.22). Burr is also presented in the play as one driven by circumstance—fear of debtor's prison—to abandon his political principles, something Hamilton would never do; the Colonel tells Mrs. Croix (later Madame Jumel) that he will become a Democrat if Jumel will pay off the $50,000 he owes his creditors. And the Colonel is shown as a man willing to forgive an enemy, even such a rival as Hamilton, who has destroyed his political career. On the field at Weehawken, as the seconds prepare for the interview, Burr writes his adversary a note, offering to forget the injury that brought them to the duelling ground. Overall, then, Smith depicts the Colonel as fully and fallibly human.

It is this rather warm portrait that saves the play from utter insipidity because, in general, Smith's technique is unperfected. His use of symbolism, for example, is heavy-handed; Burr presents Hamilton with a pair of pistols to commemorate New York's ratification of the Constitution, pistols, we suspect correctly, that will turn up with great irony later in the play. It is fortunate that Smith mentions in both the subtitle and in the foreword that his is a "poetic drama" because it might otherwise be difficult to recognize it as such. A sample of the metaphor and verse (Hamilton is speaking): "Tell Colonel Burr that this is no affair / Of ours. We are like bullets in our guns— / No more—and giant hands are aiming us / At one another" (III.4.147). Then, too, there is Smith's clumsy attempt to add a psychological dimension by portraying the relationship between Hamilton and his daughter as highly unusual; Angelica and her father are given occasional mysterious scenes in which she assumes the role of mother and he, of son.

No better is Carl Van der Voort's *Child of Nevis* (1934), another play focusing on Hamilton as principal character in depicting the relationship between the Colonel and his famous rival.[8] Like Smith, Van der Voort makes Burr a figure of contrast as he traces Hamilton's illustrious career in the Revolutionary War, in Washington's cabinet, and in the political events culminating in the duel. The image he creates, then, is that of the Colonel as total villain, although, rather surprisingly, Burr is never seen on stage. He is frequently present, however, in the conversation of the various characters, and it is clear from the start how the audience is to view him. In a discussion among Washington's aides, for example, Burr is depicted as a quitter, as one who resigns his commission as soon as the weather turns bad. But it is in the noble Hamilton's charges against him that the Colonel comes alive as stage devil. The great Federalist condemns Burr for being "a voluptuary in the extreme" and for lacking financial "probity" (III.1.22). He points to the Colonel's grand ambitions, noting that they "are always directed to his own exhaltation [sic], not to the benefit of his country," and indicates his concern about Burr's "monumental debts," suggesting that had his political enemy been elected president he would have had "to sell favors" and thus would have corrupted the nation (III.1.23). He believes that the Colonel would "wreck the country in order that he might strut the stage as king or dictator, to gratify his inordinate and insane vanity" (III.1.23).

Such a stock figure also appears in Hattie May Pavlo's *Hamilton* (1948, 1975), which, mercifully, remains unpublished.[9] In depicting Hamilton's life from his childhood on the Isle of Nevis to his preparation for the duel at Weehawken, Pavlo portrays Washington's secretary of the treasury as a great man who welds the separate states into a nation after the war and who sacrifices his health for his country. By contrast, Burr is revealed as an unscrupulous schemer. He tries, for example, to buy the presidency in 1800 with Madame Croix's money, thereby suggesting to Hamilton that he is a "Cataline [sic]" (III.2.17). In fact, Hamilton is so convinced of the Colonel's baseness that he will work to elect his political enemy Jefferson rather than see Burr become president. Of the Colonel, Hamilton declares: "Burr has neither patriotism nor principles. The reins of state in his hands and he would stop at nothing which would give him control of the United States Treasury. We have been threatened with many disasters since the infant nation was started, but with no such menace as Burr'"

(III.2.19). This Burr is also a man who considers blackmailing the prominent women he has seduced to raise enough money to avoid debtor's prison. But, worse of all, Burr is a traitor, willing to lead this time the Northern states out of the Union. In fact, one of the principal motives Hamilton has for meeting the Colonel in the duel is to ruin his conspiratorial plans and thus save the country; "if Burr kills me," Hamilton notes, "He will seal his own political doom. Of that I am certain" (III.4.36). Like others, then, Pavlo presents a noble Hamilton and a despicable Burr.

If the relationship between the two men has occupied our dramatists, so, too, has the conspiracy and the Richmond trial. Several works reflect the various ways in which American playwrights portray Burr when they deal with his alleged treason.[10] One of the earlier pieces to treat this segment of the Colonel's life is *The Conspiracy; or The Western Island* (1838), published by "A Citizen" two years after Burr's death.[11] Perhaps fearful of retaliation, the anonymous author uses fictitious names for his characters; Burr, for example, is appropriately called Colonel Hazard. Though sympathetic to the ex-vice president because of the unjust criticism he received from the press after the duel, the dramatist nonetheless depicts his protagonist as guilty of traitorous schemes. The first image of Burr in the play, however, is that of a man filled with revenge. Musing upon his situation, Colonel Hazard declares: "I am / But man, and sometimes feel as if my heart / Were like some dark and inner cave of gloom, / Where sits in moody loneliness, awake, / Remorseless and companionless revenge!" (I.1.7). It soon becomes clear just what form his retaliation will take. In a conversation with Colonel Aspen, aide to General Wild (Wilkinson), Hazard announces his treasonous plans: "We must aloft the blazing standard raise, / Quick as the meteor's flash[—]then, appeal / To all the west to rise in arms, and bid / The Allegany bound the eastern limit / To this our empire!" (I.3.13). From traitor to devil is not much of a step, and thus it is no surprise that Burr is also depicted as Satan. For example, Wade, Hazard's duped secretary, calls his deceiver "the arch fiend / And tempter" (IV.3.58). Lady Blenham (Mrs. Blennerhassett), bemoaning her situation, reinforces this image late in the play: "Had we not listen'd, ne'er had we been thus, / Our Eden had been still without a thorn, / While roses bloom'd on ev'ry little bush!" (V.3.71).

The primary image of Burr that emerges from the work, however, is that of ambitious man. In an early soliloquy, for example, Hazard portrays himself as a tough aspirant: "O I have ta'en ambition to my arms / And till I mount, must bear the pond'rous weight [of doubt] / As Atlas does the world upon his back!" (I.3.12). Ambition leads him to draw the innocent Wade into his traitorous plot: "The timid and the weak must be involv'd / In crafty webs, while brave and valiant men / Lead on to proud ambition's height" (III.2.38). And it is ambition that causes his willingness to risk his daughter's happiness—"Oh cruel father, who would drag his child / To ruin" (III.2.39), she declares—and to plan a civil war in which brother will fight brother. When Wade points out that if Hazard launches his conspiracy he will bring the country to bloodshed, the Colonel exclaims:

> Why let it bleed then or submit!
> I wage no war against my country's life,
> But I will rule, and most supremely too,
> Ere I be longer baited with the curse,
> Or made the theme of teeming scribblers, who
> But echo to the world their master[']s voice.
>
> [IV.1.52]

Overall, the play is undistinguished. The blank verse, for example, is frequently wooden ("And hark—the pattering rain 'gins to fall" [II.4.30]), a fact the author tries to mitigate in his "Prologue to the Reader": "If you are pleas'd, what matter if a word / Be long, another short, just half a third, / Or accent plac'd exactly here, or there, / To fit the verse thus smoothly to a hair" (p. 4). And the characterization is at best adequate. But the play does have the virtue of being one of the earlier pieces to use Jefferson as a figure of contrast for Burr. Here the president is a detested demagogue and vengeful foe, a man, Hazard proclaims, who "from town to town would hunt me, and / Through servile minions stab me in the dark!" (IV.1.52). Other dramatists treat Jefferson more kindly, but one-dimensional characters are common in this play.

More typical of those plays that treat the Colonel negatively is William Minturn's *Aaron Burr: A Drama in Four Acts* (1878).[12] In this work, the audience's initial perception of the main character comes

through Sambo, the stage black ("I's a cute niggah, I is"), who recounts an incident he has recently witnessed involving his master:
"Dar yest'day mornin' I's done ketch him stannin' jest here, dis way,
wid one ob dem shootin' machines in one hand, an' den he say
somethin' under his bref like, an' den he shoot away at dat ar picture
ob Mas' Hamilton tell he made a half dozen holes clean through and
through" (I.1.5). Such a suggestion of Burr as villain is fulfilled soon
after when Blennerhassett, who has innocently joined the conspiracy,
tells his wife of an ominous dream he has just had. In it, Burr is sym-
bolically depicted as an Ahab-like fiend:

> You will call me foolish; but it seemed to me while I slept that you and our
> two loved ones were in a fairy shallop, dancing upon the bright waters of a
> silver lake. Presently the rippling waves began to swell, and the fair sky above
> became overcast; then a shattered boat neared us, having within it a single
> rower, and he begged to be admitted into our vessel. As we granted his request
> the storm increased to a tempest and from a tempest to a tornado; but above
> the roar of the maddened elements rose a clear, fiendish laugh as of exulta-
> tion; when, turning, we beheld the stranger in our bark had taken the helm, and
> was pointing us out into the midst of the blackened lake! Lo! there, on its oppo-
> site shore, had arisen an edifice more magnificent than any I had ever
> imagined! It was a palace, set with many-colored brilliants, on whose lofty
> dome, surmounting all, blazed a red, fiery, fascinating meteor. As we gazed,
> enraptured, a thunderbolt—so fierce, it seemed to shatter the universal vault
> of heaven; prostrating all, it swept the brilliant structure down into the seeth-
> ing waters of our darkling lake; then, amidst the blackness of eternal despair, I
> started from my sleep.
>
> . . . .
>
> Nor was that all: as we sank below the swirling waters, our helmsman,
> assuming a demon's guise, flapped his raven wings and disappeared with a
> hideous laugh. It seemed to me prophetic.
>
> [II.1.16–17]

Following legend, Minturn also portrayed Burr as seducer, an
image that emerges primarily from the Colonel's treatment of Margaret. Her story, which the author divulges bit by bit throughout the
play, is both melodramatic and tragic. Engaged to be married, the
young woman meets the deceiver Burr by chance. Before long, however, she succumbs to his enticements and, rejecting her family and
fiancé, runs off with the Colonel to New York. Nemo, the angry young

man of the play, follows his beloved, intending to take her from her seducer. But, when he attempts to drag Margaret away, Burr cuts the youth's arm off with a sword. As usually happens, though, the Colonel soon tires of the girl and intends to leave her. She discovers Burr's plan to travel to Blennerhassett's Island and so begs to go with him. In her plea, she makes evident the power that the Colonel has over his feminine victims: "It is the one wish of my life," she tells him, "to be with you always, in safety and in danger. I would be your slave. Kill me if you will, and I will kiss the hand that strikes the blow; but do not play with my poor bursting heart as if it were a bauble of no value" (I.1.14). When the audience next sees her, she has unwisely followed the Colonel to the island, where her situation becomes acute. Burr is now in love with Alice Leighton, Blennerhassett's niece, and so, upon Margaret's arrival, casts off his former mistress. Matters worsen when Nemo, who has taken on the role of avenger, shoots at the Colonel but hits Margaret instead. Wounded, rejected, and half-crazed, the young woman wanders away from the mansion where she is recuperating, and roams the woods in search of her lover. At the end of the play, she is accidentally killed as she tries to prevent Nemo from stabbing Burr.

If Burr is a seducer and betrayer here, he is so because of his nature, for Minturn portrays his titular character as a Byronic hero of sorts. Thus, in depicting the Colonel's attempt to justify his treatment of Margaret to Alice, he has Burr make clear that he is no ordinary man: "Do not judge me hastily. The lot of genius is to be misconstrued, because misunderstood. The world can no more measure the terrible isolation, the wild yearnings of the ceaseless, consuming passions of its great men than can the placid pool of the forest appreciate the tremendous upheaval of the ocean tempest. . . . Can you wonder, then, that what may seem the extravagance of vice and cruelty may be but the natural outpourings of a soul swayed by impulses more turbulent and resistless than its fellows only because it is grander and more noble[?]" (III.2.39). But such explanations fail to satisfy Alice, who sees him for the traitor that he is, the "wily, sly, oily knave" that Wilkinson calls him (IV.2.47). Ultimately, however, Burr becomes a tragic hero straight out of Elizabethan drama. Minturn has linked him earlier in the play with Alexander the Great and with Mars, the war god, in order to increase his stature, so that now at the end, when he is arrested, he will seem to be another Macbeth. Burr points to his own classically tragic position in his final comments to Wilkinson. "You are the mean associate of greatness fallen," he tells the general, "though that greatness still remains" (IV.3.56).

Minturn's play is thus an ambitious attempt to live up to its Shakespearean ancestors—Burr even quotes the Bard at one point—but, unfortunately, a failed attempt. The curious mixture, for example, of Elizabethan and nineteenth-century dramatic techniques creates a dissonance that the author is unable to overcome. Side by side with declamatory soliloquies, ominous foreshadowings, and avenging furies (here a one-armed man!) are the antics of a bumbling Sambo, the thick-headedness of a stage Irishman, and the incongruities of a whiskey-loving chaplain. Juxtaposed with a bloody ending leaving bodies strewn about the stage is a sequence of amusing scenes that derive their humor from country dialect and down-home characters, one of whom (Aunt Patience) is the perennial unclaimed treasure. There are just too many times when the language strains for the upper register, only to slip an octave: "So, so, your most imperial majesty," Nemo says to Burr in the last act, "the owls will soon grow hoarse with hooting at your vain presumption" (IV.1.46). Thus Minturn's reach does exceed his grasp, and dramatic heaven remains secure.

Another play to treat the Colonel and his western plans negatively is Charles E. Stoaks's *Aaron Burr; or, The Kingdom of Silver* (1887).[13] There is little doubt how the author sees his main character: in the Dramatis Personae he lists Burr as "Chief Conspirator" and in the preface says his purpose is, in part, "To show that Burr's guilt lay in his intentions" (Stoaks, *Aaron Burr*, p. 3). Moreover, Stoaks is quick to fulfill his aims; he opens his work with a soliloquy in which the Colonel portrays himself as an outcast: "Ah, my countrymen, you may drive me from you as a deadly serpent—under the heat and excitement of the hour, cast me from you as an exile. You may fix the brand of Cain upon me—'tis but man against man; all men are exiles from Heaven" (I.1.6). Later in this same speech, Burr reveals his creator's conception of him as an angry, revengeful rebel: "Farewell, my native state! I have served you with devotion, but you turn from me and lick the dust from the feet of my enemies. By Heavens, my wrongs justify my actions. . . . I will build again the Kingdom of Silver [Mexico]" (I.1.6–7).

There are other roles in the play, however, that Stoaks uses to blacken the Colonel's character. He is portrayed, for example, as a subtle manipulator who gradually takes over the leadership of the conspirators without their becoming aware of his maneuvering. Crete, the only clear-sighted woman in the work, depicts him as a "polished viper, whose sting is death" (III.4.51), though neither she nor the author seems capable of linking the Colonel with Satan. Such a lost opportunity is surprising since Stoaks had earlier pictured Blennerhassett's garden as a "paradise" (II.4.31). Here, too, Burr is portrayed as a womanizer. When Wilkinson learns that Lady Blennerhassett is an active member of the conspiracy, he points to this aspect of the Colonel's portrayal: "I never knew Burr to have a big scheme but what a heroine figured a principal factor" (IV.4.60). But all these images give way to Burr as traitor. In unfolding his plans to Lady Blennerhassett, for example, he makes clear his dishonorable intentions; he will separate the western states from the Union, seize Mexico, and then establish his kingdom. In case of trouble, he will claim that his men were merely settlers who have come to farm the Bastrop lands.

Though such a presentation of Burr as villain seems intended to carry the play, it does not. Perhaps Stoaks was aware of this problem; in his preface he mentions that his "little volume is issued without claiming any great literary value" (Stoaks, *Aaron Burr*, p. 3). He was right to be so modest. Like Minturn's play, the work contains a jarring mixture of Elizabethan and nineteenth-century comedic elements. Thus, along with a witch who beats her hunchback servant, a number of ominous prophecies, and a natural world that corresponds to human events, there is the humor derived from a stage Irishman, the comedy arising from the fears expressed by superstitious common folk, and the smiles engendered by the accent of Burr's German servant, Daniel Adolphus Dummel ("Land of Goshen! I feel shoost like a vamily cistern" [I.3.12]). The play is also elaborately "decorated." "In order to compose a drama to cover the dry frame of historic fact," Stoaks indicates in his preface, "the author has dealt considerably with imagery, adding such as would connect the plot with that romance necessary to make the drama acceptable" (Stoaks, *Aaron Burr*, p. 3). Perhaps "the author" should have let history alone.

Though Stoaks seems content with a stock character, Charles Felton Pidgin is not. In his *Blennerhassett; or, The Decrees of Fate*

(1901), previously discussed in connection with the Burr-Hamilton relationship, Pidgin attempts to present a complex portrait of the Colonel.[14] He sees Burr as a man with good qualities who goes wrong and who is blasted as a result. Here is the Burr, for example, who takes in an orphan with artistic talent (Vanderlyn) and sends him to Paris to study under the masters. Here, too, is the man who devotes a good portion of his energy to the education of his daughter. "The greatest pleasure I have ever known," he notes early in the play, "was found in directing my daughter's studies" (I.1.20). But besides his interest in Theodosia, his love of a soldier's glory—another honorable trait—is a principal source of his motivation. He tells Dr. Hosack: "My love for my daughter is the best and truest part of me. My love for her and my ambition for military renown have been the moving springs of my life" (IV.1.59). This Burr is also a noble man who would never betray the women who have loved him: "I would as soon poison the springs and food that give sustenance to my enemy as divulge one fact that would injure those ladies who have trusted me" (IV.1.60).

In addition to these admirable traits, however, Pidgin recognizes Burr's darker side. He depicts the Colonel, for example, as an unscrupulously ambitious figure who will do virtually anything to achieve his aims, a portrait he suggests by likening Burr to Macbeth. Thus, in a dramatic reading of Shakespeare's play, in which the assembled company at Blennerhassett's Island takes part, the Colonel is given the titular role. Because Pidgin perceives Burr in this way, he also portrays the ex-vice president as a Catilinian deceiver. Thus Burr subtly entices the romantic Blennerhassett, first by telling him fallaciously that the Bastrop lands were purchased "in order to establish a colony of intelligent and wealthy individuals, and rear around [them] a society remarkable for the refinement of civil and social life" (II.1.32) and then by flattering the dreamy Irishman. "Your talents and acquirements," the Colonel tells him, "seem to have destined you for something more than vegetable life, and since the first hour of our acquaintance I have considered your seclusion as a fraud on society" (III.1.47). The ultimate deceiver is, of course, Satan; and Pidgin arranges matters so that Mrs. Blennerhassett, late in the play, links Burr with the arch-fiend:

Why did you ever enter our innocent, happy home? Why did not the flowers wither at your approach? Shall I tell you why you came as a destroyer and

turned our paradise into a hell? Because your mind was tortured with remorse for the unfortunate duel with Hamilton; because you were sickened by
disappointment in political preferment; because you were disgusted with
President Jefferson's just and pacific policy with all nations,—it was for these
reasons that you sought to bury the disquietudes that were tearing your soul,
by plunging into deeds of such wonderful magnitude. . . . Like the serpent in
Eden, you wound yourself into the open and unpractised heart of my unfortunate husband, and craftily, by degrees, infused into it the poison of your own
ambition. [IV.1.66–67]

The attempt to portray Burr as a multifaceted human being is not,
however, totally successful. Instead of a complex portrait, Pidgin
gives his audience a somewhat confused presentation of the Colonel,
as first admirable and then pejorative images of Burr stack up like so
many bricks in a backyard grill. Nor is the play itself finally effective.
Although the author, unlike Stoaks, believes that "The death of
Hamilton, Burr's dreams of conquest, the ruin of *Blennerhassett*, the
trial of *Burr* for treason, [and] the sad death of *Theodosia*, are the
most strikingly interesting episodes in American history, and the most
susceptible of effective dramatic treatment" (Pidgin, *Blennerhassett*,
p. [i]), he is unable to create a believable plot. The implausibility
springs in part from the fact that the historical "feature" of the piece is
"subordinated to a strong love story" (Pidgin, *Blennerhassett*, p.
[i])—Frederic and the milkmaid's. Unfortunately, these contradic-
tory impulses tend to dissipate the force of the work. In addition,
although he tries to shore up his titular character in the last act, his
focus throughout is primarily upon Burr. Hence, the dissonance engendered by special attention to the Irishman late in the play weakens
its dramatic thrust. And the grab-bag quality of the final act, in which
the author treats the six-year period in the Colonel's life beginning
with his trial and ending with the death of his daughter, is diffusive.
Still, Pidgin's attempt to create a fully human Burr, in part by using his
actual recorded comments, is noteworthy.

Unlike many plays dealing with the conspiracy and the Richmond
trial, two portray the Colonel positively. The first of these, L. France
Pierce's *Aaron Burr: A Romantic Drama in Four Acts* (1901), suggests the approaches that a number of twentieth-century playwrights
would take.[15] Here, for example, is the Colonel as a man of great
sexual power, an image that emerges in the conversation of other

characters. Thus, when Elenore Blunt, Wilkinson's niece, begs Burling not to deliver to Jefferson a cleverly doctored cipher letter that
will incriminate her lover, the general's aide makes clear Burr's attractiveness to women: "You love him like dozens of others," he tells her.
"You are blind with love for him but I am not a woman that I would
neglect my orders out of infatuation for a brilliant eye" (II.1.21). And
earlier, when the Spanish ambassador had noted that Elenore speaks
too ardently of the Colonel, Wilkinson had replied, "All women
do. . . . He knows how to manage them" (I.1.4). But such a portrayal is
only a minor aspect of Pierce's delineation of Burr.

Central, however, is the depiction of the Colonel as patriot. Burr is
no traitor in this play; when Wilkinson urges him to conquer Mexico
for himself without Jefferson's sanction, the Colonel's reply reflects
his devotion to the United States: "I want to carry the flag—my flag—
to the ramparts of Chepultepec, to the very city of Mexico, to plant it
there for the honor and glory of the country which you and I serve"
(I.1.20). In fact, he is horrified at the mere thought of committing treason: "The flag I have kissed and fought for, loved, venerated and
adored, they say, I would dishonor. The flag—oh, never, never!"
(III.1.15). In his speech at the Richmond jail to a crowd that has
called him treacherous, he reveals most fully his love of country. He
asks: "You call it treachery to wrest an empire from a sovereign power
to add to our own glory[?] You call it treachery to carry the flag for
conquest? You call it treachery to band together young bloods of New
England valleys to crush the swaggering importance of a Spanish
legion, insolent and defiant at our very threshold[?] You call it treachery that I have burned to force these swarthy weaklings to understand
the dignity of a young Republic[?]" (III.1.28). In this play, it is Wilkinson, not Burr, who is the traitor.

Also central to Pierce's depiction of the Colonel is his portrayal of
Burr as a noble man. Thus, when Bollman warns his friend that Wilkinson is an unscrupulous deceiver who may betray him, the
Colonel's reply reflects his greatness of soul: "No, no I cannot believe
it. Wilkinson has been my friend since the days of the Revolution. I
fought with him at Quebec. . . . No, Wilkinson can do no wrong. . . . I
shall ever believe in Wilkinson's honor, though he deprive me of
mine" (II.1.10). His willingness to sacrifice himself in order to free
Bollman and Blennerhassett by signing a fallacious document that

will incriminate him is admirable. He is also courageous, willing to defend his name in court rather than run away when he has the opportunity. Chief Justice Marshall makes the point, after the Colonel has been cleared: "I am happy that I may congratulate you, Mr. Burr, on your courage and dignity in the face of this ferocious conspiracy against you" (IV.1.17). But his magnanimity is most apparent in his treatment of Wilkinson and of Elenore late in the play. Even though the general has maliciously and falsely put Burr on trial for his life, the Colonel will not prosecute him because, he tells Burling, Wilkinson "was my comrade at Quebec" (IV.1.18). And he will give up Elenore for her own good, though he is deeply in love with her. He tells the general's former aide: "I am on the downward path, Burling. There is nothing ahead but chagrin and humiliation. I am an old man, and she is a maid just blossoming into womanhood. Ah! If I were young like you—But I am penniless, in debt, without credit, a suspected traitor, acquitted for want of evidence,—an outcast. What is there to crown a woman's life, except thorns. I must give her up" (IV.1.20). He even makes the break easy for Elenore by pretending he no longer loves her.

But it is as victim that Pierce primarily depicts Burr, an image later playwrights will also use. It is clear, for example, that the Colonel has been unjustly treated for duelling with Hamilton. Bollman makes this point to Lucy Blennerhassett when he notes that "Burr has been the real victim of the encounter" (II.1.1), indicating that "Hamilton did fire," despite rumors to the contrary (II.1.2). When Bollman comes to visit the Colonel in jail after Wilkinson has had the ex-vice president arrested, he again suggests that Burr is being persecuted: "They are fast depriving you of all resources for defense. Conspiracy! Speak not to me of conspiracy! This is a conspiracy against you worth the attention of the whole country" (III.1.8). It is the Colonel himself, however, who most fully reveals his basic role in the play. When Burling notes after the trial that Burr will be free but forever unjustly branded, the Colonel agrees:

I shall be free—but an unproven traitor. I shall be free to roam the wide world over, but—alone, shunned, a contaminated thing to be avoided, a scourge to be annihilated. Yes, I shall be free, free to conquer and to die for the sake of liberty and power but—I must conquer and die alone. I shall be free—but I must crawl at the feet of men, content with the crumbs they fling at me. I shall be free but I must suffer in silence their condemning glances and their brutal ep[ith]ets. I shall be free to exist in the sunlight but I am still a chained captive. I shall be free but an unconvicted criminal. I shall be free but a bleeding sore, a cancer, a rooted affliction, the first stain in the Republic's pride. Free? Yes, I shall be free, but they will never cease to lash my name through an Eternity. I shall be free, yes, free for a punishment viler than incarceration in some black hole, free to be spat upon, stoned, calumniated and made helpless to defend myself. I shall be free—but! [IV.1.18–19]

After such a speech, it comes as no surprise that Elenore should link the Colonel in the last line of the play with Western civilization's most famous victim by proclaiming: "They have crucified his soul!" (IV.1.23).

This ending is typical of the overall dreadfulness of the piece. Though Pierce like Pidgin weaves Burr's own words into her work, it takes more than cut-and-paste dramaturgy to make for success. Her dialogue, for example, is too often flat. Thus Burr's response to the declaration of faith and devotion Elenore makes in the first act suggests why the play was never published: "Fair dreamer, such sweet beliefs are a recompense for the sneers of the world. Brave little Republican! I thank you!" (I.1.25). And Elenore's expression of concern for the Colonel after Wilkinson has decided to destroy him is equally bad: "I am afraid for you, beloved! I knew it! I knew it! They are setting a trap for you. Oh beloved! Beloved!" (II.1.24). But most damaging is Pierce's introduction of a negative quality into her otherwise overwhelmingly favorable portrait of Burr, an error that a more skillful dramatist would surely have avoided. Seemingly unaware of the disastrous effect this tactic has upon her play, she momentarily turns Burr into a villain eager for power. In the second act, she has him tell Elenore: "I want power. 'Tis been my life-long dream. I want the right of conquest. I want to lead my own armies. I want sovereignty. I want a crown. I want empire" (II.1.8).

Not much better is Edward Raiden's *Mr. Jefferson's Burr* (1960), which follows Pierce's main thrust in treating the Colonel positively.[16] Focusing on the Richmond trial, the play depicts Burr again as victim, this time of the president of the United States. The author suggests what his position will be when he notes in his foreword that "History—certainly on the elementary school level—teaches us that

Aaron Burr was a traitor. This popular misconception was the opinion I held until 1950 when I discovered that Aaron Burr had been acquitted" (Raiden, *Mr. Jefferson's Burr*, p. [i]). Although Raiden demonstrates throughout that Jefferson is the villain, two somewhat lengthy speeches he contrives for Burr most fully reveal the Colonel's persecution. Thus, at the indictment hearing, he has Burr depict the illegal measures taken against him. Referring to Caesar Rodney, the U.S. attorney general, who is one of the prosecutors, the Colonel tells Chief Justice Marshall:

He must know that after a third grand jury discharged and commended me, his father, sitting as the Judge, unlawfully held me to bail. Then I learned of military orders to seize my person and destroy my property. I sought to abandon the place where the law ceased to be the sovereign power. I was illegally seized and taken over Indian trails in torrential rains for almost a thousand miles. I was forced to sleep on the muddy earth. The guard who conducted me here avoided every magistrate on the way. I was debarred the use of pen, ink and paper, and not even permitted to write to my daughter. While in this felonious captivity, passing through the State of South Carolina, I happened to see three men together and demanded the interposition of the civil authority. I wished to be delivered from military despotism, not from an investigation into my conduct, or from the operation of the laws of my country. Upon making this demand, the government agent, with a pistol in each hand, menacing all about him, forced the party on. [I.1.13–14]

The second speech, made during the trial itself, reflects the shabby case the prosecutors have brought against the Colonel, thereby suggesting that vengeance rather than justice is Jefferson's real motivation. Speaking to Marshall about the nature of the testimony given to convict him and about the witnesses who provided it, Burr again reveals his victimization:

Sir, without flights of fancy, what are the realities of proof? General Eaton, who was paid for his affidavit, claims that I told him there would be a revolution and I would lead an army to effectuate it. Commodore Truxton [sic] states that I told him I was planning an expedition against the Spanish colonies; which is not denied; and that I always said such expedition was in the event of war with Spain. The gardener knows of a few men who had arms on Blennerhassett Island and that Mr. Blennerhassett, in deep confiding secrecy told him that I was going to take Mexico. The groom saw some things on the

Island; none of them any different than might have been seen in any such place. Colonel Morgan, a senile man who sees traitors in every closet[,] tells the President I intended a revolution because I said I could drive the President out of Washington with 200 men and take New York with 500 men. And his son, who admits we were bantering when this was said, saw in the fact of my interest in Bradford, a revolution. The man hired to build a kiln on the Island, the storekeeper who told how my goods, all innocent, were taken by the authorities in violation of all rights; and several young men who saw a few boats and rifles for hunting, were called to give proof. This is the testimony out of which has been built a revolution. If these add up to an intended revolution with myself at its head, marching against the powerful array which I fought to establish, then my crime is stupidity. [II.2.88–89]

Apparently following the transcript of the trial but taking "a certain amount of dramatic license" (Raiden, *Mr. Jefferson's Burr*, p. [v]), Raiden presents an image of Burr often used in the twentieth century.

Although the Burr-Hamilton relationship and the conspiracy have preoccupied many dramatists who deal with the Colonel, some have taken a broader perspective, preferring either to focus upon several aspects of Burr's career or to treat a more protracted period of his life. Of course, the works of Dowd, Van der Voort, Pavlo, and others touch upon more than one incident in the Colonel's biography, but they have their primary interest in a single event. Two plays, however, demonstrate that it is possible to treat several elements of the vice president's history. Though separated in time by more than half a century, each explores the presidential election of 1800, the duel with Hamilton, and the conspiracy. The earlier of these, Charles Frederic Nirdlinger's *The First Lady of the Land* (1911), portrays the Colonel as a charming opportunist, an essentially positive image that arises from the various ways Burr is depicted in the work.[17] Thus, for example, Nirdlinger contrasts the unruffled Burr with an agitated Jefferson (who always plays the fiddle when he is nervous) during the House's deliberation for a new president. Here, too, is the figure of great sexual power whom Mrs. Sparkle will not even discuss while her sixteen-year-old daughter is in the room and whom another feminine character believes is a rake with half the women he meets in love with him. Even Madison, who in the end wins Dolly Todd (the "First Lady" of the title), fears that Burr will make her want to marry him: "this man your sex has always found resistless" (I.1.64). But though the Colonel has enjoyed many women, he is forever scrupulous of their reputation, an attribute that is part of his charm. Thus, when Merry, the British minister, suggests that Burr will get his loan for his western schemes once King George is informed of the Colonel's power over the future Mrs. Madison and therefore over American policy, Burr reacts strongly, telling the ambassador never to use a lady's name in such a way. Merry then indicates that he will just hint at the truth in his communiqué, but the Colonel replies: "No, sir! Not by hint, intimation, nor innuendo! Not for a world of Mexicos!" (II.1.82). Dolly makes the same point about Burr in refuting Mrs. Sparkle's claim that the Colonel "boasts his conquests": "Oh, never!" says Mrs. Todd. "If Colonel Burr kisses, he doesn't tell" (I.1.34).

Nirdlinger also portrays the vice president as a forthright man of honor in the discussion of the duel, which he moves for dramatic purposes from 1804 to 1800. Hence, when Madison endeavors to temporize by telling Burr that Hamilton may have made his troublesome remark in a jesting tone or in a context that would mitigate its sting, the Colonel retorts, "Oh, he makes it a point of grammar, a matter of syntax, elocution, the dictionary! I make it a point of honor, for him to deny or acknowledge!" (II.1.76). Yet the playwright also shows that Burr is restlessly ambitious. In answering Dolly, who has asked him if he is still considering his western plans even after being elected vice president, he replies, "Because of it! The thought of four years, possibly eight, of conspicuous insignificance appals me! And against that desert of ennui—an empire—to be had for the taking!" (II.1.103). It is precisely this ambitious nature that Nirdlinger believes leads Burr to treason; there is finally little doubt in the play that the Colonel intended to separate the western states from the Union. Overall, then, Nirdlinger portrays Burr as a charming opportunist. "This game was of my own making," he roguishly tells Mrs. Todd and Madison when Jefferson's soldiers come to arrest him. "I cut the cards, dealt them, named the stake. And well worth playing for!—If I must lose" (IV.1.201).

Though *The First Lady of the Land* is somewhat diffuse, it is generally amusing, in part because of the way Burr is presented in it. Another effective device Nirdlinger uses, however, is the employment of a comic character, here Lady Merry. Depicted throughout as a shrew, she provides much of the work's humor with her outrageous comments. Thus, for example, in expressing her annoyance with American customs, which are justified to her by invoking General Washington's name, she brings a laugh with her response:

Hell's bales! Don't you throw that man in my face! . . . For any and every complaint that one answer: "General Washington!" I tell Mrs. Todd's cook the roast is overdone and their excuse is: "General Washington has dined here." I say the Madiera's [sic] muddy, but—"General Washington didn't find it so!" They bring a pint of water for a bath and when I ask for more, " 'Twas always plenty for the General!" The beds are hard beyond endurance, but, "General Washington has slept in 'em." I'll have them know I'm not dining with General Washington, nor drinking with him, nor sl—. Well, in short, General Washington isn't paying my score! [II.1.85–86]

The audience may be surprised that even Lord Merry ever wanted to.

Though Charles A. Hallett does not make use of a termagant in his *Aaron Burr* (1964, 1969), he does deal with the same three events that Nirdlinger treats.[18] And, like his predecessor, he portrays the Colonel positively. Here, for example, is an idealistic Burr, eager to create a better world: "The new age I see," he tells Spanish Ambassador Herrara, "is one not just of new governments but [of] new concepts in government. Governments that will foster knowledge, scientific and industrial knowledge, so we can forge a new society in which all men will find happiness" (II.1.8). Here, too, is Burr as patriot. In a discussion with Herrara about his western projects, the Colonel makes clear that he is devoted to the long-term interests of his country: "Don't for a minute think that America is for sale here. On the contrary, our aim is to fulfill the American potential, create a realm where the usual legal compulsion will be a thing of the past, an empire that—well, we wish to fullfill the American dream" (II.1.7). His love for his country is so great that at the treason trial he will even risk imprisonment in order to expose the despotic Jefferson when, by following the narrowly defined charges against him, he could easily go free. "A new cause is growing in me," he tells Van Ness. "Either I expose him for the tyrant he is—perverting our democracy into a dynasty or—well, history at least will judge him for what he is. . . . When the people see his abuse of power, his contempt for law and the peril they all live in under him, they will see their mistake" (III.1.17–18).

But it is the image of Burr as a man of honor that is most pervasive in the work. Even in small matters, for example, the Colonel is rigidly high-principled. When Vanderlyn wants to paint his patron in the grand style of the day—an approach that, with an eye toward history, Burr himself favors—the Colonel refuses because he has promised Theodosia that his protégé's first painting after returning from study in Europe will be of him as he really is. "I gave my word," he tells Vanderlyn. "To a man of honor, that takes precedence over nature [the desire to be remembered by later generations]" (I.1.6). His integrity is also demonstrated during the 1800 election. To Wilkinson, he notes, "Throughout this entire sordid affair I have been strict in my observance of honor. I needn't remind you of the several times when a little more sail in the wind—a mere shift of weight—and I could have caught the current that would have brought me to the White House. But I didn't waver once" (I.6.14). And, of course, the duel, which Hallett heavily slants in Burr's favor and which like Nirdlinger he moves back to 1800, is reflective of the Colonel's sense of honor. Hamilton has slandered him, and Burr intends to vindicate his name. If he is protective of his own reputation, however, Burr is also scrupulous in caring for that of others, as the will he writes just before the duel reveals. In it, he tells his daughter: "I give my letters and papers to you. I have no other direction to give you on the subject but to request you to burn all such as would, if made public, injure any person. This is more particularly applicable to the letters of my female correspondents" (I.7.9). And at his trial for treason, he works hard to counter the accusations that have been made against him. He tells Rodney, one of the prosecutors: "Sir, your executioner may shortly put a period to all my [alleged] fantasies. But while I exist I shall not forbear to vindicate my character and motives from your aspersions. As a man to whom fame [honor] is dearer than life, I will make the last use of that life in doing justice to that reputation which is to live after me, and which is the only legacy I can leave to those I honor and love, and for whom I am proud to perish" (III.1.30).

In many ways, Hallett's *Burr* is the most sophisticated of the dramas dealing with the Colonel. The author makes skillful use, for instance, of all three of Burr's famous antagonists—Hamilton, Wilkinson, Jefferson—as dark contrasts to an admirable patriot. And, though revisionist history clearly affects the playwright, he is one of the few who brings even his secondary characters to life, notably, General Wilkinson. As Hallett portrays him, this master double-dealer, whom Vanderlyn describes as "Iago playing Falstaff" (I.1.22), finds his motivation for duplicity in the stimulation it provides. In explaining himself to a nervous aide, Wilkinson comes to life as a credible if treacherous human being:

Weeks I spend, working all the elements, mixing and brewing them, straining off the impurities, stirring it up, all for a moment like this—the essence of excitement. Reminds me of when I was a kid stealing toys. You know, I never had so much fun with the things I snitched as I had the moment I walked by the clerk with a ball or a top stuck in my shirt. You know the feeling? Rubbery legs that feel like wet noodles under you, a fist in your stomach that squeezes your guts so hard you can't breathe—and you have to curl your toes to keep from pissing in your pants. That's living, Perkins. I used to take things I didn't even like, just for that moment with the clerk. [II.4.2]

In 1974, Hallett revised the piece extensively in preparation for the first production at the American Theater Company in New York. Yet, even in its earlier form, *Aaron Burr* is the best of a generally undistinguished lot.

If Hallett and Nirdlinger before him deal with events in the Colonel's career from 1800 to 1807, three playwrights cover a more extended period of time. In *Aaron and Theodosia or The Fate of the Burrs* (1902), the earliest of these, Ben McCrary treats Burr's life from the duel with Hamilton to the Colonel's death.[19] With Shakespearean models clearly in mind, the author, like Minturn, depicts the vice president as a tragic hero, an essentially good man of high place who, because of a flaw in his character, brings himself to ruin and ends his days a pitiable wretch. There is no question in the play of the Colonel's basic nobility. He firmly believes, for example, in democratic rather than monarchical principles. When Carlos bows and starts to back out of the room after serving his master, Burr tells him: "Subjects of a monarchy imagine they have to climb a ladder to see a king, hence the habit of backing out from a royal presence. The elevation of equality has taken the place of the royal, runged ladder, that once existed in this part of America. Turn around and walk out naturally" (I.2.7). The Burr who is portrayed here has only honorable motives for his western expedition. Even the pirates who, following legend, capture Theodosia recognize that the Colonel is no traitor. Lafitte, their chief, who had seen Burr in New Orleans in 1807, makes this point when he says of the Colonel: "He was then scheming to liberate Mexico from the yoke of Spain; for his pains he was arrested under charge of treason—a farce that ended in his acquittal at Richmond" (III.2.33).

Unfortunately, however, Burr is also a man of prideful ambition, as he reveals in musing upon the cause of the duel just before he leaves for Weehawken. "The incentive," he declares, "[is] insatiable ambition[—]a disease more prevalent and incurable than insanity! A hydropathy of lust for power that makes mad dogs of men, spreading contageon [sic] with virus dripping mouths, inocculating [sic] the heart with a fevorish [sic] intent, tempered to a white heat, that it forever melts down the thrown [sic] on which well balanced reason sits" (I.2.15). It is clear, then, that the Colonel has caught the infection, and the result is a blasted life. He becomes a victim of political hatred, charged fallaciously with treason and ridiculed in the press. And his old age is a sad travail. When he is evicted from his shabby law office in 1831 because he is unable to pay the rent, he makes clear his pitiable condition: "The world has rolled over; I am beneath, crushed and crying for help! . . . No child! no home! *no country*! not a friend left, to hear me and come to my relief" (IV.1.60). It is little wonder that he often thinks of suicide.

Lest the audience miss the point, McCrary, whose technique is little better than his spelling, has Burr twice indicate his classically tragic situation. In discussing before the duel his dream of having killed Hamilton, he notes: "If the dreams that come foretell future events, 'tis done! Hamilton's earthly doom is too suddenly sealed, and mine! Wound up like a ball of yarn and started unraveling down the hill. I saw myself one step from the tiptop suddenly trip and slide down to the hard bottom below! Miserable old age, creeping on crutches; the breath of censure blowing upon my back; ever moving before the gale that this night's work will set in motion" (I.2.15). Moments before his own death, thirty-two years later, he points again to his tragic fate: "The bullet that pierced Hamilton's body opened a fountain that swept me down its course; poisoned the seed; rotted the roots[,] forever blotting out our once illustrious family tree" (V.1.69).

Such language, which McCrary no doubt intends to be poetic and to model on Shakespeare ("To do or not to do is alternative left alike to both the coward and the brave" [I.2.15]), is typical of the author's bad art. Reaching its most abysmal in the Colonel's dying words—"Thus the end and fate—of—the—Bur—r—s!" (V.1.69)—it is of a piece with an incredible plot, a band of politically sophisticated pirates who rob ships to get the latest news, and a Margaret Moncrieffe, who now as Madame Candor (Candor = frank?) is resurrected to care for Burr in his old age. McCrary even provides a loyal stage black ("I'd do anything to protect Massa Burr" [II.1.21]), who at 104 still thoughtfully brings his former owner a birthday breakfast. To date, *Aaron and Theodosia* remains unpublished.

Somewhat better in conception is Edgar Lee Masters' *Aaron Burr and Madam Jumel* (1934), which traces through discussion between the titular characters the significant events of the Colonel's life from boyhood to his second marriage.[20] Because Masters uses a modified form of Browning's celebrated technique—here the reader gets "dramatic duologues"—the overall image of Burr as a man more sinned against than sinning comes principally from the Colonel himself. He stresses to Madame Jumel that he is a man of honor. His basic reason for duelling with Hamilton, he declares, was that the arch-Federalist was showing "despotism / How to make entrance and destroy the charters / Of liberty," though he does admit that "the edge / Was his [Hamilton's] inveterate slanders" (I.1.49). As an honorable man, he notes, he refused to take the presidency from Jefferson:

> . . . I had risen
> To the very heights, lacked but a single vote
> To make me president. What's my nature, madam,
> When by this genius for the thaumaturgy
> Of politics, I might have won the prize,
> And didn't, but kept second place, respecting
> The people's choice of Jefferson?
>
> [I.1.49]

He admits, however, that he did intend to separate the western states from the Union but declares that his motives were virtuous. Hamilton was perverting democracy by building a strong central government, so he felt justified in establishing a new empire devoted to liberty. He asks: "[C]ould not I, / With sin no greater, build a separate realm / With Mexico for center, lift again / The banner of freedom on a favoring soil?" (I.1.61). Besides, he notes, times were different then; leaving the Union thirty years ago was not considered quite so horrid.

But it is as noble victim that Burr finally depicts himself. He suggests to Madame Jumel that he is "a storm driven / Eagle whom the fowlers have pursued, / And wounded" (I.1.40) and points to his life as an outcast: "I need a home, companionship. Thirty years / Of drifting and of loneliness. Ah! no words / Can tell about it" (I.1.54). He is, he believes, history's martyr, because his killing of Hamilton allowed the Federalists to break Jefferson's strength by destroying him: "History's satiric hand gave me the pistol, / And made me, one, lone, unsupported man / The pivot of a turn in Time" (I.1.59). Though he has suffered, he tells her, he has accepted his fate stoically—"I have not flinched" (I.1.41)—describing himself as a kind of Tennysonian Ulysses: "That's I: strength unexhausted, / And will to live, and hope that dreams a home; / A love that can be given, and a love / Striven for and attained" (I.1.54–55).

In essence, what Masters presents is Burr's rhetorical courtship of Madame Jumel. The Colonel comes to her mansion with some legal work he has recently completed for her and in an apparent attempt to vindicate his name from ugly slander tells her of his life. Unknown to the lady, however, Burr has instructed the Reverend Bogart to appear within a short time to marry the couple. When the clergyman arrives, Madame Jumel is at first astonished; but, moved by the tale of the Colonel's unjust suffering, she eventually puts "her head on BURR's shoulder in a gesture of surrender" (Masters, *Aaron Burr*, p. 75). An intriguing conception, this, though not entirely effective. Despite an occasional lively exchange between the two characters and the author's successful use of Hamilton and Jefferson as foils, the expository nature of the piece finally cripples its dramatic force. Masters is no Robert Browning, a fact additionally suggested by the playwright's too frequent use of inflated diction. He has Burr note that, had business interests supported his plan to establish a new empire, the country would have viewed his scheme as a "glorious phalactery" instead of as a hideous evil (I.1.64). The duel becomes a "monomachy" (I.1.53) and the Colonel's skill in public affairs, his "genius for the

thaumaturgy / Of politics" (I.1.49). On balance, then, the play does
not fulfill its promise.

The last of the works to deal with an extended period in Burr's life,
Thomas B. Sweeney's *Aaron Burr's Dream for the Southwest* (in-
appropriately titled), follows the Colonel's career from graduation
day in 1772 to his death in 1836.[21] "Published in Connection with the
Bi-Centennial Anniversary of the Birth of Aaron Burr on February 6,
1756" (Sweeney, *Aaron Burr's Dream*, title page note), the play
(1955) provides a generally favorable treatment of the Colonel. The
author, however, has a thesis, as he makes clear in his foreword: "I am
not attempting to paint Aaron Burr as a superman and certainly not as
one depraved. My hope is to produce a portrait of one of the world's
most unusual individuals, such as, for example, Leonardo da Vinci.
We are all victims of heredity. Genius and insanity are separated by a
small margin which changes in degree from age to age. Both were
present in Aaron Burr's ancestry" (Sweeney, *Aaron Burr's Dream*, p.
vi).[22] Throughout the piece, then, Sweeney frequently reminds his
readers (this is "A Drama for the Library") that heredity is responsible for the bad as well as the good qualities of his central character.

Burr is no saint here. He is a lavish spender, unable, as he himself
reveals, to live a moderate life: "My trouble is, I cannot save a
cent. / I earn tremendous fees and lose them all / In speculation,
entertaining friends— / And entertaining far beyond my means"
(III.1.105). His sexual activity is distressing. Even at sixteen, for
example, he is described as loving "the flesh pots of Egypt" (I.1.3).
There were "those village girls" in Connecticut (I.2.12), "dear Jaca-
taqua, half-caste Indian maid" during the siege of Quebec (I.2.13),
and "Mag Moncrieffe, / [who] Became [his] paramour at age fourteen" (I.2.17). Two of his bastard children estimate that they may
have "twenty or twenty-five" illegitimate brothers and sisters
(IV.4.187), and Burr himself reveals, when he discusses with friends
the cause of his marital difficulties with Madame Jumel, that he is still
a philanderer in old age:

> She has a gorgeous creature for a maid.—
> And, following my habit of a lifetime,
> One day I tried to feel her lovely leg.

> The silly girl went screaming from the room
> And told Eliza that she'd have to leave! [IV.4.193]

Yet lavishness and healthy sexuality are not diabolical failings, especially if ancestry is to blame.

Heredity is also responsible, Sweeney suggests, for Burr's good qualities, and they predominate in the play. He is, for example, properly ambitious, spending "sixteen hours a day or more" in study while he is at college (I.1.7) and completing his preparation for a legal career in six months instead of the usual three years (I.3.26). His wife also points out that "He wants to rule, or be the leading man— / Surpassing Alexander Hamilton!" (II.1.45). He himself notes that, if Jefferson would allow him to conquer Mexico for the United States, his "name would shine throughout all history / And [his] ambition then would be achieved!" (III.2.116). He is, of course, a hero at Quebec, successful in returning Montgomery's body to American lines, and his greatness is suggested throughout the play in links made between him and Frederick the Great, Caesar, Confucius, Mohammed, and even Christ. Here, too, is an idealistic Burr, a man who sees the possibility of a utopian America and who is willing to work for it. He says to Ogden:

> . . . We are not put here
> To live a life of ease, then die like dogs!
> At least I am not—I want a better world!
> No slaves, no thieves, no beggars, no murderers!
> It can be done, Matt, if we forget
> Our selfish motives and live for helpfulness!
>
> [II.2.63]

It is also a patriotic Burr who emerges from Sweeney's verse. Thus, for example, he puts his country's interest before his political career by opposing Washington's attempt to send Chief Justice John Jay as special envoy to England. Such a move, he believes, "is inexpedient and contrary to / The spirit of the Constitution itself" (II.2.58). In his western schemes, he tells Wilkinson, he intends only the fulfillment of his country's destiny, not the destruction of the Union: "You know that I am loyal / And patriotic, having one desire, / To see the United

States occupy / All of North America, in time" (III.1.102). Good as well as bad, then, Burr remains for Sweeney a pawn of heredity.

Perhaps it is this shaping of the Colonel's life around a thesis that causes part of the problem in the play; in any case, the author of such other books as *Rhymes at Odd Times* and *Life Underwriting as a Professional Career* is unable here to create a satisfying work of art. His characters, for example, too often talk in exclamations, as Theodosia Prevost does in discussing with her mother what her future husband is like and what her relationship with him will be after their marriage:

> He seems too sure! He is too sensitive!
> He will not cooperate with his friends!
> He and he alone must have the final say!
> I shall not cross him for a single word—
> That is our only chance for happiness!
> His pride of race absorbs his every thought!
> He expects a progeny of geniuses
> To carry on his name! I'll do my part!
>   [I.4.39]

But even with the frequent exclamations, the language is often flat. At an especially dramatic moment, when Burr's friends are urging him to flee for his life from the treacherous Wilkinson, the Colonel, like a wooden dummy, replies: "I will undertake escape at your advice" (III.3.129). And with the relative absence of enjambment, here a flaw, the verse is regularly stiff and halting. But on Sweeney goes, seemingly unaware, arranging Burr's life to fit his thesis. Perhaps his other works are more successful.

Sweeney's fate is, unfortunately, all too common for American dramatists who treat the Colonel. Yet the various images that emerge from their often undistinguished works are suggestive of the hold that Aaron Burr has upon the national imagination. In general, the early playwrights and those who focus upon Hamilton portray the Colonel negatively. Some depict him as a sexual predator, a satanic deceiver, or a wily traitor. Others present him as an outcast like Cain or like one of Byron's tortured heroes. Sometimes he is seen as an unscrupulous man of ambition, a Catiline, sometimes as a tragic hero who, like

Macbeth, falls from a high place because of a flaw in his character. But as the distance from the historical events in which Burr figured increases, the treatment of him becomes more positive. Perhaps this change in presentation occurs because of the favorable portrait that Parton's biography (1857) and later Wandell and Minnigerode's (1925) provide. Perhaps it results merely from the increasing sophistication of American culture, especially after World War I. Whatever the case, dramatists in the twentieth century often depict the Colonel as a noble person or a misunderstood patriot or an unmercifully hounded victim. They are sympathetic to a man whom they feel was terribly wronged.

Satan or saint, Burr is a compelling figure, and no doubt it was the attractiveness of his story alone that occasioned some of the interest in him. He is also, of course, a part of three important events in our early history—the Revolutionary War, the duel, and the western conspiracy—and the great leaders of our emerging republic people the stage along with him. But perhaps there is something else about the Colonel that accounts for his popularity as a subject for drama. May not it be that the images of him that occur again and again, those of sexual predator, of traitor, and of victim, express society's fears? In a nineteenth-century world, for example, that holds woman as chattel and as virgin, the sexual predator is seen as a frightful plunderer and a dark expression of the desire to despoil. In a new country unsure of its stability, the traitor suggests the explosive irrationality that threatens destruction and is therefore the man most abhorred. And in a modern America that fears it may be at the mercy of forces beyond its control—technology, bureaucracy, heredity—the victim becomes an obsessive if frightening fascination. In any case, Aaron Burr is a much larger part of our theatrical history than many have assumed. In American drama from the Revolution to the present, he has shown himself a man for all seasons.

Notes

1. In part because of the peculiarities of the copyright law before 1909, a number of titles were granted copyright protection, but the texts of the plays were never sent to the Copyright Office. As a result, many of them have been lost. Included in the following list of such works are the date of copyright and

the assigned identifying number: Sarah Carpenter, *Aaron Burr's Dupe*, 7 August 1901, D728; Charlotte Molyneux Holloway, *Aaron Burr*, 10 February 1900, 3793; Helen Hooker, *Aaron Burr: A Revolutionary Drama in One Act*, 27 June 1898, 39113; Anna Leach, *Aaron Burr: A Drama*, 6 June 1900, 14067; Louis O'Shaughnessy, *Aaron Burr; or, A Dream of Empire*, 6 June 1881, 8858; Marcellus Eugene Thornton, *Aaron Burr: A Tragedy in Five Acts*, 15 August 1901, D763; Marie Ida Wishaar, *Aaron Burr: A Tale of the Revolution*, 19 October 1905, D7520. A number of unpublished plays, however, are available at the U.S. Copyright Office in Washington, D.C.: Howard Wiswall Bible, *Aaron Burr: An Historical Drama in Four Acts*, 11 October 1926, D77129; Robert Goldstein, *Aaron Burr: A Play in Four Acts*, 15 November 1927, D82123; Charles A. Hallett, *Aaron Burr*, 25 April 1969, DU74165; Louis Leffer, *Aaron Burr: A Drama in Four Acts*, 21 October 1937, D52655; Louis Leiffer, *Aaron Burr*, 7 January 1939, DU61282; Ben McCrary, *Aaron and Theodosia or The Fate of the Burrs*, 29 March 1902, D1664; Leo Mishkin and William Boehnel, *Aaron Burr: A Play in Two Acts*, 3 March 1941, DU73862; Hattie May Pavlo, *Hamilton: A Drama in Three Acts*, 4 May 1948, DU14332; L. France Pierce, *Aaron Burr: A Romantic Drama in Four Acts*, 9 April 1901, D328. Recently, the Copyright Office has begun a microfilm project, the intention of which is to photocopy all plays that are not still protected by law. As of November 1976, this microfilm collection included dramas from 1901 to 1909; thus the plays of McCrary and Pierce are available on microfilm. (These two are also available on microprint cards. See *National Union Catalog: Pre-1956 Imprints* [London: Mansell Information/Publishing Limited, 1968–   ]).

2. Hugh Henry Brackenridge, *The Death of General Montgomery at the Siege of Quebec* (Philadelphia: Robert Bell, 1777).

3. To aid the reader in finding the passages cited from this play and from the other dramas discussed here, I have used page numbers instead of the more customary line numbers in my references because, in general, the plays have not been edited and therefore have been printed without line numbers. Thus II. 2. 19 refers to act II, scene 2, page 19.

4. Jerome Dowd, *Burr and Hamilton: A New York Tragedy* (New York: Geo. W. Wheat, 1884).

5. There are two earlier, extant plays: Anon., *The Conspiracy; or, The Western Island* (New York: Henry Spear, 1838), and William Russell Smith, *Aaron Burr; or, The Emperor of Mexico*, excerpted in *The Bachelor's Button* (Mobile, 1837), pp. 65–88. I discuss the first in the section on the conspiracy; the second I have been unable to secure. Another, early, anonymous *Aaron Burr* (1840) is no longer extant. See James Rees, *The Dramatic Authors of America* (Philadelphia: G. B. Zieber and Company, 1845), p. 21.

6. Charles Felton Pidgin, *Blennerhassett; or, The Decrees of Fate* (Boston: C. M. Clark, 1901). This play was also published in 1901 by C. M. Clark under the titles *Blennerhassett; or, The Irony of Fate* and *Blennerhassett: A Dramatic Romance*.

7. Chard Powers Smith, *Hamilton: A Poetic Drama* (New York: Coward-McCann, 1930).

8. Carl Van der Voort, *The Child of Nevis (Alexander Hamilton): A Play in the Old Manner* (Unpublished drama: Copyright, 1934).

9. Hattie May Pavlo, *Hamilton: A Drama in Three Acts* (Unpublished drama: Copyright, 1948, 1975).

10. Other dramatists dealing with the conspiracy include Leon Del Monte, *The Tragical History of Aaron Burr* (Cincinnati: Robert Clarke & Co., 1889); William L. O'Brien, *Aaron Burr: A Play in Four Acts* (Minneapolis: Review, 1908); and William Russell Smith, *Aaron Burr; or, The Emperor of Mexico*, excerpted in *The Bachelor's Button* (Mobile, 1837), pp. 65–88.

11. Anonymous, *The Conspiracy; or, The Western Island: A Drama in Five Acts* (New York: Henry Spear, 1838).

12. William Minturn [Defenthy Wright], *Aaron Burr: A Drama in Four Acts* (New York: Metropolitan Job Print, 1878).

13. Charles E. Stoaks, *Aaron Burr; or, The Kingdom of Silver* (Doylestown, Ohio: George A. Corbus, 1887).

14. See note 6 above for the play's bibliographical data.

15. L. France Pierce, *Aaron Burr: A Romantic Drama in Four Acts* (Unpublished drama: Copyright, 1901).

16. Edward Raiden, *Mr. Jefferson's Burr: A Play in Three Acts* (Los Angeles: Thunder, 1960).

17. Charles Frederic Nirdlinger, *The First Lady of the Land: A Play in Four Acts* (Boston: Walter H. Baker and Co., 1914). The play was first produced in 1911.

18. Charles A. Hallett, *Aaron Burr* (Unpublished drama: Copyright 1964, 1969). Extensive revisions were made in 1974 to ready the manuscript for the stage.

19. Ben McCrary, *Aaron and Theodosia or The Fate of the Burrs: A Drama in Five Acts* (Unpublished drama: Copyright, 1902).

20. Edgar Lee Masters, "Aaron Burr and Madam Jumel," in *Dramatic Duologues: Four Short Plays in Verse* (New York: Samuel French, 1934), pp. 37–75.

21. Thomas B. Sweeney, *Aaron Burr's Dream for the Southwest: A Drama for the Library* (San Antonio, Texas: Naylor, 1955).

22. Sweeney notes that some of Burr's ancestors on the Edwards side of the family were insane, a point he has Timothy Edwards make in the play:

"What a weird, incongruous lot we were, / With scars of homicidal insanity— / One killed her child; another, his sister; / Two were opium fiends, our aunt an idiot!" (I.1.3). A bit later, Burr's uncle also tells him directly: "Your tendency to go to such extremes / Is caused by the insanity which runs / In my family, and which is in your blood" (I.1.5). For a discussion of insanity in the Edwards family, see Ola Elizabeth Winslow, *Jonathan Edwards: 1703–1758* (1940; rpt. New York: Collier Books, 1961), pp. 26–28.

4. A Many-Sided, Aristocratic Jonathan _____

The image of Burr that appears in American novels and short stories is as multifaceted as that in the plays that deal with him. The vehicles used to express this diversity, however, are all too often depressingly similar; though there are some striking exceptions, the fiction depicting Burr is generally commonplace. American authors most often choose the formula romance or the shopworn historical novel as their form and tend to focus on predictable subjects: the Revolutionary War years, the conspiracy, the three major women in Burr's life, and his career from early to late. Some, however, find other types and aspects of Burr's story more appealing, and some handle the traditional forms and subjects in original ways, so there is an occasional surprise among what is typically a rather dreary lot. In any case, spanning as they do the nineteenth and twentieth centuries and ranging from moralistic condemnation to impassioned defense, the novels and stories that treat Burr, like their dramatic counterparts, depict him in a multiplicity of ways.

Representative of a miscellaneous category of fiction dealing with Burr, which uses him in unusual ways or touches upon not-often-discussed periods of his life, are three generally effective stories.[1] The first of these is James Thurber's "A Friend to Alexander" (1942).[2] In a short piece, Thurber uses the Colonel as symbolic of all the hostile, irrationally aggressive forces in modern life that bully and terrify man with their power and consequently make him feel insignificant and vulnerable. Henry Andrews, a successful architect coming unstrung, begins to have nightmares about Aaron Burr. In Henry's dreams, the Colonel is always pugnacious and provoking. One evening, for example, when Andrews sees himself talking to a beautiful woman, Burr suddenly appears, "bowing and smiling and smelling like a carnation, telling his stories about France and getting off his insults" (p. 140). Another night, as the architect talks with Alexander Hamilton, the Colonel steps up and slaps the great Federalist across the face. For Andrews, as the story progresses, Hamilton is transformed first into Henry's brother Walter, who was irrationally murdered in a cemetery by a drunkard, and after that into "practically every other guy [he] . . . ever liked" (p. 142). Then matters worsen. Burr begins "shoving Alexander around," and Hamilton "hides behind [Henry's] coattails every night, or tries to" (p. 142). Eventually, of course, the aggressor gets his man; Andrews stumbles into his wife's bedroom one morning to tell her: "The bastard got him. Alexander fired into the air, he fired in the air and smiled at him, just like Walter, and that fiend from hell took deliberate aim—I saw him—I saw him take deliberate aim—he killed him in cold blood, the foul scum!" (pp. 142–43).

In the next stage of the architect's dreams, Burr struts around, bragging that he won the duel "with his eyes closed." "He says he didn't even look," Henry tells his wife. "He claims he can hit the ace of spades at thirty paces blindfolded" (p. 145). Moreover, the murderer now turns his attention to this friend of Alexander's. Burr "jostles [Andrews] at parties" (p. 145) and taunts and bullies him continually, all the while suggesting that Henry is insignificant: "I'm beneath him," the architect remarks one morning. "I'm just anybody. I'm a man in a gray suit. 'Be on your good behavior, my good man,' he says to me, 'or I shall have one of my lackeys give you a taste of the riding crop' " (p. 147). Deeply disturbed by the progression of events in his nightmares, Henry actually begins to take target practice during his waking hours in preparation for a duel with Burr in his dreams. "It's him or me," Andrews finally proclaims. "I can't stand this forever" (p. 148).

Two days later, the architect is dead—a tragedy that puzzles Dr. Fox: "His heart was as sound as a dollar when I examined him the other day. It has just stopped as if he had been shot" (p. 153). But Mrs.

Andrews knows what has happened: "Aaron Burr killed him the way he killed Hamilton," she cries out. "Aaron Burr shot him through the heart" (p. 153). Then, with the doctor's comment that the hysterical woman is "Stark, raving crazy" (p. 153), Thurber brings to a close his chilling story that has made the reader feel anew the hostile forces of modern life—personified in Aaron Burr.

Another story to use the Colonel in a somewhat unusual way is Eudora Welty's "First Love" (1942), which deals with the mystery and inexpressibility of the emotion described in its title.[3] The unconventional aspect of the piece, however, is that twelve-year-old Joel Mayes falls in love with Aaron Burr instead of with some local Natchez belle. Yet the story is not a depiction of unnatural love or a polemic for gay power; rather it describes the usual and wholly natural feelings of a young boy in the presence of a man he admires, even adores.

To develop her theme, Welty depicts the Colonel as a being of dazzling brilliance and therefore as a seductive force. Joel's first perception of Burr, for example, is that of brightness. Awakened one night by the conversation of the Colonel and Blennerhassett, who, unaware of the boy's presence, have invaded his room to talk of their plans, Joel opens his eyes "to see the whole room shining brightly, like a brimming lake in the sun" (p. 10). As the boy watches the two men conversing, he is stunned by a graceful gesture Burr makes—a simple movement of the arm that magically illuminates the world for him: "It was like the signal to open some heavy gate or paddock, and it did open to his complete astonishment upon a panorama in his own head, about which he knew first of all that he would never be able to speak— it was nothing but brightness, as full as the brightness on which he had opened his eyes" (p. 11).

Throughout the rest of the story, Welty continues to portray the Colonel as a figure of radiance in order to suggest the effect he has upon the boy. Each night, for example, when the two conspirators return, Joel is transfixed; "there [is] something of fire in all that [happens]": "It was from Aaron Burr that the flame was springing, and it seemed to pass across the table with certain words and through the sudden nobleness of the gesture, and touch Blennerhassett" (p. 14). In a later scene, Joel unconsciously connects Burr with a striking event from the past. As he sits one night, watching the Colonel and the

Blennerhassetts, the boy momentarily slips into reverie: "Instead of the fire on the hearth, there was a mimosa tree in flower" (p. 24). In his vision, Joel remembers that back in Virginia his mother had shown him that glorious tree and had told him then the story of Princess Labam—"how she was so radiant that she sat on the roof-top at night and lighted the city" (p. 25). Feeling now the same romantic emotion that his mother's story had previously evoked, he unconsciously links the Colonel with the beautiful tree and the brilliant Asiatic princess. At Burr's trial, the Colonel is again depicted as a dazzling figure, this time as he explains away his alleged treason: "He walked back and forth elegantly in the sun, turning his wrist ever so airily in its frill. . . . All around Joel they gasped, smiled, pressed one another's arms, nodded their heads; there were tender smiles on the women's faces. They were at Aaron Burr's feet at last" (pp. 30–31).

In the story, however, Burr is not only a radiant force but also a seductive one. To highlight this aspect of Burr's portrait, Welty makes occasional use of sexual suggestion and terminology in recording Joel's response to the great conspirator. Thus the boy's first reaction to the Colonel's presence is one of "violation," of ravishment (p. 11); and Burr quickly becomes associated in the boy's mind with dark, frightening powers: "When Joel woke up again at daylight, his first thought was of Indians, his next of ghosts, and then the vision of what had happened [the sudden intrusion of Burr and Blennerhassett] came back into his head" (p. 12). In watching the Colonel skillfully draw Blennerhassett into his scheme, the boy feels that "everything in the room was conquest" (p. 15), an emotion that again highlights Burr's power and seductiveness. From Joel's perspective, there is "a kind of dominion promised in his [the Colonel's] gentlest glance" (p. 16).

"First Love," then, is a stunning achievement, reflective of its author's major talent. Welty is able to depict Burr as an object of adoration and a seducer at the same time, harmonizing these apparently antipodal roles by making the Colonel's seductiveness lie in what he is, a character of dazzling brilliance whose personal charm makes people cherish and want to support him. In addition, without in the least damaging the credibility of her story, she somehow takes the elements of a love-sick, adoring girl and transfers them to a twelve-year-old deaf mute who falls in love with an older man. And with unusual skill, she suggests and underlines the fate of Joel's love by using a background of ice and death to open and close the story. In the early paragraphs, she notes that this is "the bitterest winter of them all" (p. 3) and depicts a threatening world that kills: "Natchez people turned silently to look when a solitary man that no one had ever seen before was found and carried in through the streets, frozen the way he had crouched in a hollow tree, gray and huddled like a squirrel, with a little bundle of goods clasped to him" (pp. 4–5). And, at the end, she points out that, as Joel walks in a daze down the road Burr took to leave town, the boy "saw that the bodies of the frozen birds had fallen out of the trees" (p. 33).

Not quite so good as "First Love" is William T. Polk's "Golden Eagle Ordinary" (1956), which, however, has the value of dealing with a comparatively neglected period in Burr's life, the trip under guard to Richmond to stand trial for treason.[4] Polk's first extended description of the Colonel makes it evident that the image of Burr here will be favorable: "His brow was high and philosophically calm. His mouth was well-formed but large—the mouth of a generous, humorous man—the chin was firm, even pugnacious, but the large hazel eyes beneath the dark arched brows, they were what you noticed both first and last, sometimes full of piercing fire, and sometimes, as now, brooding and melancholy, the eyes of a poet adventurer" (p. 42).[5] No traitor in this story, Burr is instead a man with a dream of empire. His innocence and his imperial goals are made obvious in an exchange at the Golden Eagle Ordinary, a hotel and tap room in Warrenton, North Carolina, between him and Senator Gideon Bullock, who believes the Colonel guilty. Bullock charges, "You lack moral principles. You betrayed your country." But Burr interrupts: "Stop! I'm not a traitor. I never intended to take an inch of the territory of the United States—." The dialogue continues:

"But you would have taken Mexico."
"Oh well, Mexico—" Colonel Burr shrugged.
"And for what but to threaten the Union? What would you have done with it?"
"That's a secret." The colonel's voice was playful. He glanced at the girl. [P. 46]

Innocent of treason, Burr becomes a victim of Jefferson's enmity. This aspect of Burr's portrait is suggested in the Colonel's ruminations about his plight. As the stagecoach carrying him to Richmond rattles along the Carolina roads, for example, Burr reflects: "He had reason to believe that the Sage of Monticello, now wielding presidential power, would leave no juror and no witness unturned to convict him. Therefore he considered it not unlikely that due process of law would leave him in a state of suspended inanimation" (p. 42). And after his banter with Gideon Bullock, he wonders what accounts for the senator's presence in Warrenton: "Was it coincidence . . . or another sign of the meticulous vigilance of his arch enemy in the White House?" (p. 44).

Primarily, however, Polk depicts Burr as a romantic figure, as a suitable subject for larger-than-life representation. His dress, for instance, marks him as an uncommon man, setting him apart from the hoi polloi. On this particular day of his trip, the Colonel is "clothed in a long, dark purple coat, white brocaded waistcoast, knee breeches, and white stockings" (p. 44); his shoes, the author notes, are trimmed with "silver buckles" (p. 42). A chivalric hero in a democratic land, he is ever alert to feminine loveliness—"His heart leaped up, his eyes opened wide, and he bowed gallantly" when he first entered the Golden Eagle Ordinary and noticed Shirley Stewart behind the bar (p. 44)—and he is always admiring of the female form: "he bent forward drinking in the fiery-smooth brandy and the fiery-smooth beauty of the girl's face and breast above the gold-flowered, v-shaped, low-cut bodice" (p. 45). His charm is also extraordinary, a fact attested to by the love many beautiful women have given him—"debutantes of Fairfield and Litchfield, Celeste of Philadelphia, Margaret Moncrieffe of New York, Madame de Castre, the singer of Stockholm, the Indian girl on the march to Quebec, the landlady's daughter at Janina, and the Princess Louisa of Gotha" (p. 48). It is, of course, this same, still dazzling charm that leads Shirley to risk prison in order to set him free; she sneaks him out of his guarded hotel room through a secret panel in the wall.

Like a glittering character in a Sir Walter Scott novel, he also embodies the romantic attitude. Loath to leave his charming rescuer, he lectures her on the importance of experiencing to the full the occasionally dramatic moments in our humdrum, daily lives, telling her:

"This is one of life's exquisite hours, compounded of beauty and darkness,— danger and romance. So rare, so swift . . . and we let them slip through our fingers till life itself is gone! . . . Remember this, Shirley, don't let them slip past you too quickly. You must recognize them by a certain glory—they are garlanded with beauty and jewelled with peril—and you must hold tight to them with the fingertips of your body and soul. One of them is as good as a dull lifetime, two are better than a hope of heaven, and three—oh, three are worth the risk of a visit to hell." [P. 49]

It is not surprising, then, that Burr, holding such a view, acts in romantic fashion. He lingers with Shirley, for example, seizing the golden moment, but in doing so "kiss[es] away his chance of escape!" (p. 49)—the sergeants recapture him. Even when the girl turns a gun on the two guards, the Colonel refuses to leave because, gallant that he is, he realizes that only a cad would place such a courageous and beautiful girl in a situation from which prison is the likely outcome: "It won't do," he tells her. "Did you think—I could leave you—here like this? . . . Let them go, dear" (p. 50). Overall, then, the portrait of the Colonel is positive, and the story generally satisfactory.

Two novels represent the relatively few books that focus upon Burr's Revolutionary War years.[6] Together they contain the major images American authors use in depicting this formative period in the Colonel's life. The first of these, Joseph Holt Ingraham's two-volume *Burton; or, The Sieges: A Romance* (1838), aims, as the author notes in his preface, "at unfolding the steps by which a chivalrous youth, his heart beating high with honour and patriotism, became, in time, the Catiline of his country."[7] By revealing Burr's early sexual irregularities, Ingraham hopes to suggest how the "betrayer of female confidence" could later become, "by a natural and easy transition," the "betrayer of the trust reposed in him by his country" (1: x).

In Book 1, however, subtitled *The Siege of Quebec*, Ingraham provides a generally favorable treatment of Burr, here called Burton, perhaps because the novel was published only two years after the Colonel's death. Primarily, Burton is the typical romance hero—a hot-blooded but insightful youth, ardent for his country's cause and heroic in battle. Thus Ingraham depicts him early in the novel as a courageous patriot. When the Chevalier de Levi expresses dismay that Arnold has chosen "a beardless boy" as his messenger to Montgomery, Burton replies zealously: "Wisdom is not always found with gray hairs, nor is age the infallible test of experience. If devotion to the cause I have voluntarily embraced may be thrown into the scale against my youth, and if indifference to danger may be allowed to balance inexperience, then am I a fitting messenger" (1: 39).

Ingraham also depicts Burton as a shrewd judge of human nature. When he realizes, for example, that Zacharie Nicolet, his Canadian guide, has penetrated his monk's disguise, Burton decides to take Zacharie into his confidence rather than threaten him, believing that such a gesture will insure the guide's faithfulness. Of this resolution, the omniscient author notes: "The attitude assumed by the monk at this crisis not only furnished a proof of his knowledge of human nature, but did honour to his heart" (1: 82). Zacharie makes clear that Burton's assessment of him has been perceptive and wise. "Thou art the first man," he tells the American, "that ever saw [in] me other than the horned devil himself. . . . [A]nd, for treating me like a reasonable being as thou has done, instead of doing thee an injury, I would fight for thee against my mother" (1: 82).

Of course, Burton is also portrayed as a hero in battle. When Montgomery is killed during the assault on Quebec, his aide immediately assumes command and encourages the men to charge. "The soldiers," the novelist notes, ". . . inspired by the thrilling voice of the young officer, sternly grasped their weapons, and with a loud cry rallied around him. He himself was already at the foot of the bastion, ascending a scaling ladder which had been planted against it by Zacharie, who, like his shadow, kept by his side" (1: 222–23). When the foolish Colonel Campbell calls for a retreat, Burton hurries to Arnold's division to assist in the attack on the city from the other side of town. It is during his heroic efforts to storm the second barrier there that he is taken prisoner.

Ingraham, however, is careful to suggest the flaws of character that will later lead Burton to betray his country. The first full description of the titular character, for example, is mixed; the sensual aspects of his features tend to undercut the noble qualities suggested. Burton is, by his own admission, restlessly ambitious: "Why am I tortured with ambitious aspirations," he asks, "and mocked, sleeping and waking, with visions of power and empire, which, when I would grasp them, elude me? Delusive temptations, pointing me to the temple's pinnacle that my fall may be far and sure! But, stand or fall, I must fulfil[l] my destiny" (1: 18). Noting this same trait in Burton's character, the chevalier tells him that "ambition is the idol of [his] worship" and warns: "Most of all, beware of thyself" (1: 42). The chevalier also points to Burton's hotheadedness when the young major suggests that his pistols will guarantee his success in reaching Montgomery's camp: "Rash and inconsiderate," de Levi sniffs in displeasure. "There is that in the hot blood of youth which unfits them as agents in schemes that require the least grain of either caution or secrecy. . . . I would dissuade thee, on account of thy unfitness for an emprise where coolness and discretion are in demand" (1: 40).

But it is the image of libertine and seducer that is central to Ingraham's depiction of Burton's flaws. This aspect of the major's character is first revealed in the way Burton greets Jaquette Benoit, the wife of one of his peasant guides. Rather than bestowing the "kiss of sisterhood" on her cheek, the young officer, disguised as a monk, "gracefully pass[es] his arm half round her waist, and, gently drawing her towards him, press[es], instead, her lips with his own . . . with rather more warmth than beseem[s] his cloth" (1: 20–21). His predatory nature is more fully revealed, however, in his musing on his decision to convey Eugenie de Lisle to family friends without trying her virtue: "Heighho! 'tis a great temptation . . . for one to whom laurels won in love are fairer than the bays plucked in war. . . . Her extreme loveliness and naive manner have so effectually captivated me . . . that, if I do not call in honour, her orphan state, and her unsuspecting confidence, and weigh them nicely against that propensity for intrigue that is in me, she would better trust her vestal purity with a Rochester than with me. Well, women are, at last, but charming toys to amuse our leisure hours withal" (1: 135–36). Because the major falls truly in love with Eugenie, however, as he conducts her to Montgomery's camp, he is able to keep his profligate instincts in check. Overall, then, Burton is more good than bad in Book 1, though his basic flaws suggested here, especially his unscrupulousness with women, foreshadow problems for the second volume.

In Book 2, *The Siege of New-York*, Ingraham fulfills the expectations he has previously raised by depicting Burton primarily as a debaucher. Early in this part of the story, for example, he has Washington upbraid the major for his sexual transgressions: "I am not ignorant, sir, of your vanity . . . nor of the testimonials you have displayed to your brother officers, in my presence, of the weakness of the sex . . .

which it is your boast to degrade. This morning, sir . . . I overheard you shamefully boast to a group of officers of an instance of successful passion, wherein you had grossly violated the solemn bonds of friendship. It would appear, sir, that, like the Indian who preserves the scalps of his foes, you delight to cherish trophies of your victories" (2: 29–30). About midway in the volume, Ingraham himself, unable to resist moralistic comment, condemns Burton as a cold-hearted seducer. Picturing the major's reaction to the first meeting of Caroline Germaine, whom Burton has ruined, and of Eugenie de Lisle, whom he intends as his next victim, the author notes: "The dark and guilty being . . . paced the room in silence. Occasionally he glanced towards the sofa, but his thoughts were buried in schemes of conquest, alas! such conquests as degrade humanity" (2: 111).

The portrait is not entirely dark, however. When Caroline Germaine asks heavenly forgiveness for Burton with her dying breath, her exploiter feels piercing sorrow, though his pride does cause him to disguise his emotions. Echoing the image of the major presented in Book 1, Ingraham also depicts him here as still heroic in battle. During the fighting at Brooklyn Heights, Burton reveals his courage by rescuing a regiment cut off from the main body of American troops and by saving General Putnam from a British sword. Of the major's martial valor, the author exclaims: "Would that the romancer were called to unfold alone his military career! to hold up only the bright side of the shield!" (2: 263). Burton's residual nobility manifests itself near the end when he recognizes the appropriateness of Isabel Ney's revenge—she has shot him for his faithlessness to Caroline, Eugenie, and herself—and allows the girl and her British escort to get away: "Hold!" he cries to the American soldiers. "There is a female in the boat. Let them escape. I have deserved this" (2: 274). The primary image of Burton in Book 2, however, is that of predator, a portrayal attested to by the nickname "Earl," which the major now bears, linking him with the heinous seducer, the Earl of Rochester.

Though *Burton* is useful because of its depiction of Burr, the novel is artistically commonplace. The dialogue, for example, is often stilted. When Colonel Arden reveals that Burton has ruined Caroline Germaine and is therefore responsible for the girl's suffering, Eugenie woodenly exclaims: "Merciful God! how blind I am! I see, I know it all" (2: 132). Effusive language marks the treatment of true love wherever it appears. Of the relationship between Arden and Eugenie, for example, Ingraham notes: "She adored him without impiety; he worshipped her without forgetting that she was mortal. Their love was such as would bear the test of time and trial—that virtuous union of souls which earth and Heaven unite to render permanent and happy" (2: 266). The novel also presents a banal world where women are delicate and men are strong, where the pathetic fallacy is frequently in evidence, and where even the enemy recognizes the valor and nobleness of the Americans. Cornwallis, musing over the battlefield at Brooklyn Heights, makes the point: "Never will a people be conquered who . . . rise as one man, and expose their breasts as a bulwark to their liberties. From their wonderful Congress and their remarkable leader down to the lowest hind, these Americans seem to be actuated by one sentiment. It must be a long and fruitless struggle to subdue such a people!" (2: 172). Ingraham, of course, presents the usual exciting battle tableaux, where heroism is frequent, and the requisite scenes of melodrama, replete with dying girls and grim prophecies. He even provides the reader with the reason for his novel's length: "We are bound to our publishers," he comments, "to produce two respectable duodecimos, of neither less than two hundred and sixteen pages each nor more than two hundred and eighty-eight" (2: 221).

No better, unfortunately, is Charles Burdett's *The Beautiful Spy* (1865), which, however, has the distinction of being written by one of Burr's probable bastards.[8] A clerk in the Colonel's law office, Burdett presents a mixed portrait of Burr. The initial depiction of Burr, however, is generally favorable. He is described, for example, as a handsome and charming young soldier, though his eyes, the author points out, "could be likened only to those of a snake, for their fascination was irresistible" (p. 17). There are clearly noble aspects to the Colonel's character. A magnanimous man, he spends his patrimony in his country's cause and prevents needless cruelty by his troops. When the "cowboys" (Tory sympathizers) are unsuccessful in their attack upon Burr and his men as they escort Margaret Moncrieffe to General Putnam's headquarters, the Colonel refuses to allow the soldiers to put the wounded cowboys to death. He is also ambitious for an honorable fame—"My mistress is glory," he declares. "I mean to make a name—to leave my mark on the page of history" (p. 185)—and he is

courageous in battle. The author makes clear that Burr "had won im-
perishable renown by his coolness and bravery, on every occasion,
when either had been called forth"; that he "had passed waist-deep
through the snow to attack the frowning fortress of Quebec"; and that,
"when the chance shot fired by a sailor [had] carried death and desolation into the ranks of the Americans . . . [he had] refused to leave his
beloved commander who lay cold in death, but [had] staggered
through the snow, bearing his precious burden on his youthful
shoulders" (pp. 66–67).

Negative traits in Burr's character, however, tend to overshadow
his nobler instincts. Burdett portrays the Colonel here, for example, as
a faithless trifler. When he shows Burr making love to Patsy Adams,
he comments: "Perhaps she thought he came wooing, for he had often
told her how much he loved her, and she, poor fool, had believed him"
(p. 26). Burdett also likens Burr to Paris—the most famous of the
classical predators—in depicting Burr's first meeting with Margaret
Moncrieffe: "There she stood before a young officer scarcely out of
his teens, awaiting, as did Helen before Paris, the judgment she had
courted" (p. 31). And the author has Burr demonstrate the infidelity
common to his type when he shows the Colonel deciding to forsake
simple Patsy for aristocratic Margaret: "He thought what a wife she
would make, and he determined, in forgetfulness of all he had said to
Patsy, and heedless of the pangs which his faithlessness would cause
her, to make the effort to win this paragon" (p. 64).

Ironically, the deceiver becomes a victim at his own game, as the
title of Chapter 8, "Major Burr Enslaved," suggests. Burdett comments: "there was a magic in her [Margaret's] presence, a fascination
in her look, which subdued him, and rendered him powerless" (p.
333). Thus Burr succumbs to "the invincible power of the little god,
who, from the days of Adam and Eve, has ruled the world" (p. 346).
Unfortunately, such enslavement leads Burr to commit himself, at
least for a while, to Margaret's cause—she is fiercely pro-British—
and therefore to treason. In melodramatic prose, Burdett depicts the
moment of decision: "The hour had arrived when he was called upon
to sacrifice honor, name and reputation. . . . He saw before him, even
at his feet, the deep, dark abyss of crime into which he was about to
plunge, and for the moment shrunk back aghast at the spectacle thus
presented to him; but through the darkness, and gloom and despair of

that void, there beamed a bright and shining light—the eyes of Margaret lighted with love . . . and involuntarily he exclaimed, half aloud: 'Margaret, dear Margaret, you at any sacrifice' " (pp. 339–40). But in the end he remains true, refusing to go over to the British: "No, by the great God above, never; I love you, Margaret, but I will not sell my soul for you: I will not live, even for your love, to be branded as a traitor" (p. 372).

Artistically, Burdett's novel is undistinguished; like so many others, it is filled with the commonplaces of the romance. There is, for example, a beautiful heroine. Margaret is described as "tall—quite up to the standard fixed by that *arbiter elegantiorum*, Lord Chester-field—with a form fully developed in all the glory of budding woman-hood" (p. 31). The plot itself is thoroughly standard. Set during the Revolutionary War and filled with spies, traitors, and nefarious intrigues, it is a story "of decided and most desperate love at first sight" (p. 64), a narrative based upon the typical conflict between love and duty. "The alternative," Burdett notes of the Colonel's dilemma, "was now plainly presented to him, and he either must lose her [Margaret], or, in winning her, sacrifice all he had been accustomed to look upon as sacred and honorable" (p. 274). Predictably, the story also involves the ruination of virgins (Lizzie Brainard) and contains such stock scenes as the reunion of long-lost brothers (one fighting for America, the other for England). In addition, it is rife with the inflated prose of romantic fiction. A sample: "In another moment she was clasped in the arms of him to whom she had given her virgin affections; him, for whom she would have sacrificed her very soul; him, whom meaning to serve, she had betrayed and purchased with the price of her love" (p. 270). All in all, Burdett, like most novelists treating the Colonel's war years, too often nods.

By far the most popular subject for American authors depicting Burr in their fiction is the conspiracy; some eighteen works deal, in whole or in part, with the Colonel and his western schemes. Five novels, however, represent the range of images in and the various literary quality of the fictional works in which Burr appears.[9] The first of these, William Henry Venable's *A Dream of Empire or The House of Blennerhassett* (1901), provides the standard view of Burr used in many nineteenth- and early twentieth-century romances.[10] Here, then, is the fop and courtly gentleman who always dresses fastidiously, as he does, for example, when he sets out to win Wilkinson's allegiance: "Arrayed in his best cloth," Venable reports, "with boots freshly polished and face smoothly shaven, with queue and ruffles in perfect condition, a Beau Brummel[1] of exterior properties . . . Aaron Burr presented himself at the barracks" (p. 83). In social arts, he reveals himself the perfect courtier, the "American Chesterfield" (p.51). At his first dinner with the Blennerhassetts, for instance, he dazzles the company with his grace, making even young Arlington envy him. Here, too, is the skillful Lothario. "Seldom had he failed in the winning art of conversation, especially with women," the author remarks early in the novel. "Ladies were his favorite pursuit, if not his prey" (p. 74). His profligate ways are also made clear in his treatment of Salome Rosemary, whom he jilts and bilks of her inheritance, and in his trifling with Margaret Blennerhassett, whom he entices merely for sport. Venable notes: "He was reckless of consequences, vain of conquest over any woman, and scrupulous only to avoid failure in his amours. The more innocent and virtuous the victim, the keener and more careful was he in pursuit" (p. 162).

Venable also portrays Burr as a dreamer, a frequent image in the novels. As he floats down the Mississippi on the barge Wilkinson has provided him, for example, the Colonel becomes lost in a vision of empire: "He was, for the time, possessed by the sensation of being royal. He enjoyed by anticipation the prerogatives of sovereignty, the power, the luxury, the voluptuous pleasure. . . . Imaginations so extravagant, courted in solitude and fed by indolence, served to beguile the days of the long voyage fróm Fort Massac to New Orleans" (p. 120). Burr the Machiavellian schemer, another common image, is also depicted here, as he manipulates others for his own ends. In Pittsburgh, for example, before he begins his first western tour, he is careful to receive all who come to see him—"Not the humblest caller was slighted" (p. 23)—and to feign interest in everything the city fathers have to say as they show him the town sights. To win over Hugh Henry Brackenridge, he even quotes verses from the Judge's The Battle of Bunkers-Hill. When he reaches New Orleans, he employs these same techniques, of course, to conquer the people there. But Burr's manipulating is most fully revealed in his seduction of important figures. With Senator Smith of Ohio, for instance, the Colonel is especially skillful. He encourages confidential revelations, feigns interest in Smith's various affairs, and plays upon the senator's cupidity: "Adroitly did Burr shift the trend of disclosure to suit his own ends, leading the elder by plausible arguments to accept as logical the sophistry of self-love and greed" (p. 79). With Wilkinson he reaches perfection (see Chapter 8), leading the general to reflect admiringly that "Aaron Burr is a shrewd manipulator of men" (p. 93). There are even direct links made between the Colonel and Machiavelli, most notably when Burr and Blennerhassett discuss *The Prince*.

Because Venable's view of Burr is largely negative, it comes as no surprise that the principal image of him presented in *Dream* is that of traitor. Throughout the book, the author makes clear that what Burr has in mind is inimical to the United States. Early in the novel, for example, he shows the Colonel contemplating separatist schemes as he travels down the Ohio to Marietta: "Why not conquer Mexico," he muses, "make New Orleans the capital of a magnificent empire, and possibly annex the southwestern States of the severed Union. Myself the emperor of the richest realm on the globe, my daughter the crown princess and prospective queen Theodosia" (pp. 37–38). Later, as Burr continues his western tour, the author depicts him solidifying his traitorous plans and setting about his great conspiracy. By August 1806, then, this "Brutus," this "Caesar" (p. 272), is portrayed as ready to begin the dismemberment of his country.

The final image of Burr, in the novel as in life, is that of pariah. As the Colonel prepares to flee from further prosecution after his Mississippi trial, he capsulizes his own position when he remarks in a final conversation with Arlington: "I am an outcast and an outlaw" (p. 325). In the last chapter, the author has Danvers review Burr's lonely and tragic life from the time of his Richmond trial in 1807 to the present in 1815 and comment: "Burr declares himself severed from the human race, and so he is" (p. 334).

Though Venable's novel is important because it contains many of the images American authors use when they depict Burr and his conspiracy, its literary value is negligible. *Dream*'s style, for example, suffers from a variety of ills. The metaphor is often banal and elaborate, the language is frequently that of the stock romance, and the word choice is sometimes laughable. When Madam Blennerhassett, offended by Plutarch Byle's admiring glance, makes evident her annoyance, the author writes: "Speechless for the moment, but not blinded, Plutarch withdrew his optics from the imperious dame, and took an instantaneous brain-picture of her companion" (p. 15). There is as well a similar roughness in Venable's handling of other artistic elements. The obviousness of the foreshadowing and symbolism, for example, is distracting; several of the apparently important characters, notably Dr. Deville and Salome Rosemary, are never worked smoothly into the plot; and the author himself is subject to occasional lapses. Early in the book, he has Blennerhassett write separatist articles for the Ohio *Gazette*, but, at the end, he portrays the Irishman as unaware of Burr's treasonous designs. *Dream*'s major failing, however, is a disturbing lack of focus. Its subtitle, *The House of Blennerhassett*, suggests that Margaret and Harman are to be of primary importance. But the book is as much about Burr as it is about them, and the twin love stories of Arlington and Evaleen and of Danvers and Lucrece occupy much of Venable's attention. In addition, Plutarch Byle, the nosey, backwoods giant, also assumes a major role in the novel, a fact suggesting that the author is more intrigued with this character than with his announced subject. The result of such diffusion of interest, of course, is a weakened plot, the one element that might have redeemed an otherwise tiresome novel.

Another work that treats Burr negatively is Emerson Hough's *The Magnificent Adventure* (1916).[11] Like other novels touching upon the Colonel's western schemes, it depicts Burr as an ambitious conspirator. The Colonel's aspiring nature becomes obvious when he explains his aims to Theodosia: "Power, place—these are the things that strong men covet. . . . I plan for myself some greater office than second fiddle in this tawdry republic along the Atlantic. I want the first place, and in a greater field!" (p. 88). There is little doubt that Burr intends treason. To British Minister Merry and Spanish Ambassador Yrujo, he notes: "Those who march with me are in alliance with natural events. This republic is split now, at this very moment. It must follow its own fate. If the flag of Spain were west of it on the south, and the flag of Britain west of it on the north, why, then we should have the natural end of the republic's expansion. With those great powers in alliance at its back . . . it would be a simple thing, I say, to crush this republic against the wall of the Appalachians, or to drive it once more into the sea" (pp. 75–76).

Hough darkens this usual picture of Burr, however, by portraying him as willing to use his daughter's charms to further his purposes. In this book at least, if not in history, the fate of Burr's conspiracy depends upon the outcome of the Lewis and Clark expedition. Should the explorers reach the Pacific, they will have succeeded in driving a wedge between the British-controlled territory in the north and the Spanish-dominated area in the west and south. Settlers will then rapidly occupy the territory, making it impossible for the two powers to unite effectively against the United States. Merry, therefore, makes British support of Burr's scheme dependent upon his stopping the expedition.

Enter Theodosia. Burr realizes that Meriwether Lewis is still in love with Theodosia—his marriage proposal had come two weeks late; by the time Lewis arrived in New York, the girl had already agreed to become Alston's wife. Burr also knows that his daughter still secretly prefers Lewis. Hence the Colonel decides to use Theodosia to foil the expedition. He tells her that Lewis' mission is doomed to failure, that it is constitutionally impossible for Congress to ratify the illegal Louisiana Purchase and that, if Lewis joins with him in organizing the Mississippi Valley under a new government, the young man will achieve fame and wealth instead of obloquy and ruin. Knowing that his daughter will want what is best for the man she truly loves, Burr sends her to Lewis to persuade him to abandon his commitment to Jefferson. When this first attempt fails, however, Burr makes clear that he wants Theodosia to seduce the great explorer so that he will be under their control:

"Ask him no longer to return to us and opportunity. *Ask him to come back to Theodosia Burr and happiness*—do you understand?"

"Sir," said his daughter, "I think—I think I do not understand!"

He seemed not to hear her—or to toss her answer aside.

"You must try again," said he, "and with the right weapons—the old ones, my dear—the old weapons of a woman!" [Pp. 103–04]

Fortunately for the country, Lewis resists further importuning, and the conspiracy is crushed, Burr ending his days as "a broken, homeless, forsaken man" (p. 354).

Though the portrait of Burr presented here has its unusual elements, the novel as an artistic attempt does not. *Adventure*, for example, by genre an historical romance, is somewhat short on history. Though Hough's occasional footnotes and his use in the text of actual letters and proclamations suggest a careful regard for fact, the main situation is clearly fictional. The fate of the Burr conspiracy was unrelated to the success or failure of the Lewis and Clark expedition. In addition, the novel never rises above formula. *Adventure* is, for instance, blatantly celebratory. It depicts the glorious America of yesteryear, presided over by a leader (Jefferson) whose greatness matches the challenge before him and peopled by heroic men whose endurance leads to great achievement. The novel also relies upon sentimental and melodramatic scenes of the most obvious sort to hold the reader's interest. Chapter 1 consists of a tender discussion between the young Meriwether Lewis and his mother about the boy's great but painful future; Mrs. Lewis foretells tragedy in love and in life for her noble son. There is a grandly tempestuous scene as well, in which Lewis and Theodosia bid each other adieu on the morning the explorer leaves for the wilderness, Lewis momentarily succumbing to his emotions and kissing his beloved. There is a scene of great melodrama near the end when Lewis, dying from multiple wounds, struggles nobly to burn Theodosia's letters so that scandal will never taint her name. Also typical and formulaic is *Adventure*'s heavy-handed symbolism (a snake, the traditional emblem of temptation, appears at the lovers' first meeting), and, of course, the book is full of stock dialogue. An early discussion between Theodosia and Lewis makes the point:

> "You would never doubt my faith in my husband."
> "No! Of course, you love your husband. I could not look at you a second time if you did not."
> "You are a good man, Meriwether Lewis!" [P. 25]

Hough's novel, then, lacks technical ingenuity.

No better, and perhaps worse, is A. E. Dupuy's *The Conspirator* (1850), which, however, has the virtue of depicting Burr in a somewhat unconventional way.[12] Here the image of Burr (in this book, Colonel Frederick Alwin) is that of tragic hero. He is, for example, a man of high place, holding the second office in the land and having been deprived of the first only through injustice. He is basically good. Compassionate, loving, and generous, he adopts the orphaned Julie de Bourg (Natalie de Lage), raising her as his own, and devotes extraordinary attention to his daughter Isabel (Theodosia). A man of absolute personal integrity, his word is his bond. "The promise of such a man," General Zavala tells his nephew, Don Pedro, "is sufficient guarantee for the fulfil[l]ment of his word; for an honorable man, all concur in considering him" (p. 196). He is, in addition, exceptionally talented, possessing great qualities of leadership. In trying to persuade Russell (probably Charles Burdett) to join Alwin's forces, Don Pedro notes: "If determination of purpose, and constancy in the pursuit of his object, united with brilliant talent and despatch in business, can make him successful, he must be so. . . . As a leader he is invaluable" (p. 50).

Alwin is, however, also sadly flawed. He is filled with the desire for revenge against Jefferson, for example, who has stolen the presidency from him. In contemplating his future success, the Colonel makes clear his vindictive feelings: "Let me see: power, empire, renown, what more shall I require? Humiliation to *him*; aye, 'twill be sweet beyond all the rest" (p. 120). But Alwin's primary failing is an unbounded ambition. He reveals this aspect of his character in a conversation at Fitzgerald's (Blennerhassett's) island. Commenting upon the Irishman's passive existence, Alwin declares: "I could sooner die than curb my spirit down to so tame an existence; I should be like an imprisoned eagle. . . . I have often thought what a glorious sensation it must be to soar above the earth, monarch of the air, forcing all others of his tribe to yield to his power. Heavens! what a destiny—could one man possess such sway upon earth" (p. 18).

To fulfill his ambitions, the Colonel contrives a treasonous plan to revolutionize Mexico, separate the western states from the Union, and become a sovereign ruler. In attempting to carry his schemes out, though, he brings destruction upon himself and sinks into a suicidal despair. Like a typical tragic hero, he is truly a man "borne down, crushed, trampled on, [and] torn from [his] proud station" (p. 253). The final image of Alwin in the novel is that of a blasted and aged man, grieving over the death of his daughter and mourning his fate.

The depiction of Burr that Dupuy presents is noteworthy, but her literary technique is unfortunately inept. She relies too heavily, for

example, upon the stock figures of nineteenth-century formula fiction—faithful darkies, pompous civil authorities, and hateful villains.
And she too frequently indulges in tiresome sentimentality. There are
tearful letters from dying mothers, revealed at appropriate moments,
passionate love missives, full of noble sacrifice (Russell, for example,
renounces his affection for Julie because, as a bastard, he feels unworthy of her), and deathbed reunions of dying parents and long-lost
sons. In addition, Dupuy's use of symbolism is painfully obvious. The
book Margaret Fitzgerald (Madame Blennerhassett) is reading, for
example, when her husband comes to tell her that he has joined
Alwin's group, is *Paradise Lost*. And the author feels it necessary to
resort to that shopworn technique, the digression, perhaps to fulfill the
demands of her formula or perhaps to spur reader interest. Thus she
provides a horrid story of love and murder in the Legend of the Devil's
Punch Bowls (Chapter 30) and presents the grisly narrative of
Graham's killing his sister and her little boy by strangling them with
the girl's own golden hair (Chapter 22). Overall, then, *The Conspirator* is a lackluster performance.

To portray Burr as a tragic hero, as Dupuy does, is certainly not
customary for authors treating the Colonel's western affairs, but even
more unusual is the depiction of him in a positive way. Nellie Whan
Peppers uses this approach in her otherwise typical romance *The
Young Mrs. Blennerhassett* (1964), which presents a favorable delineation of Burr throughout.[13] Here, for example, is the image of him as
a vigorous and forthright man. At his first dinner with the Blennerhassetts, he impresses them with his forceful manner: "He seemed to
have an endless flow of words," Peppers notes, "and he spoke them
with authority. And while they were listening with their ears they were
seeing with their eyes a small, distinguished-looking man with flash-
ing dark eyes and a charming smile who drove home every point he
made by bringing his fist down on the table" (pp. 186–87). The Colonel demonstrates his forthrightness when he gives Blennerhassett a
full explanation of his life, once Jefferson's proclamation virtually
destroys their hopes for continuing their colonization plans. Because
Harman has steadfastly supported him, Burr feels an obligation to
make known to his friend the crushing forces that have been at work.
Such warm-hearted frankness is further manifested in Burr's treatment of the sheriff who comes to arrest him at Colonel Hinson's. Burr

readily admits who he is, and, when he learns that the officer has neglected to obtain a warrant and therefore cannot legally take him prisoner, he invites the sheriff in from the stormy night. "You'll have plenty of time to make an arrest after we have both enjoyed our hostess's fine cooking" (p. 248), he tells the rain-soaked intruder.

Peppers also depicts Burr as a man of great charm, one not unwilling to exercise it on women. A devoted father to Theodosia, he is nonetheless an active gallant, as his flirtation with Mrs. Blennerhassett makes clear. On the night of a ball at the island mansion, given to introduce him and the Alstons to Marietta society, he boldly challenges Margaret to respond to his advances. Recognizing that he has excited her with his flattery and attentions, he pursues his advantage. "Until tonight," he tells her softly, "I thought my daughter was the most beautiful woman in the world. Now I know that you are" (p. 197). Though Mrs. Blennerhassett does not succumb, her infatuation with him documents the charm he holds for the ladies. "You will always find admiration in the eyes of the women you meet" (p. 255), Theodosia tells him.

But the major image of Burr here is that of a man victimized by his enemies. Peppers shows that Hamilton, for example, actively worked against and directly harmed the Colonel. Burr notes: "I have never quite understood why Alexander Hamilton resented me as he did. I still can't. He was a brilliant man and served his country well, but he never seemed to miss an opportunity to try to discredit me. There were many times when his influence resulted in votes against me" (p. 240). The trouble Burr encounters because of his western plans is portrayed as clearly the result of political malice rather than traitorous guilt. Twice he is brought to trial without sufficient evidence, and, in each case, after the dismissal of the charges, he proves his innocence by calling for a full investigation of his conduct. In addition, he does all that he can to reveal the ridiculous nature of the continued accusations against him, as the situation worsens, including making an offer to the Mississippi authorities to search his boats. Eventually, however, because of the action of his political enemies, notably Wilkinson, Burr is forced to abandon his goal of settling the Bastrop lands and is ultimately brought to trial for treason in Richmond. There Jefferson's enmity is made clear in his direction of the prosecutor's case. "Little did I think, back in 1800, when a tie vote made us political opponents," Burr remarks, "that seven years later we would again oppose one another" (p. 251). The final touch in this portrait of victimization, however, is the jury's complete vindication of Burr; the author upgrades the actual verdict of mere acquittal to one of total exoneration. Doubtlessly influenced, then, by a later twentieth-century perspective of the country's early figures—the novel was published in 1964—Peppers provides a sympathetic treatment of Burr throughout.

Another relatively recent work, Cyril Harris' *Street of Knives* (1950), is not so kind.[14] Noteworthy for its literary qualities as well as for its image of Burr, the novel portrays the Colonel as a man of considerable powers, who, unable to make peace with the past, destroys himself because of flaws within. It is clear, for example, that Burr has great talents. He is a skillful handler of men, as the scene in which he humiliates his secretary in order to make his other followers fear and therefore blindly obey him demonstrates. His adroitness in winning the affection of a crowd is equally deft, and his ability to control women is extraordinary—the Burr portrayed here is a successful philanderer. "He's a great wielder of women," Theodosia reflects, "not a doubt in the world of it, and the handsome ones especially" (p. 142).

Burr is also, however, a man on the rack. Irritable and touchy, capable of eating only the blandest of foods (his stomach is in constant turmoil), and unable to sleep well, Burr is a sufferer whose physical ailments spring from his bitterness. Seething with anger because of the way he has been treated, the Colonel is seemingly powerless to follow Meigs's healthful advice to start afresh in Kentucky: "No, Jonathan. You are talking against the wind. They broke my back in two. They hounded me and made game of me, and after that they turned me out of doors. Now I'm quit of them and God be thanked. I'll not rest till I'm up even with them again" (p. 90).

Primarily, though, the Burr depicted here is a man who brings destruction upon himself because of his flaws. He strikes out at those nearest him when he is disappointed, unable to keep his pain within, and he is unscrupulous in his dealings with others. He does not tell Blennerhassett until it is too late for the Irishman to save himself that he plans to separate the western states from the Union, pretending instead that he is interested solely in attacking Mexico. In addition, he regularly gives his son-in-law's name as the backer of his loans without bothering to ask Alston's permission and even tries to trick Theodosia's husband into signing a note for $20,000 instead of the agreed-upon $2,000 by adding an additional zero to the pledge. "He'll make use of you," Blennerhassett comments late in the novel, "whensoever he needs you. When he doesn't, you are laid to one side" (p. 311). But Burr's greatest failing is his propensity to deceive himself with dreams of glory. A good example of this self-defeating process occurs at one of the darker moments of the conspiracy when the Colonel tells his chief supporters about the situation ahead of them. Though he knows that Jefferson has issued his proclamation condemning their expedition and that troops are waiting at Natchez to arrest them all, Burr escapes reality by slipping into his own defensive vision of the future: "I see a day coming when a new nation will rise out of our marching, built by the young and the strong and the stout of heart. Our mountain stronghold will be known once more by its ancient name. The old gods will return to its temples. Obedience and Order will be our guard against the outer and the inner enemy. That's the history we'll be making" (p. 256). Such self-deception, of course, along with his other flaws, eventually leads Burr to failure and the brink of suicide.

Harris's novel, unlike so many others treating the conspiracy, is generally quite good, having several especially effective elements. The author's use of foreshadowing, for example, is much more skillful than that of his nineteenth-century counterparts. Instead of relying upon obvious comment, Harris subtly suggests in two crucial scenes that Burr's schemes will fail. The earlier of these—the annual muster of the Ohio militia—seems initially to point to the Colonel's success, as Burr smoothly draws the soldiers into his dreams with his spirited address. But the control he has over them is shown to be transient as, one by one, they drop out of the formation he is leading when it begins to rain. In the second of the ominous scenes—the Colonel's speech to the men of Belden township—Burr becomes so haughty that the crowd rejects him, and, in that repudiation, the author suggests the fate of the conspiracy. Another effective technique is the kind of upstairs-downstairs twist Harris gives the plot with his character Hugh Shadwell, Burr's natural son. His rebellious, skirt-chasing, robust antics provide a rough parallel to those of his nobler-born parent.

Most compelling for a twentieth-century audience, however, is

Harris' exploration of the sexual needs and rivalries of the various characters. There is, of course, the randy Burr, always in pursuit of the nearest petticoat. But the author also interjects other sexual details designed to hold the reader's attention. Harris presents, for example, a contest, replete with ironic outcome, between father and son for the affections of the same woman. Burr and Hugh set out to seduce Chrissie Young, a fetching barmaid at her father's tavern in Marietta, only to find that she is a match for both of them. After playing the Colonel along for her own purposes, she turns to Hugh, for whom her feelings run deeper. In addition, Harris also explores the unnaturally possessive relationship between Theodosia and her father. Mrs. Alston is angry with Burr, for example, for taking Hugh along on the expedition. "Why did you bring that misbegotten son of yours on board the boat to stand between me and everything I love?" (p. 76), she asks, reflecting the depths of her feelings when she shrieks: "You adore him. It's written all over your face when you and he are together. . . . Oh! My heart breaks when I see the two of you together" (p. 77). Such jealousy surfaces again during the party's stay at Blennerhassett's island. When Burr openly entices Margaret Blennerhassett at dinner one evening, Theodosia contemptuously thinks to herself: "How utterly absorbed in each other they are. . . . And those two great dugs of hers next thing to spilling out over the top of her gown" (p. 142). Burr's sexual feelings for his daughter are suggested, for example, in his disdain for his son-in-law. "I would to God," he tells Theodosia, referring to his grandson, "that a better man than Joseph Alston had been at the helm when this child was got" (p. 76). With its effective techniques, then, Harris' book is untypically good.

Several writers treat Burr's relationship with the important women in his life: Mrs. Prevost, Madame Jumel, Theodosia. Representative of this category are three novels whose range of portraits is surprising.[15] The first of these, J. Aubrey Tyson's *The Stirrup Cup* (1903), focuses upon the love story of Burr and Theodosia Prevost.[16] Set during the Revolutionary War, it provides a favorable image of Burr throughout. Here, for example, is the noble military man. Major André makes the point: "As a soldier he is valiant, and he is reputed to be a commander of exceptional ability. He is a strict disciplinarian and an excellent strategist" (p. 35). Here, too, is the courageous hero

in battle. In recounting a British officer's recollection of Burr's bravery, the narrator, Abel Hartrigg, notes: "Never will I forget the effect
produced upon us when, one night, Fothergill . . . told how, on the field
of Monmouth, he had seen Colonel Aaron Burr, standing at the head
of his tattered band of heroes, face unflinchingly a withering fire which
the blunder of a well-beloved chief had compelled them to endure" (p.
127).

The primary image of Burr in the novel, however, is that of chivalrous gentleman. When Sir Edward Moreton, the British commander,
is in danger of dying from battle wounds, for example, the Colonel gallantly sends his own regimental surgeon to attend him. No less gra-
cious is Burr's willingness to spare Thornton's life after he wounds the
Englishman slightly in a duel, even though Sir Henry has needlessly
provoked and grossly insulted him. But it is as the protector of women
and their reputation that Burr most obviously distinguishes himself as
a gentleman. When, for example, an American sergeant rudely
pushes Mrs. Prevost aside in order to search her house, Burr gallantly
comes to her aid. He knocks the sergeant down, shouting at the other
soldiers, "You hounds!   Has victory so robbed you of the little
grace you have that you forget that you are men?" (p. 66). And when
he decides not to arrest the wounded British commander, who has
been taken to Mrs. Prevost's house, he does so in order that Theodosia's action in taking care of a fallen enemy officer will not jeopar-
dize her position with Washington. The measure that most fully
denotes his role as woman's protector, however, is his refusal to explain his presence behind enemy lines at Mrs. Prevost's masked ball.
Though he will be hanged at sunrise as a spy if he does not reveal his
reason for coming—he has risked execution to ask Theodosia to
marry him—he refuses to endanger Mrs. Prevost's position and reputation. Fortunately for all concerned, Theodosia saves him by announcing that he is her "affianced husband" (p. 201).

Tyson's book has little to recommend it artistically. It is a standard
romance with such stock scenes as masked balls and duels and such
lilting chapter titles as "Showing How a Tryst Was Kept in the
Shadow of a Faun." Early in the novel, Abel Hartrigg himself describes the kind of narrative he will tell: "It is the story of a stirrup cup
[a farewell drink] that was drunk many years ago, at a time when the
mountain breezes brought to the Ramapo Valley the sound of bugle-

music, the clatter of many hoof-beats, the rattle of musketry, and the sullen and deep-toned voices of distant cannon" (p. 2). And a contemporaneous reviewer noted: "Mr. Tyson's little story, *The Stirrup Cup*, is as dainty a tale of love and wartime as one need care to read. . . . [T]here is something sweet and good and pure about it."

Certainly more interesting, if only because of its image of Burr, is Edith Sessions Tupper's *Hearts Triumphant* (1906).[17] Inaccurately depicting the Colonel's suit of Madame Jumel, the novel presents an uncommon portrait of Burr. There are, to be sure, some of the usual elements in the delineation. Tupper portrays the Colonel, for example, as a man of destructive potential. Thus he is described throughout as having "sinister eyes"; and, even before he kills Hamilton, he is known as "the most famous duelist of the day" (p. 137). In addition, the author depicts Burr as a spendthrift adventurer. At one point in the novel she notes: "His tastes were extravagant, his manner of living luxurious. And friend and enemy alike knew him to be wretchedly poor. A wealthy marriage seemed the only door to the rehabilitation of his unsettled fortunes" (p. 65). And here, too, is the Colonel as rake. "This American Lovelace was an expert in the gentle art of wooing, as many women knew to their cost. His heart affairs were distinguished, not alone in this country, but in European courts. Ladies of rank, as well as those of more humble station, bore witness to his singular power of fascination. . . . He was known everywhere as a dangerous and scarred veteran of Cupid" (p. 67).

But here as well is a Burr emotionally out of control and ultimately destroyed as a result. Though he is experienced in *affaires d'amour*, his feelings for Madame Jumel utterly consume him: "I am mad," he tells her, as she pleads for Trumbell's life, "mad with rage and love and jealousy. I am a desperate, broken-hearted man, whose passion for you has burst all bounds" (pp. 139–40). Such desperation drives him, unfortunately, to ridiculous measures. Determined to make Madame Jumel his wife whether she is willing or not, he surprises her with a minister at her Christmastide festivities in an attempt to force her into marriage; if she refuses, he believes, the scandal will ruin her. Madame Jumel, however, publicly humiliates the Colonel when he demands that she give in to his desires: "Yield, sir! To you?" she cries. "I'll see you in perdition first!" (p. 235). At the end of the tumultuous scene that follows, she destroys him in front of all: "Without one moment's hesitation," Tupper explains, "madame crossed to where Burr was standing and struck him full in the face with her fan. 'Trickster, coward, liar!' she panted.—Then to the servant, with a superb gesture, 'Show Mr. Burr my door' " (p. 241).

The final image of Burr that Tupper presents is that of a broken man, begging Madame Jumel for her love. In their last interview, he falls to his knees, crying out to her: "Have pity! have mercy! I cannot live without you!" (p. 247). Catching at her gown, he grasps it "with the despair of a drowning man" (pp. 247–48). But the celebrated beauty taunts and humiliates him, avenging herself for the pain he has caused her. Then, with the magnificence for which she is famous, she dispatches him into the street (and out of the novel): "They had reached the door by now. With one supreme effort she wrenched her robe from his hands. He staggered to his feet. She flung open the great hall door, and with the strength of an infuriated lioness, taking him by the shoulders, thrust him out into the blackness of the night" (pp. 248–49).

Like Tyson's book, *Hearts Triumphant* is standard romance, abounding in all of that genre's commonplaces. The epigraph—"Therefore all hearts in love use their own tongues" (p. [iii])—typifies the fare Tupper provides, and the characters are, of course, conventional. Prudence, her name signifying the role she plays in the novel, is the requisite young maiden, ripe for suffering; Richard Trumbell, the man to whom she loses her heart, is the formulaic protector of innocence, poor but honest; and Jack Oglesby, the villain—a wealthy rake who threatens to turn Prue's father out of the family homestead if the girl refuses to marry him—is typically vulgar and boorish. The plot, too, is commonplace. Tupper employs the usual romance pattern of boy meets girl, boy loses girl, boy gets girl in the end. In addition, the banality of the complication—Richard is tempted by the alluring Madame Jumel; Prudence chooses to sacrifice herself to save her alcoholic father from being thrown out of his home—is unrelieved and wearisome, while the denouement, predictably sentimental (the lovers are triumphantly reunited), is hopelessly mechanical, as the novel moves to fulfill the promise embodied in the title.

Though *Hearts* never rises above its type, Anya Seton's *My Theodosia* (1941) generally succeeds in surmounting the limitations of its form, in part because of its focus upon Burr's unusual relationship with his daughter.[18] In what became a popular best seller, Seton presents a sympathetic, if not always laudatory, portrait of the Colonel. The Burr depicted here has his failings. He is, for example, a lavish spender, almost always in debt. This aspect, echoed throughout the book, is noted early, as Theodosia sits thinking about the diamond necklace her father has given her for her seventeenth birthday: "He was so generous—so extravagantly generous at times," she reflects, but "lately creditors had been even more pressing than usual" (p. 5). Here, too, is the notorious rake. Referring to this trait in the Colonel's character, Matthew Davis remarks: "He's a great dog with the ladies" (p. 24). Burr himself recalls that, since his wife's death, "there [have] been so many women, casual, unimportant: affairs of a few weeks or months" (p. 270). The Colonel's chief negative quality, however, is his manipulation of others. "Making up people's minds for them," he reflects, "[proves] ever an amusing occupation. With different mentalities one [uses] differing tactics" (p. 67). He conquers the wealthy Alston for Theodosia (and for himself) by making Joseph feel less insecure; he persuades his unwilling daughter to marry the Southerner by combining "tenderness and implacable purpose" (p. 71); and he gains followers for his western schemes by telling each potential recruit what will be most appealing. "One must use different nets for different fish" (p. 308), he tells Theodosia.

Seton, however, also depicts a Burr who gains the reader's admiration and sympathy. Here, for example, is the man of honor, who is justified in challenging Hamilton. For years the Colonel had ignored his rival's slanders, "disdaining to notice rumors or oblique references" (p. 267); and before he called his enemy out, he had given him every chance to save himself. Burr tells his daughter: "Before I challenged him, I gave him ample opportunity to apologize or explain. He declined to do either" (p. 296). Here, too, are the bold empire builder (no traitor in this book) and the victim of Wilkinson's duplicity and Jefferson's hatred. "It's vile horrible treachery!" Theodosia exclaims, after her father tells her that Wilkinson betrayed him for money. And Burr notes of his own situation: "My dear . . . you have read to very little purpose if you have not remarked that such things happen in all democratic governments. Was there in Greece or Rome a man of virtue and independence, and supposed to possess great talents, who was not the object of vindictive and unrelenting persecution?" (p. 340).

The major image of Burr in the novel, however, is that of a man totally, if unnaturally, in love with his daughter. There is no question of actual incest here; that would destroy the reader's sympathetic acceptance of Burr's relationship with Theodosia. But it is obvious throughout that his feelings for his daughter go beyond the normal— are, in fact, abnormal. The first indication of such aberrancy occurs early in the book when Burr reacts too strongly to a suggestion at Tammany Hall that he will use Theodosia to gain control of Joseph Alston's money. Burr leaps to his feet, reminding the assembled company that no one may slander his daughter with impunity, adding that he is "not unhandy with the pistols" (p. 24). "He's fair daft about that girl of his," the man who made the suggestion remarks. "It seems scarcely natural" (p. 24).

The incestuous nature of Burr's feelings for Theodosia becomes clearer, however, in his various reactions to her relationships with the other men in her life. He registers a "disagreeable sense of shock," for example, to her mild flirtation with and kissing of Washington Irving (p. 30). But he is "not displease[d]" when he learns that she finds Alston's advances repugnant, even though he intends to have Joseph as a son-in-law. The reader learns why: "He did not quite admit it to himself, but he would have opposed any match with a man whom she passionately desired. He had no intention of transferring her devotion from himself to another. Her worship was the sweetest thing in life" (p. 63). In addition, when he first realizes that Theodosia has been deeply affected by the handsome Meriwether Lewis, the Colonel is uncharacteristically incapable of concentrating on his work. When he finds the two alone at the Vauxhall Gardens, he is filled with rage: "Just who is this individual with whom I find you philandering in corners like a street wench?" (p. 91) he inquires angrily of his daughter. A letter to Lewis' commanding officer, asking for the cancellation of the soldier's leave and his immediate return to the frontier, follows this episode.

Several years later, when Jefferson announces at a White House dinner that he has chosen Lewis to lead an expedition into the newly acquired western territory, Burr is irritated by his daughter's reaction to the news: "He was annoyed by the flash of what looked like pure hero-worship that he had seen on Theodosia's face. And he found to his surprise that he had not overestimated his previous dislike of Lewis. It had surged back with full force" (p. 245). Much later still, at his trial in Richmond, Burr becomes visibly distraught when Lewis goes to help the fainting Theodosia, while he himself is restrained by the guards: "For a moment his face contorted. His fingers clenched, they wound themselves in the ruffled white neckcloth at his throat. There was a sharp sound of tearing linen" (p. 355).

But Burr's intense reaction when Theodosia brings Lewis to his jail cell suggests most clearly, if indirectly, his unnatural feelings for his daughter. Having learned that Lewis has come with new evidence against her father, Theodosia brings the great explorer to the Colonel in the hope that he can charm Lewis and persuade him not to testify. Instead, Burr angrily lashes out at his daughter, thereby revealing "the bitterness of his jealousy" (p. 362). She points out that the jury will pay careful attention to the national hero, but Burr viciously responds: "And you, too, listen to what he says, don't you, my dear? This Governor of Louisiana, this friend of Jefferson's, he is no doubt a far more seductive subject to listen to than a disgraced traitor, an emperor without an empire, the murderer of Alexander Hamilton, the betrayer of his country. You had better attach yourself somehow to the tail of this new comet. It's unfortunate that you happen to be married, is it not? Yet, with patience and ingenuity, perhaps even that obstacle may be surmounted" (p. 363). Though the final image of Burr in the book is that of a man crushed by events, it is as a father totally, abnormally, in love with his daughter that the reader largely remembers him.

My Theodosia is clearly one of the more compelling and effective novels that treat Burr. It is not, however, without its infelicities. Though its popular success was no doubt due to the combination of two colorful plot strands—Theodosia's passion for both her father and her frontier hero—the Lewis love story is less successful than the father-daughter relationship because it is more banal in itself and because it is more tritely handled. Seton, for example, too often lapses into the inflated language of the dime-store romance. In describing Theodosia's chance meeting with Lewis in Washington, for example, the author notes:

> They looked into each other's eyes and saw deep shadows and the call of their longing. Tears scalded her lids as she lifted her mouth to his.
> In that moment of physical communion, they escaped from themselves to become another, which was both of them and yet neither in a unity beyond time or place or thought, compact with bliss. [P. 209]

Filled with gushy metaphor—"As she met his eyes, she experienced a physical sensation of explosion in her chest as though a small musket had been fired" (p. 79)—and replete with commonplace romantic dialogue—"I know nothing of women" (p. 90)—the love story is thoroughly typical.

Other elements, however, offset the banality. Seton is successful, for example, in providing a detailed portrait of antebellum Southern life. There are the interminable discussions of crops and horseracing, the suffocating family gatherings, the tropical growth and heat, and, of course, the seemingly requisite lazy blacks. A subplot involving Joseph Alston's miscegenetic relationship with his rebellious slave, Venus, adds a titillating element to the story (Theodosia catches him *in flagrante delicto*), while Seton's weaving into the dialogue the actual words of her principal characters increases the aura of authenticity. And the use of Washington Irving as a vehicle for reporting Burr's relationship with his daughter during the treason trial is especially effective: "Why, she worships him, he thought, startled. . . . That was more like the signal of parted lovers than a look of filial affection" (p. 352). Overall, then, *My Theodosia* is one of the better works dealing with Burr.

A final category of novels that treat Burr encompasses those works that, instead of focusing on individual aspects of his history, take a broad perspective, depicting either several key events in Burr's political adventures or covering an extended period of his life. Three novels of varying quality represent this group.[19] The first, Acton Davies and Charles Nirdlinger's *The First Lady of the Land or When Dolly Todd Took Boarders* (1912), treats the 1800 election, the duel, and the conspiracy.[20] Novelized from Nirdlinger's similarly titled play (see Chapter 3), the book depicts Burr as a dangerously magnetic, many-sided man. The multifaceted nature of the Colonel's character is suggested early in the work, when Dolly defends Burr against Sally McKean's accusation that his reputation is scandalous:

"His reputation!" repeated Dolly, scornfully. "But he has so many of 'em! Think of his record as a soldier, Sally. A lad of twenty-four in the American army who had won his way to a colonelcy. Remember what he did at Quebec, on the Heights of Abraham,—he, a mere lad, carrying the dead body of that giant General Montgomery out from under the enemy's breast works into his

own camp. Then as an aide to General Washington himself—and later still
his great fame as a lawyer! . . . Oh, yes, I know Ronnie Burr's reputations,
Sally,—and all the many sides of 'em! As for his record as a heart breaker,
well, it seems to me that should prove warning enough for any woman who
isn't courting trouble. Take it from me, Sally, these so-called dangerous men
would not be half so dangerous if so many of us women didn't try to find out
the reason why." [P. 30]

Despite Dolly's underplaying, however, the Burr portrayed here is
a man of redoubtable sexual prowess—clearly a factor in his charm.
That he is attractive to women is made evident in many ways throughout the book. Sally McKean, for example, calls him "a fascinating
devil" (p. 29); Sophia Sparkle expresses the enthusiasm that Burr engenders among the schoolgirl set; and even the stable Dolly Todd
finds him seductive. Thus, in arguing about Madison with the Colonel, Dolly tells him that she will find Jefferson's secretary of state
more appealing when Burr himself is gone: "I shall [love Madison]
when you're not near me. When you are here . . . I'm little better than
the other women whom you can make do as you bid them" (p. 186).
Burr is, in fact, a rake, as a number of incidents and comments in the
novel make clear. His reputation as a reprobate is so infamous, for
example, that Mrs. Sparkle does not want to discuss "this Monster in
Human Form" in front of her fourteen-year-old daughter (p. 41);
Sally is shocked that Dolly even considers marriage to a man whom
half the women he meets fall in love with; and Mrs. Todd herself suggests to Burr that an appropriate epitaph for him would read "Rakish
to his latest day" (p. 121).
    Part of Burr's fascination, however, results from his good qualities.
He is, for example, a man of honor. Madame Jumel notes that she
"never knew him to lie" (p. 209), and Dolly points out to Mrs. Sparkle
that Burr, had he not been so high-principled, could have easily taken
the 1800 election from Jefferson: "One word from Colonel Burr—a
nod of his head, a crook of his finger, would have made him President" (p. 55). Even Jefferson is willing "to proclaim his magnanimity" (p. 98)—at least until he can discover a sinister motive for the
Colonel's actions. Burr's rigid sense of honor is perhaps best reflected, however, in the carefulness with which he guards the reputation of
the women with whom he is involved. "If Colonel Burr kisses, he
doesn't tell" (pp. 45–46), Dolly points out to Mrs. Sparkle. But Burr

has a host of other attractive qualities. He can remain cool in especially trying circumstances, pursuing his love affairs, for example,
while the House is deciding between him and Jefferson. As Hamilton
notes, he is also "the most abstemious brute in the world" (p. 124),
and, as his room at Dolly's reflects, he is a Spartan in daily life. Most
attractively, he is a fair-minded man, refusing to believe that Hamilton has slandered him. "From me," the Colonel tells Dolly, "Hamilton . . . will always have the benefit of the doubt" (p. 112).

Preeminently, however, the Burr depicted here is an ambitious
man. Sally McKean points to this greatest of his qualities in a conversation with Dolly: "Burr is a plotter, a great schemer," she tells Mrs.
Todd. "You know that as well as I. His vaulting ambition would jump
over the moon itself if he had his way" (p. 27). Burr himself admits,
"Yes, I love Mexico: to conquer her and to be her conqueror I am willing to chance my life, my future, everything in my career. For that end
I'd become an Ishmael, even a Lucifer; yes—by God—to own
Mexico I believe if it were possible I'd sell my soul" (p. 112). It is this
insatiable, Catilinian ambition, of course, that eventually leads him to
the Richmond courthouse.

Much better than Nirdlinger's play, this *First Lady* is effective
overall. It has a fast-moving and engaging plot and a vitality resulting
in part from the authors' compression of the contested election of
1800, the celebrated duel of 1804, and the infamous conspiracy of
1805–07 into a single year. There is too a careful controlling of suspense. As the story moves inexorably toward the Weehawken
heights, Davies and Nirdlinger interrupt the progress of events to
present such comic scenes as Lady Merry's tribulations with her hair-
dresser. And there is also a skillful use of history in the duel chapter.
Some of the actual documents are woven into the story so that, in general, the portrayal of the famous event and of those actions immediately preceding it are historically accurate. Other attractive techniques include the use of appropriate epigraphs for each chapter and
the employment of engaging, often witty chapter titles—conventions
popular with American novelists since the eighteenth century. One of
the epigraphs for chapter 5, in which Dolly must choose between Burr
and Madison, is a snippet from *The Beggar's Opera*: "How happy I
could be with either, / Were tother dear charmer away!" (p. 71). And
such titles as "Young Sophia Sparkle Whispers Scandal and Colonel
Burr's Leg Corroborates It" or "Lady Merry Damns Her Hair-

dresser and Holds the American Republic Responsible" please, in part, because of the ironic voice behind them.

Perhaps most compelling, however, are the marvelous characters. Besides the magnetic Burr, the authors provide a number of other engaging figures. There are, for example, the diplomatic Madison, whose typical response to difficult questions is "Yes—and—no," and the impolitic Lady Merry, whose characteristic maliciousness comes out at the most inappropriate times. Also appearing is a pert Dolly Todd who, for instance, can tell matchmaker Jefferson: "If ever I marry to go to the White House 'twill be for a double purpose;—to serve thee faithfully while you are there and get thee out as soon as possible to make way for my husband" (pp. 100–01). And, *mirabile dictu*, there is even a human Jefferson, a man who can throw pebbles at Dolly's window on the night he is elected president because he wants to talk to her, a man who can say of himself: "You see, at heart, though they call me atheist, I'm really a very superstitious man. I pick up old nails for luck and I salute the new moon over my left shoulder. But don't tell anybody! I should hate to have my enemies think that Tom Jefferson's a human being" (p. 85). In sum, then, *First Lady* is a charmer.

Treating a more protracted period in Burr's life is Charles Felton Pidgin's *Little Burr: The Warwick of America* (1905).[21] Essentially a fictional biography of the years 1775–1804, the book celebrates the Colonel throughout. Here is the ardent patriot who, even as a young law student, is ready to fight for his country; here, too, once the war begins, is the inspiring hero. He volunteers for the hazardous mission of reaching Montgomery's camp and, more noble still, rescues the body of his fallen leader when the enemy cuts the general down. Abe Budlong, the Colonel's Litchfield friend, reports: "Burr was right up side of Montgomery when he was struck, and although he was a little feller and the Gin'ral weighted more than two hundred, Little Burr jest took him up on his back and toted him out of reach of the British (p. 97). Even as a civilian wasted in health, the Colonel proves his valor when he rallies the Yale students to save New Haven from destruction.

Pidgin also portrays Burr as exemplary in other ways. The Colonel is, for example, an effective military commander. He turns Malcolm's rabble into a first-rate fighting regiment by replacing incompetent offi-

cers and by instituting rigid inspections; he quells a mutiny of militia-
men at the Gulf by severing with his sword the arm of their disgruntled leader; and he brings security to the inhabitants living along
the Westchester lines by punishing swiftly but fairly the "cowboys"
(Tory sympathizers) and "skinners" (rebel proponents) caught plundering the area. In addition, Burr is a gallant gentleman. No predator
in this book, he escorts the beautiful Adelaide Clifton through the
wilderness without a thought of attempting her virtue, and he courts
Theodosia Prevost with the most chivalrous of intentions. In fact, the
Colonel, as Pidgin depicts him, is nearly ideal. He is a learned man
who, when forced to remain for a while in the monastery at Three
Rivers, spends the time in rich conversation with the monks. He is also
a humble man who can admit past failings, as he does in one of his
meetings with Washington. "Abstemious" in food and drink, he is, in
addition, the master of his emotions—a trait that even his enemy
Hamilton admires: "There is only one thing that I envy Aaron Burr,"
he tells Billings, "and that is, his absolute control of his feelings under
all circumstances" (p. 175). And the Colonel is a stoical, even cheer-
ful man in defeat. When he is unsuccessful in his race for the New
York governorship, largely because of the machinations of Hamilton
and Jefferson, he writes his daughter: "The election is lost by a great
majority; *so much the better*" (p. 361).

Primarily, however, the Burr portrayed here is the Warwick of
America, as Pidgin's subtitle denotes. The whole of chapter 29 is devoted to this analogy, which the Colonel's daughter makes clear in a
letter to Natalie de Lage, one of Burr's orphan charges, who had
earlier made the connection between the British earl and her generous
guardian. Theodosia writes:

> So you see, my dear Natalie, your words have come true. Richard, Earl of
> Warwick, placed Edward IV. upon the throne; but when he was seated there
> and entrenched in power, he looked upon the man who had made him, as a
> possible rival, and both feared and hated him. He went deliberately to work to
> deprive the man who had made him a king, of his offices, his wealth, his
> power, and eventually brought him to his death.
>
> So, too, Thomas Jefferson, President of the United States, looks upon
> Aaron Burr, the man who made him President, as a possible rival. He both
> hates and fears him, and means to accomplish his political downfall—even as
> King Edward did that of the Earl of Warwick. [P. 359]

In other words, it is the image of Burr as victim that is foremost in Pidgin's presentation of him. To reemphasize this view, the author notes in the final paragraph of the novel that "the political and social repudiation of Aaron Burr, which was, in reality, a living death, was the result of a conspiracy conceived in the most malignant spirit and carried out in the most infamous manner. The fate of the Warwick of England—death on the battlefield—was, indeed, a happy one, compared with the unmerited political and social ostracism, which became the lot of Aaron Burr, the Warwick of America" (p. 396).

Pidgin's novel is exactly the kind of romance schoolchildren love, as the description of Burr's first night on the road from Arnold's to Montgomery's camp suggests: "The night was dark and the wind bitter—but this was the road to glory!—and Burr trod on, happy at heart and confident of success" (p. 49). *Little Burr* also contains an implausible plot, manipulated to provide as much melodrama as possible from the hackneyed situations Pidgin selects. In addition, its characters are the usual one-dimensional heroes and villains, and its assumptions are familiar and trite: God is on our side (Parson Morrison helps recruit at each town) and American women fight as well as their men (Moll[y] Pitcher fires the cannons after her husband falls in battle).

Unfortunately, Pidgin's handling of other artistic elements is no better than his treatment of plot and character. He strains to create an echo of the common man's language in Abe Budlong's speech, but his ear is flat: "Well, by gum! . . . If I warn't a member of a religious family and not used ter indulgin' in profane language, I should say there had been a h—l of a time up here" (p. 121). His metaphor is banal— Aaron and Abe are drawn to each other "Like the positive and negative poles of the magnet" (p. 9)—and his technique of opening chapters typifies his general inability. Chapter 2, for instance, begins: "COCK-A-DOODLE-DOO! The cock-a-doodle-doo given as a sonorous chant by the bright-plumaged sovereign of the henyard at the rear of the Reeve homestead, was not necessary to awaken Aaron the morning after the receipt of the news of the battle of Bunker's Hill" (p. 14). In addition, the stance of moral outrage that Pidgin takes and the preaching that occasionally slips in are wearisome. An example of the latter: "few of us in this world get our just deserts [sic], either for good or bad actions; but if we know in our hearts that we have done our best, the satisfaction that comes from that knowledge is worth more than official votes of thanks" (p. 298). *Little Burr*, then, bespeaks its author's little talent.

Another novel to deal with a protracted period of Burr's history and the last to be discussed here is Gore Vidal's first-rate *Burr* (1973).[22] Tracing the Colonel's adult life from the Revolution to his death, Vidal provides a full-length and largely favorable portrayal in which several elements predominate, especially the view of Burr as victim. Of course, many of the standard images, relatively minor and generally positive for Vidal, appear in the book. Here, for example, is Burr as Revolutionary War hero. During the Siege of Quebec, he urges the soldiers to attack after a murderous blast has killed Montgomery and several of his aides, and, when left alone—Colonel Campbell has ordered a retreat—he attempts to return the general's body to American lines. Later in the war, he saves Knox's brigade, over its commander's protest, from certain British slaughter, guiding the soldiers to the safety of Harlem Heights. As the officer in charge of Malcolm's regiment, he leads damaging night raids against the English army in New Jersey, and, as a specially appointed disciplinarian, he restores order to the mutinous militia at the Gulf.

Here, too, is Burr as skillful lawyer. Washington Irving makes this point when he recalls the apparently hopeless trial of Levi Weeks, whom the Colonel defended against the charge of murdering Elma Sands: "I was in the court-room during Colonel Burr's performance. By the time he had finished, the jury and the judge—and no doubt the devil himself—were convinced that Elma Sands was a woman of no virtue while Levi Weeks was a young Galahad" (pp. 117-18). And here is Burr as generous man, spending his inheritance on the soldiers under his command during the Revolution and, after his return from exile in Europe, dispensing the money he earns from his law practice to those in greater need than he.

Vidal also portrays Burr, however, as an effective educator. Irving highlights this aspect of the Colonel's character when he notes that Burr is a "born pedagogue": "He loves the young. He loves to teach them. After all he is the son and grandson of presidents of Princeton College" (p. 121). The most visible example of Burr's interest in educating children is, aside from Theodosia, the painter Vanderlyn, whom the Colonel discovered in poverty at Kingston, trained at his own expense, sent to Paris for further study, and even helped to get a start when he returned to the United States. In fact, Burr himself saw his interest in educating young people as his most significant achievement. "Unfortunately," he tells Charlie Schuyler when they are discussing the Colonel's Mexican schemes, "I was not able to be a king... but in my way I have been lucky for I have always been able to indulge my true passion which is to teach others, to take pleasure in bringing out the best in men and women, to make them *alive*" (p. 347).

The Burr presented here is also a man of honor, a fact most clearly reflected in his refusal to steal the presidency from Jefferson in 1800. Because his personal code includes the belief that "in politics, as in life, one ought to do what one has promised to do" (p. 194), Burr remains true to his pledge to support Jefferson. Burr tells Charlie: "Jefferson would never honour an agreement if it was inconvenient and naturally he assumed that I was like himself. But then Jefferson was not, even in Chesterfield's sense, a gentleman (of the Virginians only Madison qualified); unfortunately, I was one, or did my best to be. I worked only for what we had agreed upon at Philadelphia, the ticket of Jefferson and Burr" (p. 222). Thus, when both he and Jefferson get the same number of votes in South Carolina, the Colonel tries to prevent anyone from putting him forward as an alternative candidate. Even when Theodosia urges him to work with the Federalists to take the election, he refuses, because as he tells her: "Child, I have given my word to Jefferson" (p. 225).

The Colonel's darker side is also suggested in the novel. The flaws, however, tend to be engaging so that the ultimate effect of portraying them is to increase the reader's affection for Burr. Here, for example, he is quite clearly an adventurer. During his plotting to take Mexico, he tells those who might support him what will most likely insure their help. At a crucial point in 1805, for instance, he plays upon British Minister Merry's hopes: "I told him," Burr notes in recalling his tactics, "what he wanted to hear: that the westerners were anxious to separate from the east. As for the people of Louisiana, 'they detest the Administration,' which was the exact truth, 'and will fight, if they must, to break away,' which might have been true. 'They want me to lead them.' Again the truth. 'To set up a republic under the protection of England.' This could be made true" (p. 316). At seventy-seven, he is still scheming. To Schuyler he remarks: "For only fifty thousand dollars one can buy a principality in the Texas Territory, to be settled within a year's time by Germans, who require nothing more than passage money. . . . Charlie, do you realize that in twenty years such an investment would be worth millions?" (p. 12). To finance this latest stratagem, he marries Madame Jumel and proceeds to run through her money.

Burr's adventurism and the other aspects discussed so far are minor features in Vidal's portrait. There are, however, several additional elements that predominate. Of these, perhaps the most appealing is Burr's extraordinary relationship with women. The Burr portrayed here, for example, is a randy libertine, ever on the prowl. "I cannot—simply—be without the company of a woman" (p. 6), he tells Charlie. Mrs. Townsend's recollection of the younger Burr seemingly confirms the Colonel's statement: "There was a man!" the philosophy-reading madam of Thomas Street notes. "And how he loved the ladies!" (p. 31). Even while Burr is in jail at Richmond, he manages liaisons, and, during his exile in Europe, he frequently enjoys the company of women, once journeying seventy miles out of his way "in order to pay a call on a lady of the ducal court" at Weimar (p. 396). In his late seventies, his "satyr lips unwithered by time" (p. 77), he marries an ex-whore—largely for her money, it is true, but not without an eye for her other charms—and visits a paramour in Jersey City.

Burr's intimacy with women, however, also includes his relationship with his daughter, and here, for Vidal, there is mystery. To say that theirs was an unusual relationship is to understate. "We could say anything to one another; said everything" (p. 333), he remarks. Indeed they did, as an extract from Burr's European journal, kept for Theodosia, makes clear. For 2 May 1811, he records in detail an encounter with a Parisian prostitute: her room, he notes, was "Fairly clean (this is France). Linen passable. Spirit *brio*. We did first the *Camel*. Then an attempt at *la Tonnerre* which failed due to pique and false entry. Most pleasing, all in all. She is from Dijon in Burgandy. Her brother is a clerk in the foreign ministry (she says). I take Vanderlyn's advice based on the latest medical theory (*departement de Venise*) and after the *splendeurs de l'amour* appropriate the *vase de nuit* and take a hearty piss" (p. 67).

Madame Jumel is the first to suggest to Charlie that Burr's affection for Theodosia has an unnatural aspect to it: "She's the one he loved—his daughter, and no one else!" (p. 29), Madame notes. Then, after a moment's reflection in which she "suddenly looked grim, awed, puzzled," she adds: "Strange business, Aaron Burr and his daughter" (p. 29). Irving echoes this judgment—"He never loved anyone else, I'm certain of that" (p. 120)—and continues: "The Colonel was devastated when she married Mr. Alston who took her to live in South Carolina—so far away. I think the last time they ever saw one another was at Richmond, Virginia, during his trail for treason. I confess he was superb then! The hero of the whole affair. With Theodosia beside him like—like a consort!" (p. 120). The suggestions of incest Madame Jumel and Irving make are later seemingly confirmed when Swartwout tells Charlie just what the cause of the famous duel was, just what the "still more despicable opinion" Hamilton held entailed: "Why, he said that Aaron Burr was the lover of his own daughter, Theodosia" (p. 272), Swartwout remarks.

Another major element of the portrait Vidal presents deals with the question of Burr's western schemes. Here, however, the Colonel is clearly no traitor. In recalling the events of 1805-07, he declares flatly: "Among my numerous crimes the chief is supposed to be that I conspired to break up the union. Jefferson wanted the world to believe that when I went west I was bent on separating the new states of Kentucky, Tennessee and Ohio from their natural ruler Virginia. This was nonsense, and Jefferson knew it was nonsense" (p. 259). Actually, he tells Charlie, his "interests were, first, Mexico; second, Texas; third, the Floridas. I never saw myself as King of Kentucky" (p. 286). In a later memoir he elaborates:

> Our plan was this: a force of 5,000 men from all over the United States would assemble in small groups at various points along the Mississippi. Should there be war with Spain these men would immediately become a frontier American army. Under my leadership, we would cross the Sabine River and, with American naval support at Vera Cruz, liberate Texas and Mexico.
> In the event that there was no war with Spain, then a British fleet would replace the American, and we would assemble our army at New Orleans. With the support of the leading Creoles of that city, we would set out by both land and sea. [P. 306]

In fact, his purpose, he notes, was idealistic: "To make a civilization on this God-forsaken continent!" "I can assure you," he remarks to

Charlie, "that that early republic of ours was no place for a man who wanted to live in a good world, who wanted to make a true civilization and to share it with a host of choice spirits, such as I meant to establish in Mexico" (p. 347).

Instead of a traitor, then, Burr was a victim. Indeed, this is the final and all-encompassing image that emerges from the novel. Washington victimizes him by blocking his rise in the army, Hamilton by slandering him and helping to destroy his political career, and Wilkinson by lying to the president and even by sending assassins to kill him. But it is Jefferson who is the major villain. His ill treatment of the Colonel begins in 1796 when he hypocritically breaks his word and refuses to support Burr for the vice presidency. It is after the 1800 election, however, that his outright attack begins. "Six months after our inauguration," Burr tells Charlie, "Jefferson joined forces with the Clintons to eliminate me from politics not only in the nation, but, rather more seriously, in New York state" (p. 241). Using Cheetham to destroy the Colonel as he had employed Callender to attack Hamilton, Jefferson waged the most vicious kind of internecine warfare.

Once the conspiracy charges begin, however, the president shows his ugliest side. Jackson makes the point and accurately predicts the future in a conversation with Burr in December 1806: "By the time Jefferson gets through with you," he tells the Colonel, "every one will think you're the greatest traitor since Benedict Arnold" (p. 339). Fulfilling Old Hickory's prophecy, Jefferson sends to Congress the very next month a message about the western plot in which he declares Burr "the principal actor, whose guilt is placed beyond question" (p. 350). Once the treason trial begins, Jefferson handles the case from Washington: "Day after day he sent messengers to the west to collect (or create) evidence and witnesses" (p. 354), the Colonel recalls. Later, when his position is shown to be questionable, the president tries to prove Burr guilty of treason "*by construction*." The Colonel's comment on this procedure reveals his victimization: "May I say that the entire concept of *constructive treason* is unconstitutional and was known to be so by every lawyer in the United States, save Jefferson. But he was desperate. Although he had assembled nearly fifty witnesses to denounce me (of whom more than half perjured themselves), there was never any proof that I had levied war against the United States, or advised the thirty men on Blennerhassett's Island to levy such a war" (p. 371). The image of Burr as victim, then, is the major element in Vidal's portrait.

In what is clearly the best novel to treat Burr, Vidal easily outstrips his competitors with his deftness of technique. The setting of situation, time, and place, for example, emerges unobtrusively from an opening dispatch to the *New York Evening Post* announcing Burr's marriage in 1833 to Madame Jumel and from the narrator's comment on it. "I don't seem able to catch the right tone," Charlie Schuyler explains, "but since William Leggett has invited me to write about Colonel Burr for the *Evening Post*, I shall put in everything, and look forward to his response" (p. 4). No florid description of countryside here or romanticized depiction of a stereotypical heroine. Instead, Vidal provides a quick shot of a rather startling event, given the characters involved, and then moves smoothly into his tale.

It is clear from the start, then, that the kind of narrative Vidal presents is much more sophisticated than the typical historical romance. For here the author uses the story-within-a-story technique employed frequently in modern fiction to provide the added subtlety of several perspectives. Thus what the reader has in front of him is the notebook of Charles Schuyler (the character is based on Charles Burdett). A clerk and student in Burr's law office, Charlie, who also happens to be one of the Colonel's bastards but is unaware of that fact, sees in his jottings a way out of drudgery. By accepting William Leggett's offer to write an anonymous pamphlet that will prove that Aaron Burr is Martin Van Buren's father, Schuyler hopes to gain enough money to launch his literary career and to fulfill, at least for a while, his various other needs. So Charlie keeps a journal, containing his notes on Burr, of course, but also recording his own reflections on what he is doing and on who he is—or is becoming. "Do I betray the Colonel?" he wonders, after he has agreed to Leggett's scheme. "In a small way, yes. Do I hurt him? No. An anonymous pamphlet maintaining that he was the devil would distress him not at all. Much worse has been written about him by such supremely non-anonymous figures as Jefferson and Hamilton" (p. 20).

What the reader gets, then, are two stories—Burr's and Schuyler's—woven together so skillfully that he is as interested in Charlie's struggles (how like his own!) as he is in the Colonel's explanation of his tumultuous life. The viewpoint is often Burr's, of course, as

Charlie records the Colonel's memoirs—of the Revolution, Burr's political life, his western affairs, and the key figures in his personal drama—so the tale of former times has a suspicious slant. But if such a perspective is not always accurate, it nonetheless makes for compelling reading. A sample—one of the Colonel's comments on Washington: "I have never known a man so concerned with the trifles and show of wealth and position as Washington. But then it was his genius always to look the part he was called upon to play, and it is not possible to create a grand illusion without the most painstaking attention to detail. Much of his presidential day was occupied with designing monograms and liveries and stately carriages, not to mention inventing, with Hamilton's aid, elaborate court protocols" (p. 148).

Other effective techniques Vidal uses include the skillful variation of present and past time and of outer and inner stories. In the middle section of the novel, for example, the reader gets great chunks of Burr's life in memoir form, provided with only the briefest of introductions to keep him aware of the frame story—the fortunes of Charlie. But just as he tires of the exploration of the past, Vidal switches to present time for a while (chapters 22 through 24 of 1834), reviving his interest in Schuyler's betrayal of his father and in his attempted destruction of his brother (yes, here at least, Van Buren is Burr's son). There is also an element of suspense employed as Charlie tracks down Hamilton's "still more despicable opinion."

Vidal's greatest achievement, however, is his creation of character. From the charming Aaron Burr to the sodomitic William de la Touche Clancey, he provides a cast that bubbles with life. Of course, most intriguing, after the full-length portrait of Burr, is the dazzling, though jaundiced, depiction of Jefferson. Here is the hypocritical spellbinder who can work his magic on even such a wary man as the Colonel. Burr tells Charlie: "There was something in Jefferson's manner that *held* me as no other man was ever able to do. Even after I came to know well his recklessness with the truth, I never failed to respond to that hushed voice, to those bright child's eyes, to his every fanatical notion, to his every rich slander. He was a kind of wizard, no doubt of it" (p. 156). Here, too, is the great civil libertarian who denies equality to blacks and plunders their women. Burr again: "It was a curious sensation to look about Monticello and see everywhere so many replicas of Jefferson and his father-in-law. It was as if we had all of us been transformed into dogs, and as a single male dog can re-create in his own image an entire canine community, so Jefferson and his family had grafted their powerful strain upon these slave Africans" (p. 201).

The president is also depicted as a political gutter fighter who pays the vicious Callender to slander Washington, Adams, and Hamilton and as a man without principle who connives with the Federalists to win the presidency in 1800. In addition, Vidal presents the shocking image of a great Republican leader who does not believe in the First Amendment and who subverts the Constitution by bringing Justice Chase to trial so that he can frighten his political enemies in the judiciary, notably Marshall. Most of all, however, it is the picture of Jefferson as tyrant determined to crush Burr, a portrait discussed earlier, that appears here. Possibly the president is even deranged as he works madly and vindictively to bring the Colonel to the gallows. Such, at least, is Burr's view: "Jefferson's headaches and irascible outbursts combined with his extraordinary expenditure of money to produce or create evidence against me (Jefferson *never* spent public money) was proof to me of his irrationality that season. Certainly it was not the act of a sane man to rest the government's case against me on the evidence of someone he knew to be a Spanish agent [Wilkinson]" (p. 358).

Besides the striking image of Jefferson, however, there are other marvellous portraits, characters like Jackson or Davy Crocket or Madame Jumel, who reveal themselves in the book primarily through their speech. The depiction of Old Hickory, for example, emerges from such set pieces as his musings on the Burr-Hamilton duel:

Never read such a damned lot of nonsense as the press has been writing! All that hypocritical caterwauling for that Creole bastard who fought you of his own free will, just like a gentleman which he wasn't, if you'll forgive me, Colonel! I know you couldn't have met him unless you *thought* he was one, but he was not, Sir. He was the worst man in this union, as you, Sir, are the best. The best and that goes for that pusillanimous spotted caitiff of a president we got. I only fear—aside from the damage it's done you, Sir, and that we'll undo quick enough—I fear that duelling will be stamped out and where would we all be then, I ask you? Why, there's a number of men right here in Nashville that one day I know I'll take a gun to, even if I am a poor shot, and that's the truth. [P. 308]

Madame Jumel comes alive in such multilingual outbursts as her comment to Charlie about Burr's selling her stock in a Hartford toll bridge and then insisting that the money be sewn into his jacket:

" '*Ma foi!*' I said to him. 'It will be better to sew the money into *my* petticoat. After all, those shares belong to me, *non?*' We were in our bedroom in the house *du Gouverneur* and I wanted to make no scene. *Naturellement.* So what did he say to that? Why, damn him for a bastard in hell, he said, 'I am your master, Madame. Your husband, and under law what you have is mine!' *Under law!* . . . Well, I know the law forward and back and if he wants to play at litigation with me there are a hundred lawyers in this city I can put to work, and beat him in every court!" [Pp. 24–25]

Jefferson, Jackson, Madame Jumel—these along with a host of other choice spirits like the consumptive Leggett, the moralistic Bryant, and, of course, the uncertain Charlie Schuyler, groping his way to maturity (security?)—make *Burr* the best of the novels dealing with the Colonel and a critical delight throughout.

Thus, over and over again, American novelists and short story writers turn to the figure of Aaron Burr in their works, presenting him in a wide variety of ways. Nonetheless, certain depictions appear with enough regularity to suggest that there is something strangely compelling about this character from America's early national history. Nineteenth-century authors tend to focus upon Burr as traitor and sexual predator, whereas in the twentieth century another image also emerges. In our time, the view of Burr as victim seems to hold special fascination for American authors. Not surprisingly, perhaps, these are the same three portraits that the playwrights presented when they chose to use the Colonel in their works. It is probable, therefore, that the same reasons account for the emergence of these images in both drama and fiction. No doubt, the restoration of Burr's name, which Davis and Parton began and Wandell and Minnigerode continued, has something to do with the shift in attitude toward Burr that occurs over the years. But perhaps there is something else as well that occasions the change. The nineteenth century seems to have seen in Burr some of the very things it feared most—the possibility of the dismemberment of the Union and of the plundering of its women—whereas the twentieth century seems to find in him a reflection of one of its greatest anxieties—the threat of victimization. It may be, then, that Burr becomes for American culture a vehicle that authors use to express the fears that plague society and by so doing help Americans to deal with their common nightmares.

Notes

1. Other works in this miscellaneous category are *The Amorous Intrigues and Adventures of Aaron Burr* (New York: Published for the Proprietors, [184–]); Grace MacGowan Cooke and Annie Booth McKinney, *Mistress Joy: A Tale of Natchez in 1798* (New York: Century, 1901); Mary Dillon, *Miss Livingston's Companion: A Love Story of Old New York* (New York: Century, 1911); Edgar Fawcett, *A Romance of Old New York* (Philadelphia: J. B. Lippincott, 1897); Willard Rouse Jillson, *The Lost Letter of Aaron Burr, 1805: A Tale of Early Lexington* (Frankfort, Ky.: Roberts Printing, 1946); Leonora Sansay, *Secret History; or, The Horrors of St. Domingo* (Philadelphia: Bradford & Inskeep, 1808); Charles Woodcock Savage, *A Lady in Waiting* (New York: D. Appleton and Company, 1906); Harriet Beecher Stowe, *The Minister's Wooing* (Boston: Houghton, Mifflin and Company, 1887); George Alfred Townsend, *Mrs. Reynolds and Hamilton* (New York: E. G. Bonaventure, 1890); and George Ethelbert Walsh, *Allin Winfield* (New York: F. M. Buckles & Company, 1902).

2. James Thurber, "A Friend to Alexander," in *My World—And Welcome to It* (New York: Harcourt, Brace and Company, 1942), pp. 139–53.

3. Eudora Welty, "First Love," in *The Wide Net and Other Stories* (New York: Harcourt, Brace and Company, 1943), pp. 3–33.

4. William T. Polk, "Golden Eagle Ordinary," in *The Fallen Angel and Other Stories* (Chapel Hill: University of North Carolina Press, 1956), pp. 41–51.

5. It is worth noting that most of the authors treating Burr make reference to his extraordinary eyes. They evidently contributed no small part to his personal attractiveness, especially to women.

6. Others primarily treating Burr's exploits in the Revolution are Lindley Murray Hubbard, *An Express of '76: A Chronicle of the Town of York in the War for Independence* (Boston: Little, Brown, and Company, 1906); Kenneth Roberts, *Arundel* (1930; rpt. Greenwich, Conn.: Fawcett, 1976); and Emma Gelders Sterne, *Drums of Monmouth* (New York: Dodd, Mead & Company, 1935).

7. Joseph Holt Ingraham, *Burton; or, The Sieges: A Romance*, 2 vols. (New York: Harper & Brothers, 1838), 1: ix.

8. Charles Burdett, *The Beautiful Spy: An Exciting Story of Army and High Life in New York in 1776* (Philadelphia: John E. Potter and Company,

1865). This novel was also published under the title, *Margaret Moncrieffe, the First Love of Aaron Burr: A Romance of the Revolution.* For a discussion of Burdett's parentage, see Chapter 1.

9. Others dealing with the Colonel and his conspiracy are Marguerite Allis, *To Keep Us Free* (New York: G. P. Putnam's Sons, 1953); *The Conspiracy of Col. Aaron Burr* (New York: G. W. Simmons, 1854); Carlen Bateson, *The Man in the Camlet Cloak* (Akron, Ohio: Saalfield, 1903); Robert Ames Bennet, *A Volunteer with Pike* (Chicago: A. C. McClurg & Co., 1909); Emerson Bennett, *The Traitor; or, The Fate of Ambition* (Cincinnati: U. P. James, 1860); Edwin Lassetter Bynner, *Zachary Phips* (Boston: Houghton, Mifflin and Company, 1892); Edward Everett Hale, "The Man without a Country," *The Man without a Country and Other Stories* (Boston: Little, Brown, and Company, 1918), pp. 21–60; Marion Boyd Havighurst, *Strange Island* (New York: World, 1957); Mary Johnston, *Lewis Rand* (Boston: Houghton Mifflin Company, 1908); Clark McMeekin [Isabel McLennan McMeekin and Dorothy Park Clark], *Reckon with the River* (New York: D. Appleton-Century, 1941); Edward Stanley, *The Rock Cried Out* (New York: Duell, Sloan and Pearce, 1949); Elizabeth Brandon Stanton, *"Fata Morgana": A Vision of Empire* (Crowley, La.: Signal, 1917); and James W. Taylor, *The Victim of Intrigue* (Cincinnati: Robinson & Jones, 1847).

10. William Henry Venable, *A Dream of Empire or The House of Blennerhassett* (New York: Dodd, Mead and Company, 1901).

11. Emerson Hough, *The Magnificent Adventure* (New York: D. Appleton and Company, 1916).

12. A. E. [Eliza Ann] Dupuy, *The Conspirator* (New York: D. Appleton & Company, 1850).

13. Nellie Whan Peppers, *The Young Mrs. Blennerhassett: A Novel of Early Days in West Virginia* (New York: Exposition Press, 1964).

14. Cyril Harris, *Street of Knives* (Boston: Little, Brown and Company, 1950).

15. Others treating Burr's relationship with his important women are Anne Colver, *Theodosia: Daughter of Aaron Burr* (New York: Farrar & Rinehart, 1941) and Rupert Hughes, *The Golden Ladder* (New York: A. L. Burt, 1924).

16. J. Aubrey Tyson, *The Stirrup Cup* (New York: D. Appleton & Co., 1903).

17. Edith Sessions Tupper, *Hearts Triumphant* (New York: D. Appleton and Company, 1906).

18. Anya Seton, *My Theodosia* (Boston: Houghton Mifflin, 1941).

19. Others belonging in this category are Jacob George Bragin, *The Life of*

Aaron Burr (n.p., [New York], 1938); Jeremiah Clemens, *The Rivals* (Philadelphia: J. B. Lippincott & Co., 1860); Addison Lewis, *The Gadfly* (St. Paul: Webb, 1948); Charles Felton Pidgin, *Blennerhassett; or, The Decrees of Fate* (Boston: C. M. Clark, 1901); and Charles Felton Pidgin, *The Climax; or, What Might Have Been* (Boston: C. M. Clark, 1902).

20. Acton Davies and Charles Nirdlinger, *The First Lady of the Land or When Dolly Todd Took Boarders* (New York: H. K. Fly, 1912).

21. Charles Felton Pidgin, *Little Burr: The Warwick of America* (Boston: Robinson Luce, 1905). One of Burr's early twentieth-century proponents, Pidgin worked hard in his writings and in other ways to restore Burr's good name. Unfortunately, his works are generally undistinguished and, as is the case with his drama *Blennerhassett*, sometimes ambiguous. For the bibliographical data of his other major works dealing with Burr, see note 19 above and note 6 in Chapter 3.

22. Gore Vidal, *Burr: A Novel* (New York: Random House, 1973).

5. American Symbol—American Fears

> The task of the cultural analyst is not to discover sim-
> plicity, or even to discover unity, for simplicity and unity
> do not exist, but to drive a wedge of rationality through the
> pathetic indecisions of social thought.
>
> Louis Hartz, *The Liberal Tradition in America*[1]

Aaron Burr has provoked an interest for American authors that is surprising in its strength and pervasiveness. Thirty-three dramatists and
forty-nine writers of fiction have used him in their works; in addition,
the partisan press and various popular poets have found in him a
fitting subject for their sometimes vitriolic pieces. From all of this
prodigious literary activity, three images of Burr emerge: conspirator-
traitor, sexual predator, and suffering victim. American authors have
also provided historical or literary analogues for each of these depictions, seeing the Colonel as an American Catiline, an American
Lovelace, or an American Warwick. The stories of these major
figures with whom Burr is identified highlight the Colonel's qualities
that writers have found most important and compelling. By linking
him with these characters from the past, they have, in effect, raised
Burr to the level of American symbol, made him, that is, a representative of elements in American life that, in this case, are profoundly disturbing. Thus Burr becomes for our culture the emblem of traitorous
conspiracy, dark spoliation of women, and terrifying victimization. In
him, some of American society's deepest fears are dramatically reflected.

That Burr would be depicted as an American Catiline seems hardly
surprising. The similarity in character and in deed that many writers

found between the great Roman conspirator and his latter-'day American counterpart is suggested in Catiline's story.[2] Descended from an ancient Roman family, Lucius Sergius Catilina, born about 108 B.C., reached maturity during the tumultuous times of the Roman Revolution—one hundred years of internal strife between the conservative *optimates*, the party of the nobility, and the more democratic *populares*. He probably fought against the insurgent tribes in the Social War of 91–88 and most likely supported Sulla, an optimatist, in the civil feud of 88–82. Although after Sulla's victory he was charged with murdering a number of the opposition including his own brother-in-law and the influential Gratidianus, the accusations were evidently made to embarrass Catiline during his consular campaign of 64; he was tried and acquitted after the election, which he lost. His enemies also claimed at various times that his early years had been marred by shocking depravity, notably incest, adultery, seduction of Roman youth, and debauchery with a vestal virgin. But, though he was infamous for his sexual affairs, the variety and multiplicity of these charges suggest political exaggeration at work.

Elected praetor in 69 and again in 68, Catiline became propraetor of Africa the next year. By the summer months of 66, however, he was back in Rome, where he found that the political situation had greatly changed during his absence. As a consequence, he switched to the *populares*, becoming a leader of that faction and determining to run for consul in the next election. L. Volcacius Tullus, then consul, blocked the former propraetor's candidacy, however, because, while Catiline was still in Africa, envoys from that province had accused him before the Senate of extortion, a charge that was still pending and that therefore made him legally ineligible to run for office. Angered by what some believe was an optimatist plot to prevent his election, Catiline may have launched a conspiracy in late 66 with the support of Crassus and Caesar. The aim of this so-called First Catilinian Conspiracy (66–65 B.C.) was to seize control of the government by murdering the two new consuls, Cotta and Torquatus, who were to be replaced by Autronius and Catiline. Piso was also to be dispatched with an army to take Spain. The plot, however, was discovered; somewhat mysteriously, the Senate did not condemn the alleged conspirators. In fact, the entire matter seems to have been kept quiet. It may be that Catiline had played only a small part in this planned upheaval, or perhaps none at all, because when his trial for extortion finally occurred in late 65, Torquatus—the man whom Catiline wanted, according to his enemies, to kill—appeared as a friendly witness and helped to secure an acquittal.

Prevented by these legal affairs from being a candidate in 65, Catiline did run for consul the next year, but Cicero and Antonius defeated him in an election tainted by bribery on all sides. It was during this campaign that Cicero made his vicious attack in the *Oratio in Toga Candida* on his opponent's moral and political life. Undeterred, however, by his loss and by his trial later that year for the murders of Gratidianus and others which had occurred during the Sullan proscriptions—he was acquitted—Catiline ran for consul again in 63, promising that he would abrogate all debts and reallocate the country's wealth. Though former supporters of Sulla came to Rome to give him their votes, Cicero and the *optimates* bought the election for Silanus and Murena. Having thus been disappointed for the fourth time in his bid for office, Catiline turned to rebellion.

Calling together a group of friends sometime after the election, he told them of his plan to break the tyranny that imperiled the state and promised them various kinds of emoluments for their support. It is at least possible that both Crassus and Caesar were involved in the beginning phases of this conspiracy, though, if they were, they later removed themselves from it. In any case, there was widespread sympathy from many quarters for the revolt that Catiline now set in motion. He planned to have Manlius raise troops in Etruria and begin a march against Rome on 27 October 63. On that day, there was to be insurrection in other parts of the country and, on 28 October, a riot in Rome itself, during which Cicero and other prominent noblemen were to be killed. Through Fulvia and Quintus Curius, however, Cicero learned of the plot and, after gathering evidence, presented his discoveries to the Senate, which passed a "last decree" on 21 October, giving Cicero the power to protect the city—an action that caused Catiline to change his timetable.

Charged with violating the law, the conspirator voluntarily placed himself in the custody of M. Metellus while he awaited trial, knowing that he had great popular support. Then, on the night of 6 November, he held a clandestine meeting of his associates at Laeca's house and further revised his plans. He and a few compatriots would flee to

Etruria to hasten the march on Rome, while others would create uprisings in various areas of the country. Those left behind would murder prominent political figures and set fire to particular districts in the city. In fact, they would begin their terrorism by killing Cicero the next morning. All of this information, however, was conveyed to the consul who, after spoiling the murder plot, called the Senate into session at the Temple of Jupiter Stator on 7 November. With Catiline listening, Cicero exposed the conspirator's new plans in what came to be called the First Catilinian Oration (he was to make four), urging the traitor to go into exile. When the accused began his defense, he was interrupted by cries that he was a public enemy and a parricide, and he angrily withdrew from the temple. That night he left the city, purportedly for exile in Marseilles but in fact for Etruria to join Manlius. Others under the command of Publius Lentulus and Gaius Cethegus were to remain behind to put the revised program into effect.

In Etruria, Catiline worked to build up his forces and proceeded to move toward Rome. When the Senate learned of these actions, he and Manlius were officially declared public enemies. About this same time, Lentulus made a grave mistake in trying to gain the support of the Allobroges, a Transalpine tribe whose ambassadors had arrived in Rome to protest the abuses of their governor. The envoys betrayed Lentulus to Cicero and worked with the consul to gain indisputable evidence against the conspirators. When he had convincing proof against them, Cicero arrested the principal traitors in the city and presented his case to the Senate. Subsequently, on 5 December, he persuaded that body, with Cato's help, to pass an illegal death sentence for the five in custody and that night had them killed in one of the Roman prisons.

When Catiline's troops learned of these events, many of them deserted. Their leader then marched those remaining to Pistoria, hoping to flee from that city into Transalpine Gaul; but he soon found himself trapped by Celer to the north and by Antonius to the south, who had been sent to capture or crush him. Recognizing his desperate plight, he decided to surprise Antonius's army, which was closest to him. He rallied his men with an inspiring speech and then led them heroically into battle, demonstrating both his courage and his military skill. His forces, however, unable to withstand their larger and better-equipped adversary, died valiantly on the field, and Catiline himself fell among them. Thus, with the dispatch of the traitor's head to Rome as a symbol of victory, the Catilinian Conspiracy came essentially to an end in January 62 B.C.

As this sketch suggests, the parallels between the despised Roman and the no-less-detested Aaron Burr are striking. The principal similarity, of course, is that both men, frustrated in their drive for power, launched conspiracies in order to regain it. But there are other correspondences. Both were talented and courageous military leaders who served their country in times of crisis and who later went bad. Both were men of great political ambition who, early in their careers, switched from a conservative party with which by birth they were naturally allied to a more democratic faction in whose struggles they saw the possibility of attaining their own ends. And both were hated and attacked, often with good reason, by powerful opponents who tried to destroy them—Cicero in Catiline's case, Hamilton and Jefferson in Burr's. The subjects of gossip about their sexual affairs, the two were notable for their immorality; incontinent behavior marked their adult lives. Both were also suspected of political misdeeds—Catiline of extortion when he was propraetor of Africa and Burr of attempting to steal the presidency from Jefferson. In addition, both paid dearly for their conspiratorial schemes—the Roman with his head, the American with twenty-nine years of contumely and disgrace. And both, of course, were legendary figures, linked inextricably with the darker side of life. It is little wonder, then, that for one reason or another American authors saw Burr as an American Catiline.

When writers looked to the past to find an analogue for the Colonel as libertine, however, they usually turned to fiction rather than to history. In Richardson's profligate Lovelace, they found the basic similarity they were seeking. His story, of course, is the story of *Clarissa*.[3] Intended for Clarissa's older sister, Arabella, the aristocratic but rakish Robert Lovelace became a frequent visitor at the Harlowe estate. However, finding Clarissa more appealing, he contrived to have Arabella reject him so that he could pursue his own inclinations. Jealous of her younger sister, Arabella with her brother, James, who was envious of Clarissa because their grandfather had left her the greater part of his fortune, then worked to spoil the girl's happiness. Using a former quarrel as a pretext, James challenged the haughty Lovelace to a duel in which young Harlowe was slightly wounded, his opponent generously sparing his life. The result of this encounter, however, was that the Harlowe family turned against and insulted James's rival and forbade Clarissa to see him, especially after she spoke in his behalf. Fearing renewed violence, the girl hesitantly agreed to a secret correspondence with Lovelace in order to ameliorate the situation. But James immediately introduced the rich though unattractive Mr. Solmes as a new suitor for Clarissa's hand. With Arabella, James hoped to provoke a split between the family and his younger sister because he feared that his uncles would favor the girl in their wills just as his grandfather had done.

James's plan worked. When Clarissa rejected Solmes, Mr. Harlowe, who had hoped to raise the social and financial standing of the family through marriage, was enraged; he determined to bend the disobedient girl's will to his own. Despite Clarissa's offer to stay single for life, if only her parents would not insist upon her accepting this latest beau, the family remained intransigent, in part because they believed she still favored Lovelace, whom they detested. She, in fact, continued to correspond with him because she feared he might provoke bloodshed if she refused. All this time, however, Lovelace, who had sworn with wounded pride to avenge himself upon as many women as possible because his first love had jilted him, had been attempting to gain Clarissa's confidence and affection. He intended that she should fly to him when her situation became intolerable, and he therefore worked to increase the pressure on her. As her family became more and more insistent and cruel, he suggested that she put herself under the protection of his relatives. When Clarissa realized that she would shortly be forced to marry Solmes, Lovelace tricked her into going off with him, ostensibly to be made independent of both him and her family.

Lodging her at Mrs. Sinclair's brothel, Lovelace set out to seduce her as he had so many other young women. Putting into effect a number of elaborate intrigues, which he relished, he intended to try the virtue of this exemplar of her sex and, if she survived the test, to marry her. Such reasoning, at least, provided the rationalization he apparently needed to hold the girl a virtual prisoner and to increase her suffering. Clarissa's only contact with her former life came through Anna Howe, a dear friend, with whom the unhappy victim continued to correspond. More worldly-wise than Clarissa, Miss Howe recom-

mended immediate marriage so that her friend's reputation would not
be further sullied. Even though she detested the scheming libertine,
Anna felt that matrimony was now Clarissa's only hope.

Lovelace, of course, sought to bring the girl to his bed without
taking the intermediate step to the altar. But, as he continued his machinations, he found that his admiration for the noble sufferer increased and that his love for her deepened—facts he made clear to his
brother rake, John Belford, with whom he regularly corresponded.
Thus, in his frequent interviews with the girl, Lovelace would occasionally be overcome and offer marriage, but Clarissa still refused to
accept him, fearing that, if she did, she might ruin her chances of reconciliation with her family. Indeed, her father, upon hearing that she
had fled with Lovelace, had uttered a furious curse, damning her in
this world and in the next; and the entire family, incited by James and
Arabella, refused to have anything to do with her. Lovelace, however,
continued to pursue his cruel stratagems, seeking all the while to lead
Clarissa astray; but, though the girl occasionally waivered in her resolution not to marry him, she was able to withstand his further en-
treaties and seductive ploys.

After the villain began to take increasing liberties with her, though,
Clarissa tried to escape and reached Hampstead, where, unfortunately, Lovelace was successful in recapturing her. Then, by having two
women from Mrs. Sinclair's impersonate his aunt and his cousin, the
rake was able to induce Clarissa to leave with the two frauds. Lovelace told the girl that she would be taken to London and there would
come under the protection of his relatives; but, in fact, he had her returned to her former apartment in the brothel. Then, with the help of
Mrs. Sinclair, who secretly administered drugs to the girl, Lovelace
raped her, leaving her stupefied with narcotics and overcome by grief.
Repentant afterwards, the libertine again proposed marriage, but
Clarissa utterly rejected him and tried frequently to escape. At last,
after Lovelace had left to attend his sick relative, Lord M., the girl succeeded in fleeing and lodged herself at Smith's in Covent Garden. But
Mrs. Sinclair soon discovered where Clarissa was staying, and,
hoping for a reward from the rich despoiler, had her arrested for supposed debts.

Lovelace, however, was shocked at Mrs. Sinclair's action. Fearing
that if he went himself to save the girl she would think that he had con-

trived the entire affair, he sent Belford to release and comfort her. Lovelace's friend returned Clarissa to Smith's; but the indignity of having been taken for debt proved a final blow to the young woman's health, and, no longer wishing to live, she went into decline. Attended by both an apothecary and Dr. H. and nursed by the Widow Lovick, Clarissa prepared herself for death, all the while seeking not a reconciliation with her family but only the removal of her father's curse and a last blessing. The Harlowes, however, thought that the girl was merely feigning illness in order to restore herself to favor and therefore remained implacable. Lovelace, on the other hand, was constantly pleading for Clarissa to marry him. But, though she did convey through Belford the forgiveness of her destroyer, she firmly refused to see him.

Returning from abroad, Colonel Morden, Clarissa's cousin, took up the girl's cause without seeing her and worked to bring about a rapprochement with the family. He also called upon Lovelace and Lord M. to assure himself that the rake would marry Clarissa if she would have him. Then, after receiving the shocking news from Belford that the innocent sufferer could not live long, the colonel rushed to his cousin in time to hear her dying requests. In the interim, having been informed by Dr. H. that their lovely relative was, in fact, desperately ill, the Harlowes finally made overtures to the girl. But their letters arrived too late; Clarissa had already expired. All this time, Lovelace, forbidden to see his victim, was wracked by guilt and tortured by thoughts that his beloved might die. When he received word of her demise, the grief-stricken seducer went off to the Continent in hopes of recovering his spirits. Having learned, however, that Morden had expressed a desire to avenge his cousin's death, Lovelace wrote the colonel a note, which led directly to a challenge. In the duel that followed, Morden killed the man who had destroyed the most lovely flower of young womanhood.

As this précis of *Clarissa* suggests, there are several similarities between Lovelace and Burr, most of them, of course, involving the relationship the two had with women. Each, for example, was a sexual predator of great charm, whom the ladies found irresistible. Leslie Fiedler makes this point about Lovelace. In his discussion of Richardson's villain as an archetypal figure, Fiedler speaks of Clarissa's seducer as having "an absolute, almost magical, ability to compel love,"[4] a trait apparent in his many conquests. Davis had noted earlier this same quality in Burr when he had remarked upon the Colonel's dazzling attractiveness and had mentioned his "fascinating power almost peculiar to himself" of maintaining the affection of those he had seduced.[5] Each man also loved intrigue—was, in Fiedler's terms, "a Machiavelli of the boudoir" (Fiedler, *Love and Death*, p. 63)—and each gloried in subduing his prey, though Lovelace, of course, was much more hostilely aggressive in his amours than Burr; the Colonel never used force. In addition, each was inordinately vain about his conquests. Burr, for example, kept letters from his mistresses; Lovelace, on the other hand, kept rough score, boasting to Belford of the "hectacomb" of women he had offered in sacrifice to his Nemesis (Richardson, *Clarissa*, 1: 145). Finally, each was an aristocrat who, except where ladies were concerned, believed in the gentleman's code and fought duels when it was breached. And though Lovelace fell on the field of honor, Burr's fate was no less ruinous. After he killed Hamilton, he had few happy and many miserable days. Thus the various parallels between Richardson's libertine and the fascinating Aaron Burr led some writers to see the Colonel as an American Lovelace.

When American authors represented Burr as victim, however, they usually did not provide a literary or historical analogue, though the reasons why they neglected to do so are unclear. To associate the Colonel with Christ, the archetypal victim, was generally unthinkable; and other, more appropriate figures seem not to have occurred to them. The sad fact apparently is that, in most cases, their imaginations—never especially keen anyway—simply failed them.[6] Charles Felton Pidgin, however, Burr's prolific celebrator in belles-lettres, was more successful than his colleagues; he found in Warwick the Kingmaker the essential similarity other writers had overlooked.[7]

Born 28 November 1428, Richard Neville, the Earl of Warwick by 1449, allied himself from the beginning with his father, the Earl of Salisbury, and his uncle Richard, Duke of York, against the weak Lancastrian Henry VI and his haughty wife, Margaret of Anjou. In the spring of 1455, when his kinsmen took up arms against the king, Warwick joined them. His heroic action at the Battle of St. Albans, which followed, led to a Yorkist victory and to immediate personal fame; as a reward for his bravery, he was made Captain of Calais when his uncle, now controlling the king and ruling in his name, formed a new government. In that post, Neville increased his renown with great exploits at sea, restoring England's diminished naval honor and protecting his country's shipping. He also developed a taste for statesmanship and intrigue; with masterful skill, he negotiated an alliance with Philip of Burgundy that was to serve his family well in the continual struggle for power at home.

In the summer of 1459, when Margaret and her noblemen decided to try to break Yorkist ascendancy, Warwick led six hundred men from Calais to his uncle's camp at Ludlow, where the Duke was preparing for battle. But the Queen's forces were numerically superior, and, when under Andrew Trollope the greater part of Neville's contingent deserted, York and his kinsmen fled, Warwick himself returning to Calais. There he decided he would continue to work for the reforms his uncle had sought but in his own way; he would no longer be subservient to his family. By June 1460, he was back in England with a force of two thousand men to rid the country of a corrupt court faction. Beloved by the people since his heroism at St. Albans, he had little trouble taking London, which capitulated without a fight. He then defeated the Lancastrians at Northampton, captured the king, returned him to London, and set up a Neville government. The Duke of York, however, had his own plans for the new regime. Joined by his sons Edmund, Earl of Rutland, and Edward, Earl of March, he came to the capital to have himself crowned king. Skillfully, with Edward's help, Warwick persuaded his uncle of the folly of such an attempt and then diplomatically worked out an agreement with the Lords and the Commons that insured York's succession to the throne after Henry's death.

Meanwhile, the Lancastrians had gathered strength in the north. Recognizing the necessity of again meeting their enemies, Warwick and his family formed their plans. York and Salisbury, Neville's father, would engage Margaret's forces; Warwick himself would remain in London to govern the realm. But matters did not turn out as all had hoped. At Wakefield, the Yorkist army was crushed, Warwick's father, uncle, and cousin Edmund all losing their lives. The earl then took his forces north to meet the advancing Lancastrians, who were marching on the capital. Taking the king with him, Warwick set up his defenses at St. Albans. But, on 16 February 1461, he was badly routed, losing Henry to his enemies, and fled to join Edward of York, who was hurrying from the west to bring reinforcements. When the two kinsmen met, Warwick boldly suggested that Edward claim the throne, a proposal Edward found attractive. As a result, they hurried to London, where Neville's brother rallied the people to their cause; and then, on 4 March 1461, Warwick had his cousin proclaimed Edward IV, King of England.

After the two smashed the Lancastrians in a battle at Towton that left ten thousand dead, Warwick decided to remain in the north to restore order and to check any new advances that Margaret and Henry, who had escaped to Scotland, might make. For the next three years, he was content to work in the northern area of the country destroying for a time the remaining Lancastrian influence—Henry was eventually captured and imprisoned in the Tower; Margaret fled to the Continent—and sharing the governance of England with his protégé Edward. But in 1464, the situation changed. Enticed by Louis XI of France, who wanted a peace and an alliance with England so that he could crush his disruptive barons, Warwick proposed a French marriage for Edward with Bona of Savoy, Louis's sister-in-law. The king, however, who had lately been showing increasing independence, mysteriously temporized. Though he did nothing to prevent Warwick's continued correspondence with Louis on the issue, he found various reasons for delay, finally suggesting that such a serious matter of state should be submitted to the Great Council for approval before the earl journeyed to France to make final arrangements. When the council met in September, Edward revealed to a shocked assembly that he had already wed the Lancastrian widow Elizabeth Woodville, Lord Rivers's daughter, that previous May. Whatever his reasons for not telling his cousin earlier, he had allowed the man who had raised him to the throne to make a fool of himself before his countrymen and the king of France. Though there was a reconciliation of sorts before Warwick left for Middleham Castle in the north, the earl had been badly betrayed. The relationship between the two men had been fractured beyond repair.

Warwick busied himself for the next two years with affairs of state, journeying several times to the Continent to secure for England the best possible arrangement with the squabbling factions abroad. But as he assessed his own political situation, he saw that his future lay with the king of France and therefore worked to support an Anglo-French alliance, although Edward favored the Burgundians, Louis's enemies. And because the king was raising the Woodvilles to places of eminence in an attempt to break Neville's power, Warwick also began to recruit friends at home. These included, among others, his brother George, chancellor and archbishop, and the Duke of Clarence, Edward's brother. But after the king removed George Neville as chancellor and renewed a treaty with Charles of Burgundy, both actions occurring while the earl was in France negotiating for Edward with Louis, Warwick knew that he would have to fight to regain supremacy. In May 1469, he fomented a rebellion in the north through his follower Robin of Redesdale and by August had captured the king, who agreed to do as he was bidden. Because the people refused to support Warwick, however, he was forced to release Edward two months later. A formal accommodation followed, but both men recognized its shallowness.

Determined to avenge himself on his betrayer, Warwick then attempted in early 1470 to put the Duke of Clarence on the throne and govern through him; but, when that plan failed, the earl fled to France. There, anxious to regain power, he sought Louis's aid to return Henry VI—the man he had deposed nine years before—to his kingship. In exchange for a peace treaty and an English alliance against Charles of Burgundy, Louis agreed to help and persuaded a reluctant Margaret of Anjou to ally herself with her most detested enemy. Then, having been provided with troops and a fleet by Louis, Warwick set out for England on 9 September 1470, arriving four days later at Dartmouth and Plymouth and marching immediately thereafter to meet Edward's forces. When John Neville, Marquess of Montagu, gave his support to his older brother, the king fled to Burgundy, and Warwick was once again in control of his country. He quickly freed Henry VI from the Tower and in mid-October returned the House of Lancaster to the throne.

Warwick's task now was to gain popular support and establish his power so firmly that when Edward made his inevitable attempt to regain the crown, the earl would be able to withstand the challenge. His most difficult problem in achieving these goals was to persuade his countrymen to ratify the bargain he had made with Louis to support France against Burgundy. Ancient hatreds and economic interests were obstacles to such action, but Warwick worked tirelessly to convince Parliament that England's good lay with Louis XI. Although the earl was unsuccessful in gaining a declaration of war against the Burgundians, he did persuade the Lords and the Commons to conclude a ten-year truce with France, during which time neither side was to aid the enemies of the other. This pact, Warwick knew, was his guarantee of the future; in return for the alliance, Louis held out the promise to Neville of a realm of his own—Holland and Zeeland—should he ever lose his power in England.

Ultimately, in his attempt to establish complete control of the country, Warwick could not gain the support of the people. They found the treaty with France onerous and were slow to respond to the earl's authority. After all, he was not the king. Thus, when Edward landed at Ravenspur in March 1471 with two thousand Burgundians, Warwick knew he was in trouble. He rushed to the north to raise troops, sparred with Edward at Conventry, saw his brother George desert him, and, finally, on Easter Sunday, 14 April 1471, met the invaders at Barnet. A thick fog, which made his artillery useless and caused confusion at a crucial moment in the battle, led to his downfall. As he tried to mount his horse after his forces had given way before the onslaught, the Earl of Warwick was thrown to the ground and fatally stabbed in the throat. Edward immediately shipped his body to London where, naked except for a loin cloth, it lay exposed for two days in St. Paul's cathedral. Thus the man who had made his cousin king died in battle against that same kinsman who much earlier had betrayed him.

As Warwick's story suggests, the basic similarity Pidgin saw between Neville and Burr is that both were victimized—the earl by his ungrateful protégé Edward, who allowed Warwick to embarrass himself before the world, who inexorably rid the court of Neville supporters, and who finally fought his cousin in a battle that led to his death; the Colonel by a suspicious Jefferson, who never trusted Burr after the 1800 election, who helped to destroy him politically, and who worked behind the scenes at Richmond to hang him. But there are additional parallels that Pidgin no doubt had in mind. Both Warwick and Burr, for instance, were heroic military leaders who earned fame early. Both were magnetic personalities to whom, until late in their political careers, the people rallied almost instinctively. And both were bold adventurers, men of ambition who were at home in the

world of intrigue. Each was also an adept politician who worked in-
defatigably and skillfully to persuade others of his viewpoint, as, for
example, Warwick did in convincing his uncle, the Duke of York, that
his intention to have himself crowned king in 1460 was a mistake and
as Burr did in cajoling the New York electorate to vote for Jefferson in
1800. In addition, each was a man who refused to accept defeat.
Warwick restored Henry VI to the throne after Edward had humili-
ated the earl and forced him to flee to France; Burr turned to his western schemes after Jefferson's odious Cheetham had ruined the vice
president in national politics. Finally, each man was, as Kendall says
of Warwick, a "fierce prisoner of his vision of himself, the victim as
well as subject" of his individual legend (Kendall, *Warwick*, p. 239).
Because of these many correspondences, then, it is appropriate that
Pidgin depicted Burr as an American Warwick. Like other American
writers, who as a group gave depth and resonance to the figure of
Aaron Burr by repeatedly representing the Colonel as conspirator,
predator, and victim and by often providing historical or literary analogues for those portrayals, Pidgin helps to raise Burr to emblematic
stature.

Burr, however, becomes something more than just a complex
American symbol. The three images of him that predominate in
imaginative literature suggest that he is related to American culture in
a more subtle but also more meaningful way. In choosing, no doubt
intuitively and perhaps unconsciously, to highlight the particular
aspects of the Colonel that they did, American writers seem to use him
as a vehicle to express society's fears and therefore in some way to
purge them.[8]

In a nineteenth-century world that was unsure of its own stability,
one of the views of Burr American authors naturally emphasized was
that of conspiring traitor. The scoundrel Cheetham was the first to see
the Colonel in this way, portraying him in his *Narrative, View, Nine
Letters*, and newspaper as a political traitor, a Catiline who attempted
to steal the presidency from Jefferson. In the 1804 New York gubernatorial election, Cheetham and others continued to highlight Burr's
Catilinian qualities, one anonymous rhymster even seeing him as a
traitorously ambitious, biblical Aaron. Then after the Colonel shot
Hamilton, this view of him as Catiline was again raised, though often

in conjunction with other equally opprobrious images. And both during and after the treason trial in Richmond, of course, the newspapers branded him a thorough-going traitor.

American playwrights and novelists were quick to seize upon this image. The ubiquitous Anon., for example, portrayed Burr as an ambitious traitor in *The Conspiracy*, a verse drama of doubtful merit. Fellow playwright William Minturn depicted the Colonel as an Ahab-like traitor in his *Aaron Burr*, and Charles E. Stoaks saw his main character as an angry, revengeful rebel and "Chief Conspirator" in a similarly titled play. In his tedious, two-part novel *Burton*, Joseph Holt Ingraham traced the stages of Burr's progress from patriot to Catiline, and in the equally bad *Conspirator* A. E. Dupuy saw the Colonel as a traitorous tragic hero. These and a host of other nineteenth-century writers—novelists Emerson Bennett, Edwin Lassetter Bynner, and James W. Taylor among them—reflected the uneasiness of their times in their depiction of Burr as traitor.

But these authors were not alone in their anxiety about the country's stability. Many Americans of the past century feared disloyalty and the possible destruction of the bond that held the states together, a fact reflected most clearly in the pervasive glorification and calls for the preservation of the Union that occurred, especially from the 1830s on. Thus Congressman Owen Lovejoy of Illinois could note in 1861 that "every nation has some nucleus thought, some central idea, which they enshrine" and that for the United States it was the concept of Union to which Americans adhered "with a spirit of superstitious idolatry." He therefore felt it unwise "to tamper with that holy instrument around which all American hearts cluster, and to which they cling with the tenacity of a semi-religious attachment."[9]

But it was Daniel Webster who had earlier established this notion in the American consciousness. In the moving conclusion of his second reply to Hayne in 1830 on Foot's resolution, the great orator had revealed his reverence for the Union and had urged his listeners to preserve it:

While the Union lasts, we have high, exciting, gratifying prospects spread out before us, for us and our children. Beyond that I seek not to penetrate the veil. God grant that in my day, at least, that curtain may not rise! God grant that on my vision never may be opened what lies behind! When my eyes shall be turned to behold for the last time the sun in heaven, may I not see him shining on the broken and dishonored fragments of a once glorious Union; on States dissevered, discordant, belligerent; on a land rent with civil feuds, or drenched, it may be, in fraternal blood! Let their last feeble and lingering glance rather behold the glorious ensign of the republic, now known and honored throughout the earth, still full high advanced, its arms and trophies streaming in their original lustre, not a stripe erased or polluted, nor a single star obscured, bearing for its motto, no such miserable interrogatory as "What is all this worth?" nor those other words of delusion and folly, "Liberty first and Union afterwards"; but everywhere, spread all over in characters of living light, blazing on all its ample folds, as they float over the sea and over the land, and in every wind under the whole heavens, that other sentiment, dear to every true American heart,—Liberty *and* Union, now and forever, one and inseparable![10]

After that speech, feeling for the Union grew especially strong, and the expression of reverence for and the calls to sustain it became frequent. In the 1832 presidential campaign, for example, Amos Kendall, one of Jackson's organizers, echoed Webster's sentiments, though somewhat less eloquently: "With us," he proclaimed, ". . . the Union is *sacred*. Its preservation is the *only* means of preserving our civil liberties."[11] Old Hickory himself made a vigorous appeal that same year for maintaining the Union with his proclamation to the people of South Carolina, some of whom had proposed nullification. In concluding, he begged God's help to prevent dismemberment: "May the Great Ruler of Nations grant that the signal blessings with which He has favored ours may not, by the madness of party or personal ambition, be disregarded and lost; and may His wise providence bring those who have produced this crisis to see the folly before they feel the misery of civil strife, and inspire a returning veneration for that Union which, if we may dare to penetrate His designs, He has chosen as the only means of attaining the high destinies to which we may reasonably aspire."[12] In 1849, Longfellow made a similar if poetic plea in his famous "The Building of the Ship." Near the end of the piece, he wrote: "Sail on, O UNION, strong and great! / Humanity with all its fears, / With all the hopes of future years, / Is hanging breathless on thy fate!"[13] And Webster thrilled a packed Senate chamber on 7 March 1850, when he delivered his great speech for "the Constitution and the Union," which he began: "I wish to speak to-day, not as a

Massachusetts man, nor as a Northern man, but as an American. . . . I speak to-day for the preservation of the Union. 'Hear me for my cause' " (Webster, *Writings and Speeches*, 10: 57–58).

With this sentiment widespread, therefore, any threat of dissolution was likely to be seen as evil and to be intensely feared. "The Union became so powerful a concept," Nagel notes, "that Americans looked with horror on the violence, desolation, and darkness which dismemberment would bring."[14] As early as 1815, for example, a Charleston lecturer discussing "The Permanency of the American Union" proclaimed: "Next to the frown of Deity the loss of union would be our most awful visitation."[15] Speaking in the Senate fifteen years later, Edward Livingston expressed more intense fears: "Disunion!" he cried, "the thought itself, the means by which it may be effected, its frightful and degrading consequences, the idea, the very mention of it, ought to be banished from our debates, from our minds. God deliver us from this worst, this greatest evil."[16] In his 1832 proclamation Jackson declared that "compared to disunion all other evils are light, because that brings with it an accumulation of all" (Jackson, *Messages*, 2: 655). And in 1842 Clay saw "the dissolution of the union of these States" as "the greatest of all possible calamities which could befall this people."[17] Eight years later, in his great compromise speech of 5–6 February 1850, he pointed out that disunion would lead only "to certain and irretrievable destruction."[18]

It seems natural, then, that, in a nineteenth-century society that was uncertain of its cohesiveness and terrified of the misery and chaos that dismemberment would bring, one of the images of Burr that American writers would elect to emphasize would be that of traitor. Over and over again in their plays, novels, and stories, they show the Colonel scheming to separate the western states from the Union and to crown himself emperor of a new country. No doubt sharing the uneasiness of their contemporaries, they seem to have felt the rightness of such a portrayal for their time.[19]

Nineteenth-century authors, however, also stress the depiction of Burr as dark despoiler, and this for reasons analogous to those just noted. In a society that held as one of its primary images of woman the view of her as untainted virgin and that consequently feared the sexual predator, it is not surprising that writers would choose to portray the Colonel as rake. The political hacks, for example, lost no time in depicting him in this way. Cheetham, of course, labelled him a latter-day Solomon "with three hundred wives and concubines" in the Burrite Creed, a campaign poster described him as a man debauched, and a Federalist handbill spoke of his "abandoned profligacy" in detailing his many sexual intrigues. But our literary artists also portrayed the Colonel as predator. In "Aaron Burr's Wooing," Stedman wondered in verse if there were a "widow or maid" who "long would resist" the Colonel's charms when he came "a-wooing." And dramatists William Minturn and Charles E. Stoaks, representative of the many playwrights who saw Burr negatively, depicted him as a dangerous rake. Thus, in *Aaron Burr: A Drama in Four Acts*, Minturn highlighted this image of the Colonel by showing in full his faithless treatment of the innocent Margaret, and, in *Aaron Burr; or, The Kingdom of Silver*, Stoaks called attention to the Colonel's womanizing by having Wilkinson comment specifically upon it. Typical of the many nineteenth-century novelists who treated Burr as rake, Ingraham in *Burton* devoted much of his second volume to the Colonel's sexual transgressions, and Burdett in *The Beautiful Spy* likened his probable father to Paris in his characterization of Burr as utter trifler. But in their portrayal of the Colonel, our writers were merely reflecting the common view of American women as spotless virgins and the societal horror of the sexual predator.

There is, of course, little doubt that our progenitors frequently pictured their women, especially in sentimental fiction, as unsullied maidens. Earnest makes the point: "The sentimental novelists represented their heroines as delicate flowers, emotional rather than intellectual, given to fainting and to moral and religious preachments, and, of course, chaste in thought and deed. As William Wasserstrom says, 'Womanliness came to mean sexlessness.' "[20] In her study of the nineteenth-century novel, Judith Fryer, echoing Earnest, calls this character the "American Princess"—"Eve before the Fall": "Delicately beautiful and innocent, she is the psychosexual opposite of the Temptress."[21] Fryer also notes that such a figure is not limited to the works of minor artists: "She is the 'pale maiden' of Hawthorne and Melville—Priscilla, Hilda, Lucy—and Henry James's Daisy Miller, Isabel Archer, Milly Theale, Maggie Verver" (pp. 24–25). And, in discussing the Clarissa archetype and the many heroines in American fiction derived from it, Leslie Fiedler brilliantly captures the essence of this figure: "She is feeling without passion, and her love climax is tears. She is a Protestant virgin, proper to a society that destroyed the splendid images of the Mother of God, but she is also the product of anti-metaphysical Sentimentalism, which found it easier to believe that the human could achieve divinity than that the divine could descend into the human. It is as Pure Maiden that she offers salvation, and upon her maintenance of that purity depends not only her own essential bliss but that of the male who attempts to destroy it" (Fielder, *Love and Death*, p. 67).

This character, however, was a creature of fact as well as fiction. In the old South, for example, as Osterweis observes, "woman was a being made of finer clay than man, someone to be admired, adored, and protected."[22] W. J. Cash describes her as "the South's Palladium, this Southern woman—the shield-bearing Athena gleaming whitely in the clouds, the standard for its rallying, the mystic symbol of its nationality in face of the foe. She was the lily-pure maid of Astolat and the hunting goddess of the Boeotian hill. And—she was the pitiful Mother of God."[23] No strictly regional figure, however, she was elsewhere "the lady"—one of the results of American industrialization. Lerner describes her existence and how she came to be:

As class distinctions sharpened, social attitudes toward women became polarized. The image of "the lady" was elevated to the accepted ideal of femininity toward which all women would strive. In this formulation of values lower class women were simply ignored. The actual lady was, of course, nothing new on the American scene; she had been present ever since colonial days. What was new in the 1830's was the cult of the lady, her elevation to a status symbol. The advancing prosperity of the early nineteenth century made it possible for middle class women to aspire to the status formerly reserved for upper class women. The "cult of true womanhood" of the 1830's became a vehicle for such aspirations. Mass circulation newspapers and magazines made it possible to teach every woman how to elevate the status of her family by setting "proper" standards of behavior, dress and literary tastes. *Godey's Lady's Book* and innumerable gift books and tracts of the period all preach the same gospel of "true womanhood"—piety, purity, domesticity.[24]

Hogeland gives further testimony that this figure actually existed, categorizing her as "ornamental" in his study of feminine life styles possible between 1820 and 1860.[25] In discussing the sentimentalization of women that occurred in American fiction—the positing that "woman in general and some women in particular are absolutely pure"—Fiedler notes that this perception of womanhood became, in fact, a reality: "With no counter-tradition, cynical or idealizing, to challenge it, the sentimental view came to be accepted as quite *literally* true, was imposed upon actual woman as a required role and responded to by men as if it were a fact of life rather than of fancy" (Fiedler, *Love and Death*, p. 80).

It is not surprising, then, that in such a world the predator should be one of the men most feared, a fact reflected in our literature where he appears with numbing regularity and where his name is legion. From Mrs. Rowson's Montraville to Theodore Dreiser's Drouet, he threatens our pale ladies with his dazzling, phallic charm until he is either converted to virtue or dismissed from sight. Hence, for many of our nineteenth-century writers treating Burr, it was natural to highlight the Colonel's role as Lovelace, to focus on his sexual plundering, when they used him in their works. For them, he became the expression of one of society's most frightening nightmares.

Though the images of traitor and of libertine remain important in the twentieth century,[26] the depiction of Burr as victim also emerges in the literature of our time. Once again societal fears are involved. In a world that feels threatened by the complex forces of modern life that act to crush the individual, it is perhaps not unexpected that American writers would turn to this portrayal of the Colonel. Two early twentieth-century poets, for example, saw Burr as victim. In "Colonel Aaron Burr" Law pictured him as a noble man, victimized by jealousy and slander; and in "A Plea" Farrell called for a restoration of the innocent sufferer's reputation. Like the poets, dramatists Pierce, McCrary, Masters, Raiden, and Hallett also portrayed the Colonel as unjustly treated. In *Aaron Burr*, Pierce depicted his titular character as a victim of circumstances and events, whereas in *Aaron and Theodosia* McCrary suggested that, though Burr was overly ambitious, he was nonetheless a victim of political hatred, falsely charged with treason. Masters portrayed him as history's martyr in *Aaron Burr and Madam Jumel*, Raiden saw him as a victim of Jefferson's hatred in *Mr. Jefferson's Burr*, and Hallett showed him as a man of honor ruined by Hamilton, Wilkinson, and Jefferson. Charles Felton Pidgin expressed the sentiments of many modern novelists when he viewed the Colonel as victim in *Little Burr*. Seeing his hero as the Warwick of America, Pidgin condemned Jefferson as an ingrate and persecutor. Though her primary focus was elsewhere, Anya Seton followed this depiction in part, by portraying Burr in *My Theodosia* as a martyr to Jefferson's hatred and Wilkinson's duplicity. And in *The Young Mrs. Blennerhassett*, Nellie Whan Peppers characterized the Colonel as a forthright man of great charm who was destroyed by his enemies. Gore Vidal, of course, took the revisionist viewpoint in *Burr* by treating the Colonel as sufferer at the hands of Washington, Hamilton, Wilkinson, and Jefferson. Thus, in seeing Burr as victim, these writers reflected the anxieties that modern Americans experience as they confront their complex and threatening world.

There is, of course, little doubt that twentieth-century Americans often see themselves as, and fear being, victims, as is suggested by the pervasiveness of this image in American literary works. Commenting upon the American novel, Hassan, for example, notes that "the ideas of victimization, rebellion, and alienation remain at the center of Western literature since—and perhaps before—the turn of the century."[27] Indeed, any sampling of American well-known fiction from 1893 to the present reveals the extent to which the depiction of man as victim haunts modern consciousness.[28]

Such a portrayal first becomes commonplace in the works of the early naturalists. Crane's *Maggie*, for instance, shows the crushing effects of environment on its main character, portraying her dismal life and inevitable slide into prostitution and suicide. Dreiser's *An American Tragedy* provides another example in its picturing of Clyde Griffiths's pathetic struggles as the foreordained result of social and biological forces over which the passive youth has no control. Of course, this image of man as martyr is everywhere in our military fiction. In *Three Soldiers*, Dos Passos depicts the brutalizing effects of war on Fuselli, Chrisfield, and Andrews, each of whom is dehumanized and, in one way or another, destroyed. Hemingway reveals the stoical suffering of Frederic Henry, who, though he can leave the battlefield behind, cannot make a separate peace with a world that breaks everyone in the end. And Dalton Trumbo describes the excruciating agony of Joe Bonham, who, left by the war without face and limbs, has become, in effect, little more than a human slab of meat. In *From Here to Eternity*, James Jones shows that the peacetime military is no less effective than the army at war in victimizing those under its control; Prewitt and his fellows are as mercilessly crushed as their battle-weary counterparts in such books as Mailer's *The Naked and the Dead*. There Lieutenant Hearn and Red Valsen succumb to the ruthlessness of General Cummings and Sergeant Croft and to the fierce heat of a killing jungle. And Heller, of course, points to the meaningless butchery of war in *Catch-22*, capsulizing in Yossarian's reflection that "every victim [is] a culprit, every culprit a victim" both the helplessness that is the essence of modern life and the bitterly ironic lot that is man's fate—he is at once martyr and persecutor.[29] Speaking for all the sufferers in our military fiction, Frederic Henry aptly expresses the victimization every one of them feels: "That was what you did," he notes. "You died. You did not know what it was about. You never had time to learn. They threw you in and told you the rules and the first time they caught you off base they killed you."[30]

American authors who treat modern man's struggles against the compelling forces of corporate life voice essentially the same, if somewhat more muted, sentiments. In *Point of No Return*, for example, John P. Marquand portrays the vapidness and soul-shriveling anxiety that afflict and dehumanize Charles Gray as he contends for the vice presidency of the Stuyvesant Bank. Sloan Wilson details the grinding pressures for conformity in his incisive depiction of Tom Rath's career, providing in *The Man in the Gray Flannel Suit* a metaphor and a label for a generation of postwar organization men. And, more recently, in *Something Happened*, Joseph Heller documents that in fact nothing occurs in the modern corporation but a gradual leaching away of the individuality and health of those caught up in it; Bob Slocum and his contemporaries· live in a state of constant fear and worry that destroys their relationships with their families and their co-workers and that leaves them enervated and irritable.

The image of man as victim is, of course, also prevalent in black and Jewish fiction. Richard Wright's explosive *Native Son*, for example, pictures in Bigger Thomas the pathological result of a society's vicious hatred and exploitation of its black people. And Ralph Ellison's *Invisible Man* dramatizes the history, plight, and pathos of the black man in an America which, while attempting to "Keep This Nigger-Boy Running," has denied him his identity and humanity. Saul Bellow and his contemporaries also treat modern man as tormented and persecuted in their writings. In *The Victim*, for instance, Bellow portrays the tortured consciousness of Asa Levanthal, who suffers from the feeling that he is both preyed upon by others and yet in some way culpable for their woes. J. D. Salinger details in *The Catcher in the Rye* how Holden Caulfield, unable to adjust to life at Pencey Prep and elsewhere, is broken on the wheel of adolescence. And Bernard Malamud in *The Assistant* depicts the anguish of a poor Jewish grocer, Morris Bober, in a world unfit for his gentle goodness.

Such a portrayal, however, is not limited to subgenres or to the novels of racial and cultural minorities but is pervasive in what used to be called the mainstream of American fiction. Sherwood Anderson's grotesques in *Winesburg, Ohio*, for example, are all victims of the truths they try to live by. The Hemingway hero in his various forms from Nick Adams to Santiago is destroyed, if not defeated, trapped by a world in which, as Philip Young notes, "things do not grow and bear fruit, but explode, break, decompose, or are eaten away."[31] And the members of the Compson family in Faulkner's *The Sound and the Fury*, especially Benjy, Caddy, Quentin, and Jason, are all bedeviled by their biological or private demons. In *Tender Is the Night*, Fitzgerald depicts the slow disintegration of Dick Diver, whose talent and identity cannot withstand the crushing force of his wife's money. Dos Passos portrays a host of characters in *U.S.A.* who are, in a broad sense, victims of life, and Steinbeck, first in *In Dubious Battle* and then more powerfully in *The Grapes of Wrath*, shows the frightening effect on human beings of an unjust economic system in collapse.

In the contemporary novel, Hassan notes that "the victim has a thousand faces," is, in fact, "the representative hero of our time" (Hassan, *Innocence*, p. 69); he appears in the works of such diverse authors as Jean Stafford, Flannery O'Connor, Henry Miller, James Baldwin, Gore Vidal, and Jack Kerouac. Weinberg adds support for such a view by pointing out in her study of the Kafkan mode in recent fiction that the absurdist novel "has at its center the victim of worldly circumstances."[32] And in his analysis of the past decade, Morris Dickstein discerns in the fiction of the sixties a pessimism "which sees individual life as manipulated and controlled from without," a "sense of impotence and fatality" that marks one side of the sensibility of those tumultuous years.[33]

Such a portrait, however, is not limited to imaginative literature. In

their works, social scientists and other cultural critics point out that
the view of the human condition American novelists hold is, in fact,
the reality of American life. These observers speak of modern man as
a victim of war, poverty, and crime. They see him helpless before the
crippling forces of environment, heredity, and society and exploited
by an ever-growing bureaucracy, an uncaring government, and a
rapacious business community. They note that his institutions have
failed him, that advertising continues to manipulate him, and that
consumer fraud is a constant threat. And they show him succumbing
with increasing frequency to alcoholism, drug addition, and mental
illness. Former New York City mental health commissioner, Dr. J.
Herbert Fill, for example, believes that the *majority* of Americans,
victims of a dehumanizing society, are, in fact, on the verge of emotional collapse: "We are surely witnessing the mental breakdown of a
nation," he proclaims, "the tragic result of centuries of mental conditioning to a man-estranged world view."[34]

Other social commentators speak variously of a pervasive alienation, rootlessness, atomization, loss of identity, depersonalization,
and sense of powerlessness in modern life, all grim reminders of our
unhappy plight. In his study of the societal forces that lead men to
become "other-directed" instead of "autonomous," David Riesman,
for example, notes that "the helplessness foreseen by a few thinkers,
and sensed even in the earlier age of frontiers by many who failed, has
become the common attribute of the mass of men."[35] William H.
Whyte, Jr., in his analysis of the organization man, perceives a similar
feeling among corporate managers. He observes: "Once people liked
to think, at least, that they were in control of their destinies, but few of
the younger organization people cherish such notions. Most see themselves as objects more acted upon than acting—and their future,
therefore, determined as much by the system as by themselves."[36]
And, in his discussion of living and working in the city, John Helmer
documents the common "experience of fatefulness in everyday urban
life" that leaves city people feeling helpless and fearful.[37]

The amount of attention this condition of victimization receives
from imaginative writers and sociologists suggests, of course, the
anxiety that modern man has about it. Fear of being a victim is, in fact,
strong in American life, as both writers and commentators agree. In
his study of American fiction written between 1950 and 1970, Tony

Tanner, for example, finds in recent literature "an abiding . . . dread that someone else is patterning your life, that there are all sorts of invisible plots afoot to rob you of your autonomy of thought and action, that conditioning is ubiquitous."[38] "The possible nightmare of being totally controlled by unseen agencies and powers," he adds, "is never far away in contemporary American fiction" (Tanner, *City of Words*, p. 16). And Morris Dickstein makes a similar point in his discussion of the past decade: "By the end of the sixties—in both fiction and reality—this confidence [that history could be comprehended and shaped] was displaced by a sense that history was out of control, or that the Others had their hands on the wheel and were preparing to do us in completely" (Dickstein, *Gates*, p. 127).

In a society, then, that fears it may be at the mercy of forces over which it has no control, forces whose seemingly inevitable end is the destruction or brutalizing of the individual, it is little wonder that various authors choose to portray Burr as victim. Sometimes they see him as unfortunately misunderstood by Washington or as secretly hounded and defamed by Hamilton; sometimes they show him as innocent but cruelly deceived and betrayed by the duplicitous Wilkinson; and sometimes they depict him as vengefully pursued by an angry Jefferson, who can never forget that the Colonel could have taken the presidency from him had the New Yorker wanted to. Whatever the case, they return repeatedly to the image of Burr as victim, linking him intuitively with one of our most gnawing anxieties.

The Aaron Burr emerging from our literature, then, is a complex figure whom American authors use for reasons not necessarily apparent at first glance. Again and again when they choose to treat the Colonel in their works, they turn to the images of traitor, predator, and victim, suggesting thereby that he is connected with American culture in a more meaningful way than the popular conception of him as the detestable murderer of Hamilton or as the rival in infamy of Benedict Arnold might indicate. By their repeated use of him in their plays, novels, and stories and by their selection of appropriate analogues for him, they give Burr new stature as an American symbol. Thus, in his various roles as an American Catiline, Lovelace, and Warwick, he comes to represent aspects of American life that are intensely distressing, touches, that is, upon our most terrifying nightmares of societal chaos, of phallic plundering of our women, and of helpless victimization. And because these anxieties—sometimes buried, sometimes so insistent that they lead to overreaction—haunt our national imagination, our writers seek to give them artistic expression and thus to exorcise them. In their search for suitable vehicles to do so, they turn frequently to the gigantic figure of Aaron Burr, who, as Vidal's recent best seller demonstrates, remains still dazzling, still mysterious, wedded apparently forever to our deepest fears.

Notes

1. Louis Hartz, *The Liberal Tradition in America: An Interpretation of American Political Thought since the Revolution* (New York: Harcourt, Brace and Company, 1955), p. 63.

2. In the sketch of Catiline's life, I follow primarily Arthur Kaplan's *Catiline: The Man and His Role in the Roman Revolution* (New York: Exposition Press, 1968). Though Kaplan is more sympathetic to Catiline than many, he is one of the very few to give a complete biography of the great Roman revolutionary; authors generally concentrate on the conspiracy itself. In addition, his chronology is accurate and his presentation of the story clear. For a discriminating treatment of the conspiracy proper, see E. G. Hardy, *The Catilinarian Conspiracy in Its Context: A Re-study of the Evidence* (Oxford: Basil Blackwell, 1924), still the standard discussion in English.

3. An accessible text is Samuel Richardson, *Clarissa, or, The History of a Young Lady*, Everyman ed., 4 vols. (1932; rpt. London: J. M. Dent & Sons, 1962). Hereafter cited as *Clarissa*.

4. Leslie A. Fiedler, *Love and Death in the American Novel*, rev. ed. (New York: Stein and Day, 1966), p. 65. Hereafter referred to as *Love and Death*.

5. Matthew L. Davis, *Memoirs of Aaron Burr*, vol. 1 (New York: Harper & Brothers, 1836–37), p. 92.

6. It is possible, of course, that the reason most American writers did not associate Burr with some figure in either history or literature is that they preferred not to do so. These same authors, however, had no hesitancy in linking the Colonel with Catiline or with Lovelace, and it therefore seems logical that they would have provided an analogue for Burr as victim if they had thought of one.

7. In the sketch of Warwick's life, I follow Paul Murray Kendall's *Warwick the Kingmaker* (New York: W. W. Norton & Company, 1957), the

standard biography, which supersedes Charles W. Oman's *Warwick: The Kingmaker* (London: Macmillan and Co., 1891). Kendall's book is hereafter cited as *Warwick*.

8. See Simon O. Lesser, *Fiction and the Unconscious* (Boston: Beacon Press, 1957), for an insightful discussion of how literature expresses unconscious fears.

9. Owen Lovejoy, ["Speech on the State of the Union"], in U.S. Congress, *Congressional Globe*, 36th Cong., 2d sess., 1861, appendix, p. 87.

10. Daniel Webster, *The Writings and Speeches of Daniel Webster*, national ed., 18 vols (Boston: Little, Brown, & Company, 1903), 6: 75. Hereafter referred to as *Writings and Speeches*.

11. Amos Kendall, *Autobiography of Amos Kendall*, ed. William Stickney (1872; rpt. New York: Peter Smith, 1949), p. 430.

12. Andrew Jackson, "Proclamation," in *A Compilation of the Messages and Papers of the Presidents, 1789–1897*, ed. James D. Richardson, vol. 2 (Washington, D.C.: Government Printing Office, 1896), p. 656. Hereafter referred to as *Messages*.

13. Henry Wadsworth Longfellow, "The Building of the Ship," in *Complete Poetical and Prose Works*, ed. Horace E. Scudder, vol. 1 (Boston: Houghton Mifflin, 1893), p. 257.

14. Paul C. Nagel, *One Nation Indivisible: The Union in American Thought 1776–1861* (New York: Oxford University Press, 1964), p. 281. Hereafter referred to as *Nation*.

15. "The Permanency of the American Union," *Niles' Weekly Register* 12 (7 June 1817): 230.

16. Edward Livingston, ["Speech on Foot's Resolution"], in *Register of Debates in Congress*, 6, pt. 1 (Washington, D.C.: Gales & Seaton, 1830), p. 271.

17. Henry Clay, ["Henry Clay to Jacob Gibson, 25 July 1842"], in *The Private Correspondence of Henry Clay*, ed. Calvin Colton (Boston: Frederick Parker, 1856), p. 466.

18. Henry Clay, "Speech of Mr. Clay," in U.S. Congress, *Congressional Globe*, 31st Cong., 1st sess., 1850, appendix, p. 127.

19. Fears of instability and disloyalty in the nineteenth century and consequently of the conspirator-traitor did not end at Appomattox. See David Brion Davis, ed., *The Fear of Conspiracy* (Ithaca, N.Y.: Cornell University Press, 1971), especially pp. 149–204; Ralph Henry Gabriel, *The Course of American Democratic Thought*, 2nd ed. (New York: Ronald Press, 1956), pp. 138–48; and Merle Curti, *The Roots of American Loyalty* (1946; rpt. New York: Russell & Russell, 1967), pp. 173–99.

20. Ernest Earnest, *The American Eve in Fact and Fiction, 1775–1914* (Urbana: University of Illinois Press, 1974), p. 62.

21. Judith Fryer, *The Faces of Eve: Women in the Nineteenth Century American Novel* (New York: Oxford University Press, 1976), p. 24.

22. Rollin G. Osterweis, *Romanticism and Nationalism in the Old South* (New Haven: Yale University Press, 1949), p. 88.

23. W. J. Cash, *The Mind of the South* (New York: Alfred A. Knopf, 1940), p. 86.

24. Gerda Lerner, "The Lady and the Mill Girl: Changes in the Status of Women in the Age of Jackson," in *Our American Sisters: Women in American Life and Thought*, ed. Jean E. Friedman and William G. Shade, 2nd ed. (Boston: Allyn and Bacon, 1976), p. 127.

25. Ronald W. Hogeland, " 'The Female Appendage': Feminine Life-Styles in America, 1820–1860," in *Our American Sisters: Women in American Life and Thought*, ed. Jean E. Friedman and William G. Shade, pp. 134–36.

26. Modern writers see Burr as conspirator-traitor for essentially the same reason that their nineteenth-century counterparts did; fear of disloyalty is still strong in our time. See David Brion Davis, ed., *The Fear of Conspiracy*, especially pp. 205–360, and the titular essay in Richard Hofstadter's *The Paranoid Style in American Politics and Other Essays* (New York: Alfred A. Knopf, 1966), pp. 3–40. There are, however, two reasons why twentieth-century authors depict Burr as sexual predator. The first involves the same anxieties felt by earlier Americans: because the despoiler is still a man to be feared in our time, it seems likely that writers persist in using Burr as a vehicle to express that apprehension. No doubt, too, as the sexual sophistication of the country increased over the years, authors also chose to portray the Colonel as libertine in order to titillate their readers.

27. Ihab Hassan, *Radical Innocence: Studies in the Contemporary American Novel* (Princeton: Princeton University Press, 1961), p. 9. Hereafter referred to as *Innocence*.

28. The case could be made just as convincingly with modern American drama or poetry.

29. Joseph Heller, *Catch-22* (New York: Simon and Schuster, 1961), p. 396.

30. Ernest Hemingway, *A Farewell to Arms* (New York: Charles Scribner's Sons, 1929), p. 350.

31. Philip Young, *Ernest Hemingway* (Minneapolis: University of Minnesota Press, 1959), p. 40.

32. Helen Weinberg, *The New Novel in America: The Kafkan Mode in Contemporary Fiction* (Ithaca, N.Y.: Cornell University Press, 1970), pp. x–xi.

33. Morris Dickstein, *Gates of Eden: American Culture in the Sixties* (New York: Basic Books, 1977), p. 99. Hereafter cited as *Gates*.

34. J. Herbert Fill, *The Mental Breakdown of a Nation* (New York: New Viewpoints, 1974), p. 4.

35. David Riesman, "The Saving Remnant: An Examination of Character Structure," in *Individualism Reconsidered and Other Essays* (Glencoe, Ill.: Free Press, 1954), p. 103.

36. William H. Whyte, Jr., *The Organization Man* (New York: Simon and Schuster, 1956), p. 395.

37. John Helmer, "Introduction," in *Urbanman: The Psychology of Urban Survival*, ed. John Helmer and Neil A. Eddington (New York: Free Press, 1973), p. viii.

38. Tony Tanner, *City of Words: American Fiction 1950–1970* (New York: Harper & Row, 1971), p. 15.

Selected Bibliography

Drama

Aaron Burr. 1840. [Lost].

Bible, Howard Wiswall. *Aaron Burr: An Historical Drama in Four Acts*. Unpublished drama. Copyright: Howard Wiswall Bible, 11 October 1926, D77129. Held at U.S. Copyright Office.

Brackenridge, Hugh Henry. *The Death of General Montgomery at the Siege of Quebec* Philadelphia: Robert Bell, 1777.

Carpenter, Sarah. *Aaron Burr's Dupe*. Unpublished drama. Copyright: Sarah Carpenter, 7 August 1901, D728. [Lost].

The Conspiracy; or, The Western Island: A Drama in Five Acts. New York: Henry Spear, 1838.

Del Monte, Leon. *The Tragical History of Aaron Burr*. Cincinnati: Robert Clarke & Co., 1889.

Dowd, Jerome. *Burr and Hamilton: A New York Tragedy*. New York: Geo. W. Wheat, 1884.

Goldstein, Robert. *Aaron Burr: A Play in Four Acts*. Unpublished drama. Copyright: Robert Goldstein, 15 November 1927, D82123. Held at U.S. Copyright Office.

Hallett, Charles A. *Aaron Burr*. Unpublished drama. Copyright: Charles A. Hallett, 1964, 25 April 1969, DU74165. Held at U.S. Copyright Office.

Holloway, Charlotte Molyneux. *Aaron Burr*. Unpublished drama. Copyright: Charlotte Molyneux Holloway, 10 February 1900, 3793. [Lost].

Hooker, Helen. *Aaron Burr: A Revolutionary Drama in One Act*. Unpublished drama. Copyright: Helen Hooker, 27 June 1898, 39113. [Lost].

Leach, Anna. *Aaron Burr: A Drama*. Unpublished drama. Copyright: Anna Leach, 6 June 1900, 14067. [Lost].

Leffer, Louis. *Aaron Burr: A Drama in Four Acts*. Unpublished drama. Copyright: Louis Leffer, 21 October 1937, D52655. Held at U.S. Copyright Office.

Leiffer, Louis. *Aaron Burr*. Unpublished drama. Copyright: Louis Leiffer, 7 January 1939, DU61282. Held at U.S. Copyright Office.

McCrary, Ben. *Aaron and Theodosia or The Fate of the Burrs: A Drama in Five Acts*. Unpublished drama. Copyright: Ben McCrary, 29 March 1902, D1664. Held at U.S. Copyright Office.

Masters, Edgar Lee. "Aaron Burr and Madam Jumel." In *Dramatic Duologues: Four Short Plays in Verse*, pp. 37–75. New York: Samuel French, 1934.

Minturn, William [Defenthy Wright]. *Aaron Burr: A Drama in Four Acts*. New York: Metropolitan Job Print, 1878.

Mishkin, Leo, and William Boehnel. *Aaron Burr: A Play in Two Acts*. Unpublished drama. Copyright: Leo Mishkin, 3 March 1941, DU73862. Held at U.S. Copyright Office.

Nirdlinger, Charles Frederic. *The First Lady of the Land: A Play in Four Acts*. Boston: Walter H. Baker and Co., 1914.

O'Brien, William L. *Aaron Burr: A Play in Four Acts*. Minneapolis: Review, 1908.

O'Shaughnessy, Louis. *Aaron Burr; or, A Dream of Empire*. Unpublished drama. Copyright: Louis O'Shaughnessy, 6 June 1881, 8858. [Lost].

Pavlo, Hattie May. *Hamilton: A Drama in Three Acts*. Unpublished drama. Copyright: Hattie May Pavlo, 4 May 1948, DU14332. Held at U.S. Copyright Office.

Pidgin, Charles Felton. *Blennerhassett; or, The Decrees of Fate*. Boston: C. M. Clark, 1901.

Pierce, L. France. *Aaron Burr: A Romantic Drama in Four Acts*. Unpublished drama. Copyright: L. France Pierce, 9 April 1901, D328. Held at U.S. Copyright Office.

Raiden, Edward. *Mr. Jefferson's Burr: A Play in Three Acts*. Los Angeles: Thunder, 1960.

Smith, Chard Powers. *Hamilton: A Poetic Drama*. New York: Coward-McCann, 1930.

Smith, William Russell. *Aaron Burr, or, The Emperor of Mexico*. Excerpted in *The Bachelor's Button*, pp. 65–88. Mobile, 1837.

Stoaks, Charles E. *Aaron Burr; or, The Kingdom of Silver.* Doylestown, Ohio: George A. Corbus, 1887.

Sweeney, Thomas B. *Aaron Burr's Dream for the Southwest: A Drama for the Library.* San Antonio, Texas: The Naylor Company, 1955.

Tarkington, Booth. *The Aromatic Aaron Burr.* Unpublished drama. 1931. Held in the Manuscript Division, Princeton University Libraries.

Thornton, Marcellus Eugene. *Aaron Burr: A Tragedy in Five Acts.* Unpublished drama. Copyright: Marcellus Eugene Thornton, 15 August 1901, D763. [Lost].

Van der Voort, Carl. *The Child of Nevis (Alexander Hamilton): A Play in the Old Manner.* Unpublished drama. Copyright: Carl Van der Voort, 1934, D29697. Held at the Library of Congress.

Wishaar, Marie Ida. *Aaron Burr: A Tale of the Revolution.* Unpublished drama. Copyright: Marie Ida Wishaar, 19 October 1905, D7520. [Lost].

Fiction

Allis, Marguerite. *To Keep Us Free.* New York: G. P. Putnam's Sons, 1953.

The Amorous Intrigues and Adventures of Aaron Burr. New York: Published for the Proprietors, [184–].

Bateson, Carlen. *The Man in the Camlet Cloak: Being an Old Writing Transcribed and Edited.* Akron, Ohio: Saalfield, 1903.

Bennet, Robert Ames. *A Volunteer with Pike: The True Narrative of One Dr. John Robinson and of His Love for the Fair Señorita Vallois.* Chicago: A. C. McClurg & Co., 1909.

Bennett, Emerson. *The Traitor; or, The Fate of Ambition.* Cincinnati: U. P. James, 1860.

Bragin, Jacob George. *The Life of Aaron Burr: An Original Romantic Story Based on the Life of Aaron Burr.* [n.p. New York], 1938.

Burdett, Charles. *The Beautiful Spy: An Exciting Story of Army and High Life in New York in 1776.* Philadelphia: John E. Potter and Company, 1865.

Bynner, Edwin Lassetter. *Zachary Phips.* Boston: Houghton, Miflin and Company, 1892.

Clemens, Jeremiah. *The Rivals: A Tale of the Times of Aaron Burr and Alexander Hamilton.* Philadelphia: J. B. Lippincott & Co., 1860.

Colver, Anne. *Theodosia: Daughter of Aaron Burr.* New York: Farrar & Rinehart, 1941.

The Conspiracy of Col. Aaron Burr: A Historical Romance. New York: G. W. Simmons, 1854.

Cooke, Grace MacGowan, and McKinney, Annie Booth. *Mistress Joy: A Tale of Natchez in 1798.* New York: Century, 1901.

Davies, Acton, and Nirdlinger, Charles. *The First Lady of the Land or When Dolly Todd Took Boarders.* New York: H. K. Fly, 1912.

Dillon, Mary. *Miss Livingston's Companion: A Love Story of Old New York.* New York: Century, 1911.

Dupuy, A. E. [Eliza Ann Dupuy]. *The Conspirator.* New York: D. Appleton & Company, 1850.

Fawcett, Edgar. *A Romance of Old New York.* Philadelphia: J. B. Lippincott, 1897.

Hale, Edward Everett. "The Man without a Country." In *The Man without a Country and Other Stories*, pp. 21–60. Boston: Little, Brown, and Company, 1918.

Harris, Cyril. *Street of Knives.* Boston: Little, Brown and Company, 1950.

Havighurst, Marion Boyd. *Strange Island.* New York: World, 1957.

Hough, Emerson. *The Magnificent Adventure: This Being the Story of the World's Greatest Exploration, and the Romance of a Very Gallant Gentleman.* New York: D. Appleton and Company, 1916.

Hubbard, Lindley Murray. *An Express of '76: A Chronicle of the Town of York in the War for Independence.* Boston: Little, Brown and Company, 1906.

Hughes, Rupert. *The Golden Ladder.* New York: A. L. Burt, 1924.

Ingraham, Joseph Holt. *Burton; or, The Sieges: A Romance.* 2 vols. New York: Harper & Brothers, 1838.

Jillson, Willard Rouse. *The Lost Letter of Aaron Burr, 1805: A Tale of Early Lexington.* Frankfort, Ky.: Roberts Printing, 1946.

Johnston, Mary. *Lewis Rand.* Boston: Houghton Mifflin Company, 1908.

Lewis, Addison. *The Gadfly: A Portrait in Action.* Saint Paul: Webb, 1948.

McMeekin, Clark [Isabel McLennan McMeekin and Dorothy Park Clark]. *Reckon with the River.* New York: D. Appleton-Century, 1941.

Peppers, Nellie Whan. *The Young Mrs. Blennerhassett: A Novel of Early Days in West Virginia.* New York: Exposition Press, 1964.

Pidgin, Charles Felton. *Blennerhassett; or, The Decrees of Fate: A Romance Founded upon Events of American History.* Boston: C. M. Clark, 1901.

————. *The Climax; or, What Might Have Been: A Romance of the Great Republic.* Boston: C. M. Clark, 1902.

————. *Little Burr: The Warwick of America.* Boston: Robinson Luce, 1905.

Polk, William T. "Golden Eagle Ordinary." In *The Fallen Angel and Other Stories*, pp. 41–51. Chapel Hill: University of North Carolina Press, 1956.

Roberts, Kenneth. *Arundel*. 1930. Reprint. Greenwich, Conn.: Fawcett, 1976.

Sansay, Leonora. *Secret History; or, The Horrors of St. Domingo, in a Series of Letters, Written by a Lady at Cape Francois, to Colonel Burr, Late Vice-President of the United States, Principally during the Command of General Rochambeau*. Philadelphia: Bradford & Inskeep, 1808.

Savage, Charles Woodcock. *A Lady in Waiting: Being Extracts from the Diary of Julie de Chesnil, Sometime Lady in Waiting to Her Majesty Queen Marie Antoinette*. New York: D. Appleton and Company, 1906.

Seton, Anya. *My Theodosia*. Boston: Houghton Mifflin, 1941.

Stanley, Edward. *The Rock Cried Out*. New York: Duell, Sloan and Pearce, 1949.

Stanton, Elizabeth Brandon. *"Fata Morgana": A Vision of Empire—The Burr Conspiracy in Mississippi Territory and the Great Southwest—Natchez Love Story of Ex-Vice President Aaron Burr*. Crowley, La.: Signal, 1947.

Sterne, Emma Gelders. *Drums of Monmouth*. New York: Dodd, Mead & Company, 1935.

Stowe, Harriet Beecher. *The Minister's Wooing*. Boston: Houghton, Mifflin and Company, 1887.

Taylor, James W. *The Victim of Intrigue: A Tale of Burr's Conspiracy*. Cincinnati: Robinson & Jones, 1847.

Thurber, James. "A Friend to Alexander." In *My World—And Welcome to It*, pp. 139–53. New York: Harcourt, Brace and Company, 1942.

Townsend, George Alfred. *Mrs. Reynolds and Hamilton*. New York: E. G. Bonaventure, 1890.

Tupper, Edith Sessions. *Hearts Triumphant*. New York: D. Appleton and Company, 1906.

Tyson, J. Aubrey. *The Stirrup Cup*. New York: D. Appleton and Company, 1903.

Venable, William Henry. *A Dream of Empire or The House of Blennerhassett*. New York: Dodd, Mead and Company, 1901.

Vidal, Gore. *Burr: A Novel*. New York: Random House, 1973.

Walsh, George Ethelbert. *Allin Winfield: A Romance*. New York: F. M. Buckles & Company, 1902.

Welty, Eudora. "First Love." In *The Wide Net and Other Stories*, pp. 3–33. New York: Harcourt, Brace and Company, 1943.

Other Works

"Aaron Burr!" *American Citizen*, 28 April 1804.

Abernethy, Thomas Perkins. *The Burr Conspiracy*. New York: Oxford University Press, 1954.

Adams, Charles Francis, ed. *Memoirs of John Quincy Adams*. 12 vols. Philadelphia: J. B. Lippincott & Co., 1874–77.

Adams, Henry. *History of the United States of America*. 9 vols. New York: Charles Scribner's Sons, 1889–91.

Aristides [William Peter Van Ness]. *An Examination of the Various Charges Exhibited Against Aaron Burr, Esq. Vice-President of the United States; and a Development of the Characters and Views of His Political Opponents*. New York: Ward and Gould, 1803.

Atherton, Gertrude. *The Conqueror: A Dramatized Biography of Alexander Hamilton*. 1902. Reprint. New York: Frederick A. Stokes, 1930.

Beirne, Francis F. *Shout Treason: The Trial of Aaron Burr*. New York: Hastings House, 1959.

Benedict, Frank Lee. "Aaron Burr." In *The Rivals: A Tale of the Times of Aaron Burr and Alexander Hamilton*, by Jeremiah Clemens, p. xi. Philadelphia: J. B. Lippincott & Co., 1860.

Beveridge, Albert J. *The Life of John Marshall*. 4 vols. Boston: Houghton Mifflin, 1916–19.

Biddle, Charles. *Autobiography of Charles Biddle*. Philadelphia: E. Claxton and Company, 1883.

Bronson, Enos. ["Burr Victimized"]. *United States' Gazette*, 19 August 1807.

Bruce, William Cabell. *John Randolph of Roanoke, 1773–1833*. 2nd ed., rev. 2 vols. in 1. New York: G. P. Putnam's Sons, 1922.

Bryant, William Cullen. "Funeral of Aaron Burr." *New York Evening Post*, 19 September 1836.

Bullough, Vern L. *The Subordinate Sex: A History of Attitudes toward Women*. Urbana: University of Illinois Press, 1973.

Burdett, Charles. "Reminiscences." Newspaper Clipping. New York Public Library. Reprinted in part in Samuel H. Wandell, *Aaron Burr in Literature*, pp. 44–47. 1936. Reprint. Port Washington, N.Y.: Kennikat Press, 1972.

Burr, Aaron. *The Private Journal of Aaron Burr*. Ed. William K. Bixby. 2 vols. Rochester: The Genesee Press, 1903.

————. Aaron Burr to Thomas Jefferson, 23 December 1800. Jefferson Papers. Library of Congress.

————. Aaron Burr to Thomas Jefferson, 12 February 1801. Jefferson Papers. Library of Congress.

————. ["Burr's Farewell Address to the Senate"]. *Washington Federalist*,

13 March 1805. Cited in Matthew L. Davis, *Memoirs of Aaron Burr*, 2: 362. 2 vols. New York: Harper & Brothers, 1836–37.

Burr, Samuel Engle, Jr. *Colonel Aaron Burr: The American Phoenix*. New York: Exposition Press, 1964.

———. *The Influence of His Wife and His Daughter on the Life and Career of Col. Aaron Burr: An Address*. Linden, Va.: Burr, 1975.

———. *Napoleon's Dossier on Aaron Burr*. San Antonio, Texas: Naylor, 1969.

Burr, Theodosia. Letter to Tapping Reeve and Sarah Burr Reeve, n.d. Park Family Papers. Yale University Library.

["Burr's Death"]. *New York Star*, 14 September 1836. Reprinted in the *Richmond Enquirer*, 20 September 1836.

Cady, Edwin Harrison. *The Gentleman in America: A Literary Study in American Culture*. Syracuse: Syracuse University Press, 1949.

Campaign poster. Burr-Lewis, 1804. New York Public Library.

Campbell, Angus; Converse, Philip E.; and Rodgers, Willard L. *The Quality of American Life: Perceptions, Evaluations, and Satisfactions*. New York: Russell Sage Foundation, 1976.

Carrington, Frank G. *The Victims*. New Rochelle, N.Y.: Arlington House, 1975.

Cash, W. J. *The Mind of the South*. New York: Alfred A. Knopf, 1940.

Chandler, Joseph R. "Aaron Burr." *United States' Gazette*, 16 September 1836.

Cheetham, James. "Burr and Wilkinson." *American Citizen*, 25 September 1807.

———. ["Conduct of Aaron Burr"]. *American Citizen*, 26 March 1804.

———. "The Creed." *American Citizen*, 30 March 1804.

———. "General Hamilton's Death." *American Citizen*, 21 July 1804.

———. *"General Hamilton's Death." American Citizen*, 27 July 1804.

———. "A Good Joke." *American Citizen*, 20 March 1804.

———. ["Man without Principle"]. *American Citizen*, 3 April 1804.

———. "Mr. Burr's Trial." *American Citizen*, 20 June 1807.

———. *Narrative of the Suppression by Col. Burr, of the History of the Administration of John Adams, Late President of the United States*. 2nd ed., rev. and corrected. New York: Denniston and Cheetham, 1802.

———. *Nine Letters on the Subject of Aaron Burr's Political Defection, with an Appendix*. New York: Denniston & Cheetham, 1803.

———. *"Same subject continued* [General Hamilton's Death]." *American Citizen*, 30 July 1804.

———. *A View of the Political Conduct of Aaron Burr, Esq., Vice-President of the United States*. New York: Denniston & Cheetham, 1802.

Clay, Henry. [Henry Clay to Jacob Gibson, 25 July 1842], pp. 463–66. In
    The Private Correspondence of Henry Clay. Ed. Calvin Colton.
    Boston: Frederick Parker, 1856.
———. "Speech of Mr. Clay." *Congressional Globe*. 31st Cong., 1st sess.,
    1850, appendix, pp. 115–27.
Coffin, Alexander, Jr. *The Death of General Montgomery, or, The Storming
    of Quebec: A Poem*. New York: Printed for the Author, 1814.
Coleman, William. ["Burr's Conspiracy to Kill Hamilton"]. *New York
    Evening Post*, 3 August 1804.
Colton, Calvin, ed. *The Private Correspondence of Henry Clay*. Boston:
    Frederick Parker, 1856.
"Communication." *American Citizen*, 29 March 1804.
"Communication ['Hamilton's Death']." *American Citizen*, 14 July 1804.
Coombs, J. J., comp. *The Trial of Aaron Burr for High Treason*. Washing-
    ton, D.C.: W. H. & O. H. Morrison, 1864.
"Correspondence." *American Citizen*, 24 March 1804.
C[ox], I[saac] J[oslin]. "Burr, Aaron." *Dictionary of American Biography*.
    Edited by Dumas Malone. New York: Charles Scribner's Sons,
    1928–37.
Crawford, Charles. *A Poem on the Death of Montgomery*. Philadelphia:
    Robert Aitken, 1783.
Curti, Merle. *The Roots of American Loyalty*. 1946. Reprint. New York:
    Russell & Russell, 1967.
Daniels, Jonathan. *Ordeal of Ambition: Jefferson, Hamilton, Burr*. New
    York: Doubleday & Company, 1970.
Davis, David Brion, ed. *The Fear of Conspiracy: Images of Un-American
    Subversion from the Revolution to the Present*. Ithaca, N.Y.: Cornell
    University Press, 1971.
———. "Introduction," pp. xiii–xxiv. In *The Fear of Conspiracy: Images of
    Un-American Subversion from the Revolution to the Present*. Ed.
    David Brion Davis. Ithaca, N.Y.: Cornell University Press, 1971.
Davis, Matthew L. *Memoirs of Aaron Burr*. 2 vols. New York: Harper &
    Brothers, 1836–37.
["The Death of Hamilton"]. *American Citizen*, 18 July 1804.
Dickstein, Morris. *Gates of Eden: American Culture in the Sixties*. New
    York: Basic Books, 1977.
Duane, William. ["The Persecution of Burr"]. *Aurora General Advertiser*,
    12 June 1807.
———. ["Proceedings of Burr's Case"]. *Aurora General Advertiser*, 23 June
    1807.
Duer, William A. *Reminiscences of an Old Yorker*. New York: W. L.
    Andrews, 1867.

Dunlap, William. *A History of the American Theatre.* New York: J. & J. Harper, 1832.

Earnest, Ernest. *The American Eve in Fact and Fiction, 1775–1914.* Urbana: University of Illinois Press, 1974.

Epaminondas [Augustus Brevoort Woodward]. *To the Federal Members of the House of Representatives of the United States.* New York: Hopkins for Lang, 1801.

Farrell, John H. "A Plea," p. 21. In *The Aaron Burr Memorial.* Ed. Grand Camp of the Aaron Burr Legion. Boston: Mount Vernon Book & Music, 1903.

Fiedler, Leslie A. *Love and Death in the American Novel.* Rev. ed. New York: Stein and Day, 1966.

Fill, J. Herbert. *The Mental Breakdown of a Nation.* New York: New Viewpoints, 1974.

Fisher, Josephine. "The Journal of Esther Burr." *New England Quarterly* 3 (1930): 297–315.

"A Fragment." *American Citizen,* 20 March 1804.

Friedman, Jean E., and Shade, William G., eds. *Our American Sisters*: *Women in American Life and Thought.* 2nd ed. Boston: Allyn and Bacon, 1976.

Fryer, Judith. *The Faces of Eve: Women in the Nineteenth Century American Novel.* New York: Oxford University Press, 1976.

"Funeral of Col. Burr." *New York Courier and Enquirer.* Reprinted in the *United States' Gazette,* 20 September 1836.

Gabriel, Ralph Henry. *The Course of American Democratic Thought.* 2nd ed. New York: Ronald Press, 1956.

Hamilton, John C., ed. *The Works of Alexander Hamilton.* 7 vols. New York: J. F. Trow, 1850–51.

"Hand-bill." *American Citizen,* 12 March 1804.

Hardy, E. G. *The Catilinarian Conspiracy in Its Context: A Re-Study of the Evidence.* Oxford: Basil Blackwell, 1924.

Hartz, Louis. *The Liberal Tradition in America: An Interpretation of American Political Thought since the Revolution.* New York: Harcourt, Brace and Company, 1955.

Hassan, Ihab. *Radical Innocence: Studies in the Contemporary American Novel.* Princeton: Princeton University Press, 1961.

Heller, Joseph. *Catch-22.* New York: Simon and Schuster, 1961.

Helmer, John. "Introduction," pp. vii–xii. In *Urbanman: The Psychology of Urban Survival.* Eds. John Helmer and Neil A. Eddington. New York: Free Press, 1973.

Hemingway, Ernest. *A Farewell to Arms.* New York: Charles Scribner's Sons, 1929.

Hofstadter, Richard. "The Paranoid Style in American Politics," pp. 3–40. In *The Paranoid Style in American Politics and Other Essays*. New York: Alfred A. Knopf, 1966.

Hogeland, Ronald W. " 'The Female Appendage': Feminine Life-Styles in America, 1820–1860," pp. 133–48. In *Our American Sisters: Women in American Life and Thought*. Eds. Jean E. Friedman and William G. Shade. 2nd ed. Boston: Allyn and Bacon, 1976.

Hopkins, Joseph R. *Hamiltoniad: or, The Effects of Discord*. Philadelphia: D. Hogan, 1804.

Hopkins, Lemuel. *The Democratiad: A Poem in Retaliation for the* Philadelphia Jockey Club. Philadelphia: Thomas Bradford, 1795.

Irving, Peter. ["Burr Justified"]. *Morning Chronicle*, 16 July 1804. Reprinted in the *New York Evening Post*, 17 July 1804.

Irving, Pierre M., ed. *The Life and Letters of Washington Irving*. 4 vols. London: Richard Bentley, 1862–64.

Jackson, Andrew. "Proclamation," 1: 640–56. In *A Compilation of the Messages and Papers of the Presidents, 1789–1897*. Ed. James D. Richardson. 10 vols. Washington, D.C.: Government Printing Office, 1896–99.

The Jeffersoniad: or, An Echo to the Groans of an Expiring Faction. Fredericktown, Md.: Bartgis, 1801.

Jung, Carl G. "Approaching the Unconscious." In *Man and His Symbols*. Eds. Carl G. Jung and M–L von Franz. London: Aldus Books, 1964.

Kaplan, Arthur. *Catiline: The Man and His Role in the Roman Revolution*. New York: Exposition Press, 1968.

Kazin, Alfred. *On Native Grounds: An Interpretation of Modern American Prose Literature*. New York: Harcourt, Brace & World, 1942.

Kendall, Amos. *Autobiography of Amos Kendall*. Ed. William Stickney. 1872. Reprint. New York: Peter Smith, 1949.

Kendall, Paul Murray. *Warwick the Kingmaker*. New York: W. W. Norton & Company, 1957.

Kent, William. *Memoirs and Letters of James Kent, LL.D*. Boston: Little, Brown, and Company, 1898.

Law, Marion Laird. "Colonel Aaron Burr," p. 1. In *The Aaron Burr Memorial*. Ed. Grand Camp of the Aaron Burr Legion. Boston: Mount Vernon Book & Music, 1903.

Lerner, Gerda. "The Lady and the Mill Girl: Changes in the Status of Women in the Age of Jackson," pp. 120–32. In *Our American Sisters: Women in American Life and Thought*. Eds. Jean E. Friedman and William G. Shade. 2nd ed. Boston: Allyn and Bacon, 1976.

Lesser, Simon O. *Fiction and the Unconscious*. Boston: Beacon Press, 1957.

Lewis, Alfred Henry. *Richard Croker.* New York: Life, 1901.

Lindsay, Merrill. "Pistols Shed Light on Famed Duel." *Smithsonian* 7, no. 8 (1976): 94–98.

Livingston, Edward. ["Speech on Foot's Resolution"], vol. 6, pt. 1, pp. 247–72. *Register of Debates in Congress.* 29 pts. in 14 vols. Washington, D.C.: Gales & Seaton, 1825–37.

Lodge, Henry Cabot, ed. *The Works of Alexander Hamilton.* 12 vols. New York: G. P. Putnam's Sons, 1904.

Lomask, Milton. *Aaron Burr: The Years from Princeton to Vice President, 1756–1805.* New York: Farrar, Straus & Giroux, 1979.

Longfellow, Henry Wadsworth. "The Building of the Ship," 1. 245–57. In *Complete Poetical and Prose Works.* Ed. Horace E. Scudder. 6 vols. Boston: Houghton Mifflin, 1889–93.

Lovejoy, Owen. ["Speech on the State of the Union"]. *Congressional Globe.* 36th Cong., 2nd sess., 1861, appendix, pp. 84–87.

McCaleb, Walter Flavius. *The Aaron Burr Conspiracy.* Expanded ed. 1936. Reprint. New York: Argosy-Antiquarian, 1966.

_____. *A New Light on Aaron Burr.* 1963. Reprint. New York: Argosy-Antiquarian, 1966.

Martin, Luther. "Correspondence." In *Baltimore Federal Gazette,* 23 July 1807. Reprinted in the *United States' Gazette,* 31 July 1807.

Mason, J[ohn] M[itchell]. *An Oration, Commemorative of the Late Major-General Alexander Hamilton; Pronounced before the New-York State Society of the Cincinnati, on Tuesday, the 31st July, 1804.* New York: Hopkins and Seymour, 1804.

Mitchell, Broadus. *Alexander Hamilton: The National Adventure 1788–1804.* New York: Macmillan, 1962.

Morison, Samuel Eliot. *The Oxford History of the American People.* New York: Oxford University Press, 1965.

Morris, Gouverneur. *The Diary and Letters of Gouverneur Morris.* Ed. Anne Cary Morris. 2 vols. New York: Charles Scribner's Sons, 1888.

Nagel, Paul C. *One Nation Indivisible: The Union in American Thought 1776–1861.* New York: Oxford University Press, 1964.

The National Union Catalogue: Pre-1956 Imprints. London: Mansell Information/Publishing, 1968–.

Nott, Eliphalet. *A Discourse Delivered in the North Dutch Church, in the City of Albany, Occasioned by the Ever to be Lamented Death of General Alexander Hamilton, July 29, 1804.* Albany: Charles R. and George Webster, 1804.

Odell, George C. D. *Annals of the New York Stage.* 15 vols. New York: Columbia University Press, 1949.

Oman, Charles W. *Warwick: The Kingmaker*. London: Macmillan and Co., 1891.

"On the Death of General Hamilton." *American Citizen*, 4 August 1804.

"On the Murder of Hamilton: A Scotch Ballad." *The Western Telegraph*. Reprinted in Samuel H. Wandell, *Aaron Burr in Literature*. 1936. Reprint. Port Washington, N.Y.: Kennikat Press, 1972.

Osterweis, Rollin G. *Romanticism and Nationalism in the Old South*. New Haven: Yale University Press, 1949.

Parmet, Herbert S., and Hecht, Marie B. *Aaron Burr: Portrait of an Ambitious Man*. New York: Macmillan, 1967.

Parton, James. *The Life and Times of Aaron Burr*. Enlarged ed. 2 vols. Boston: Ticknor and Fields, 1867.

"The Permanency of the American Union." *Niles' Weekly Register* 12 (7 June 1817): 228–30.

Philanthropos [William Ladd]. *A Letter to Aaron Burr, Vice-President of the United States of America, on the Barbarous Origin, the Criminal Nature and the Baneful Effects of Duels; Occasioned by His Late Fatal Interview with the Deceased and Much Lamented General Alexander Hamilton*. New York: John Low, William Barlas, and John Reid, 1804.

Plumer, William. *William Plumer's Memorandum of Proceedings in the United States Senate, 1803–1807*. Edited by Everett Sommerville Brown. New York: Macmillan, 1923.

A Poem on the Death of Genl. Alexander Hamilton. Baltimore: Wane & Murphy, n.d.

Pool, Bettie Freshwater. "The Nag's Head Picture of Theodosia Burr," pp. 18–25. In *The Eyrie and Other Southern Stories*. New York: Broadway, 1905.

"Portrait of Aaron Burr." *Richmond Enquirer*. Reprinted in the *National Intelligencer & Washington Advertiser*, 4 November 1807.

Quinn, Arthur Hobson. *A History of the American Drama from the Beginning to the Civil War*. 2nd ed. New York: F. S. Crofts & Co., 1943.

――――. *A History of the American Drama from the Civil War to the Present Day*. New York: Harper & Brothers, 1927.

Rees, James. *The Dramatic Authors of America*. Philadelphia: G. B. Zieber and Company, 1845.

"Republicans Won't Let Him Rule O'er the Nation." *New York Evening Post*, 3 April 1804.

Richardson, James D., ed. *A Compilation of the Messages and Papers of the Presidents, 1789–1897*. 10 vols. Washington, D.C.: Government Printing Office, 1896–99.

Richardson, Samuel. *Clarissa, or, The History of a Young Lady*. Everyman ed. 4 vols. 1932. Reprint. London: J. M. Dent & Sons, 1962.

Riesman, David. "The Saving Remnant: An Examination of Character Structure." In *Individualism Reconsidered and Other Essays*. Glencoe, Ill.: Free Press, 1954.

"Rise! Rise Columbians, Make Your Stand." Broadside. New York Public Library.

Robertson, David. *Reports of the Trials of Colonel Aaron Burr*. 2 vols. Philadelphia: Hopkins and Earle, 1808.

Roden, Robert F., comp. *Later American Plays: 1831–1900*. 1900. Reprint. New York: Burt Franklin, 1964.

Safford, William H. *The Blennerhassett Papers*. Cincinnati: Robert Clarke & Co., 1891.

_____. *The Life of Harman Blennerhassett*. Chillicothe, Ohio: Ely, Allen & Looker, 1850.

Schachner, Nathan. *Aaron Burr: A Biography*. New York: Frederick A. Stokes, 1937.

Soniat du Fossat, E. *The Invitation: A Poem Addressed to General Wilkinson, Commander in Chief of the United States Army*. Natchez, Miss.: Andrew Marschalk, [1807].

Stedman, Edmund Clarence. "Aaron Burr's Wooing." *Harper's New Monthly Magazine* 75 (1887); 666–67.

Syrett, Harold C., and Cooke, Jean G., eds. *Interview in Weehawken: The Burr-Hamilton Duel as told in the Original Documents*. Middletown, Conn.: Wesleyan University Press, 1960.

Tanner, Tony. *City of Words: American Fiction 1950–1970*. New York: Harper & Row, 1971.

"To Aaron Burr, Vice-President of the United States." *American Citizen*, 26 July 1804.

"To the Memory of Gen. Hamilton." *American Citizen*, 8 August 1804.

["A Toast to Aaron Burr"]. Cited in Luther Martin's letter, 23 July 1807. *Baltimore Federal Gazette*. Reprinted in the *United States' Gazette*, 31 July 1807.

Towne, Benjamin. ["The Siege of Quebec"]. *Pennsylvania Evening Post*, 23 January 1776.

Truax, C. H. "Judicial Organization and Legal Administration from 1776 to the Constitution of 1846." In *History of the Bench and Bar of New York*. Ed. David McAdam et al. 2 vols. New York: New York History, 1897–99.

"Two Songs on the Brave General Montgomery, and Others, Who Fell within the Walls of Quebec, Dec. 31, 1775." n.p.: Danvers, 1776.

Wandell, Samuel H. *Aaron Burr in Literature.* 1936. Reprint. Port Washington, N.Y.: Kennikat Press, 1972.

————, and Minnigerode, Meade. *Aaron Burr.* 2 vols. New York: G. P. Putnam's Sons, 1925.

Webb, Mrs. Joshua. "To One Whom the World Reviled." Reprinted in James Parton, *The Life and Times of Aaron Burr*, 2: 333. Enlarged ed. 2 vols. Boston: Ticknor and Fields, 1867.

Webster, Daniel. *The Writings and Speeches of Daniel Webster.* National ed. 18 vols. Boston: Little, Brown, & Company, 1903.

Wegelin, Oscar, comp. *Early American Plays: 1714–1830.* New York: Dunlap Society, 1900.

Weinberg, Helen. *The New Novel in America: The Kafkan Mode in Contemporary Fiction.* Ithaca, N.Y.: Cornell University Press, 1970.

Whyte, William H., Jr. *The Organization Man.* New York: Simon and Schuster, 1956.

Wilkinson, James. *Memoirs of My Own Times.* 3 vols. Philadelphia: Abraham Small, 1816.

Williams, John Mason. *The Hamiltoniad: or, An Extinguisher for the Royal Faction of New-England.* Boston: Independent Chronicle Office, [1804].

Williams, William Carlos. "The Virtue of History," pp. 188–207. In *In the American Grain.* 1933. Reprint. New York: New Directions, 1956.

Winslow, Ola Elizabeth. *Jonathan Edwards: 1703–1758.* 1940. Reprint. New York: Collier Books, 1961.

Woodruff, Hezekiah N. *The Danger of Ambition Considered, in a Sermon, Preached at Scipio, N. Y. Lord's Day, August 12, 1804; Occasioned by the Death of General Alexander Hamilton, Who Fell in a Duel with Aaron Burr, Vice-President of the United States of America, on the 11th July, 1804.* Albany: Charles R. and George Webster, 1804.

Young, Philip. *Ernest Hemingway.* Minneapolis: University of Minnesota Press, 1959.

————. *Three Bags Full: Essays in American Fiction.* New York: Harcourt Brace Jovanovich, 1973.

Index

Aaron and Theodosia or The Fate of the Burrs (McCrary), 98-100, 176
Aaron Burr (Hallett), 96-98, 176
"Aaron Burr" (handbill), 57-58, 69
Aaron Burr (Pierce), 89-92, 176
Aaron Burr (Stoaks), 86-87, 171, 174
Aaron Burr (Wright), 83-86, 171, 174
Aaron Burr and Madam Jumel (Masters), 100-102, 176
Aaron Burr's Dream for the Southwest (Sweeney), 102-4
"Aaron Burr's Wooing" (Stedman), 48, 174
Adair, John, 32
Adams, John, 11, 33, 152
Adams, John Quincy, 40
Albany Register, The, 15
Allbright, Jacob, 34
Alston, Aaron Burr (grandson), 20, 37, 42
Alston, Joseph (son-in-law of Aaron Burr), 13, 20, 29, 35, 38, 125, 129, 130-31, 132, 136, 137, 139, 148
Alston, Theodosia Burr (daughter), 13, 28, 35, 37, 39, 42, 83, 88, 89, 93, 97, 99, 123, 124, 125, 126, 127, 129, 130, 132, 136, 139, 143, 145, 146; death of, 37; letter to father during his sojourn in Europe, 38; relationship with father, 132, 137-38, 139, 147-48
American Tragedy, An (Dreiser), 177
Anderson, Sherwood, 179
André, Major John, 132
Antonius, C., 159, 160
Aristides. *See* Van Ness, William Peter, as author
Arnold, Benedict, 6, 47, 52, 115, 149, 181
Assistant, The (Malamud), 179
Autronius, P., 158

Baldwin, James, 179
Bastrop lands, 88, 129
Bayard, James A., 12
Beautiful Spy, The (Burdett), 119-21, 174
Behrens, Albrecht, 56
Belcher, Jonathan, 4
Bellow, Saul, 178-79

Benedict, Frank Lee, 69, 70
Bennett, Emerson, 171
Bentham, Jeremy, 37
Biddle, Charles, 24
Blennerhassett, Harman, 26, 28, 29, 35, 84, 88, 89, 90, 93, 111, 112, 122, 123, 124, 127, 128, 130, 131
Blennerhassett, Margaret (Mrs. Harman), 26, 32, 82, 87, 88, 112, 122, 123-24, 128, 129, 132
Blennerhassett: A Dramatic Romance (Pidgin), 107 n.6
Blennerhassett; or, The Decrees of Fate (Pidgin), 79, 87-89
Blennerhassett; or, The Irony of Fate (Pidgin), 107 n.6
Blennerhassett's Island, 26, 32, 35, 85, 88, 93, 94, 127, 132, 149
Blodgett, Rebecca, 40-41
Bollman, Eric, 29, 32, 34, 90
Bona of Savoy, 167
Bowen, George Washington, 41
Brackenridge, Hugh Henry, 6, 71 n.2, 76-77, 122
Brown, Andrew, 15
Browning, Robert, 100, 101
Bryant, William Cullen, 153
"Building of the Ship, The" (Longfellow), 172
Bunker's Hill, 6
Burdett, Charles, 40, 119-21, 127, 150, 174
Burgundy, Charles the Rash, Duke of, 168
Burgundy, Philip the Good, Duke of, 166
Burr, Aaron: actions immediately following duel, 4, 23-24; acquitted in Frankfort, 32; acquitted of treason, 36; admitted to bar, 8; appeals for waiver to take law examination, 8; appointed lieutenant colonel, 7; appointed state attorney general, 8; arrested in Mississippi, 32; asks to subpoena Jefferson, 34; as assemblyman, 8; in Battle of Monmouth, 7; as *bête noir*, xiii; Biddle fears suicide of, 36; birth of, 4; buys Bastrop lands, 29; as Cain, 47, 59, 60-62, 65, 70, 86, 104; calls on Jefferson after western trip, 28; captured by Gaines, 33; as Catiline, 47, 50, 51, 52, 55, 61, 63, 70, 81, 88, 104, 115, 141, 157, 161, 170, 171, 181; comments on Texas independence, 38; conspiracy, 25-36 passim; controls Westchester lines, 7; death of, 43; divorce of, 43; divorce proceedings of, 41-42; duel correspondence, 15-18 passim; duel with Hamilton, 3-4, 15-22, 95, 97, 99, 110, 141; early press speculations on conspiracy, 27; 1800 presidential election, 12-13; elected senator, 9; elected vice president, 13; essay on the passions, 5; evacuation of New York, 6; events leading to duel, 15-18; extraordinary eyes, 154 n.5; farewell address to Senate, 25; final days of, 42-43; flees New York after duel, 24; generosity of, 38; graduation address of, 5; gubernatorial candidate in 1792, 9; gubernatorial candidate in 1804, 14-15; handles mutinous soldiers, 7; indicted for murder, 24; indicted for treason and misdemeanor, 35; indictment hearings in Richmond, 34-35; involvement with the Bank of Manhattan, 12; as ladies' man, 77, 89-90 (*see also* Burr,

Aaron: relationship with women; Burr, Aaron: as sexual predator); land speculation of, 12; as law student, 5, 8; as lawyer, 8; learns of Jefferson's proclamation, 32; leaves East in 1806 to begin conspiracy, 30; letter from prison to daughter, 35; letters to Alston after duel, 23-24; letters to Jefferson, 13; letter to Alston before duel, 20; letter to daughter before duel, 19-20; life after return from Europe, 38-43; as Lovelace, 134, 157, 161, 164-65, 176, 181; marital difficulties of, 41-42; marriage to Eliza B. Jumel, 41; marriage to Theodosia Prevost, 8; meets with Wilkinson in 1805, 26-27; as ministerial student, 5; as murderer, xiii, 47, 59-65, 110, 111; natural children of, 40; offered direction of Mexican revolution, 38; as political opportunist, 47, 49, 50, 51, 53, 55 (see also Burr, Aaron: as Catiline); possibility of rigged pistols of, 22; presides at Chase trial, 25; at Princeton, 5; *The Private Journal* of, 39; proposals to Merry after western trip, 28; proposals to Merry in 1804, 26; proposals to Truxtun, 29; proposals to Yrujo, 28; Quebec expedition of, 6; reception in South after duel, 24; reelected to state legislature in 1800, 12; relationship with daughter, 10-11, 132, 137-38, 139, 147-48; relationship with women, 39-42 (see also Burr, Aaron: as ladies' man; Burr, Aaron: as sexual predator); remarks to Morgan, 30; reopens law practice, 37; replaced by Clinton as vice presidential candidate in 1804, 14; resigns commission, 7; in Richmond prison, 35; runs away from home, 5; as Satan, 35-36, 82, 88-89; sends cipher letter to Wilkinson, 29-30; as sexual predator, 39, 47, 48, 57-58, 70, 84-85, 87, 94-95, 102, 104, 105, 112, 114, 115, 117-18, 120, 122, 130, 132, 134, 136, 140, 147, 153, 157, 161, 164-65, 170, 173-74, 176, 181, 184 n.26 (see also Burr, Aaron: as ladies' man; Burr, Aaron: relationship with women); sojourn abroad after trial, 36-37; support from Catholic authorities in New Orleans for, 27; as traitor, xiii, 47, 66-68, 70, 82, 85, 86-87, 95, 104, 105, 123, 124-25, 127, 153, 157, 161, 170-71, 173, 176, 181, 184 n.26; trial in Frankfort, 31, 32; trial in Mississippi, 33; trial in Richmond, 35-36; trip to Richmond under arrest, 33; troubles with Washington, 5-6, 7; as U.S. senator, 9-11; vice presidential candidate in 1796, 11; vice presidential possibility in 1792, 9; vice presidential years, 13-14; as victim, 47, 67-68, 69-70, 78, 79, 91-92, 92-94, 99, 101, 102-4, 105, 113-14, 129-30, 136, 138, 143-44, 145, 148-50, 152, 153, 157, 165, 169-70, 176-77, 181; in war as civilian, 7; as Warwick, 143-44, 157, 169-70, 177, 181; western tour in 1805 of, 26-28; withstands religious revival, 5

Burr, Aaron Columbus (natural son), 40

Burr, Eliza B. *See* Jumel, Eliza B.

Burr, Esther Edwards (mother), 4
Burr, Reverend Aaron (father), 4
Burr, Sarah. *See* Reeve, Sarah Burr
Burr, Theodosia Prevost (wife), 8, 10, 48, 103, 104, 132, 133, 143
Burr (Vidal), 145-53, 177, 182
Burr and Hamilton (Dowd), 77-79
Burrites, 14, 55
Burton; or, The Sieges (Ingraham), 115-19, 171, 174
Bynner, Edwin Lassetter, 171
Byron, George Gordon, Lord, 104

Caesar, Gaius Julius, 158, 159
Callendar, James Thompson, 149, 152
Campbell, Colonel, 6, 116, 145
Carleton, General Guy, 76
Cash, W. J., 175
Catcher in the Rye, The (Salinger), 179
Catch-22 (Heller), 178
Catilina, Lucius Sergius. *See* Catiline
Catiline, 158-61
Cato, M. Porcius, 160
Celer, Q. Metellus, 160
Cethegus, Gaius, 160
Chase, Samuel, 24-25, 152
Cheetham, James, 14, 49-53, 54, 55, 56, 57, 58, 59, 66, 149, 170, 174
Child of Nevis (Van der Voort), 80-81
Church, John B., 22
Cicero, Marcus Tullius, 159, 160, 161
Clarence, George, Duke of, 168
Clarissa (Richardson), 161-65
Clay, Henry, 32, 173
Clinton, De Witt, 14, 54
Clinton, George, 8, 14, 58
Coleman, William, 60
College of New Jersey. *See* Princeton

"Colonel Aaron Burr" (Law), 69-70, 176
Conspiracy; or The Western Island, The (Anon.), 82-83, 171
Conspirator, The (Dupuy), 126-28, 171
Cooper, Charles D., 15, 16, 17
Cornwallis, General Charles, 119
Cotta, Lucius Aurelius, 158
"Cowboys," 119, 143
Crane, Stephen, 177
Crassus, Marcus Licinius, 158, 159
Crocket, Davy, 152
Curius, Quintus, 159

Danger of Ambition Considered, The (Woodruff), 62
Daveiss, Joseph, 31, 32
Davies, Acton, 139-42
Davis, Matthew, 5, 39, 42, 165
Dayton, Jonathan, 26, 28
Death of General Montgomery at the Siege of Quebec, The (Brackenridge), 6, 76-77
De Lage, Natalie, 127, 143
Democratiad, The (Hopkins), 49
Dickstein, Morris, 179, 181
Discourse Delivered in the North Dutch Church, A (Nott), 62
Dos Passos, John, 177, 179
Dowd, Jerome, 77-79, 94
Dream of Empire or The House of Blennerhassett, A (Venable), 121-24
Dreiser, Theodore, 176, 177
Duane, William, 66
Dupuy, A. E. [Eliza Ann], 126-28, 171

Earnest, Ernest, 174
Eaton, William, 28, 93

Edward IV, 143, 166, 167, 168, 169
Edwards, Esther. *See* Burr, Esther Edwards
Edwards, Jonathan (grandfather of Aaron Burr), 4
Edwards, Ogden (cousin of Aaron Burr), 42
Edwards, Timothy (uncle and guardian of Aaron Burr), 4, 107-8 n.22
Ellison, Ralph, 178
Epaminondas. *See* Woodward, Augustus Brevoort
Examination of the Various Charges Exhibited Against Aaron Burr, An (Van Ness), 14, 53-54

Farewell to Arms, A (Hemingway), 177, 178
Farrell, John H., 70, 176
Faulkner, William, 179
Fiedler, Leslie, 164, 165, 174-75, 176
Fill, J. Herbert, 180
First Lady of the Land, The (Nirdlinger, drama), 94-96
First Lady of the Land or When Dolly Todd Took Boarders, The (Davies and Nirdlinger, novel), 139-42
"First Love" (Welty), 111-13
Fitzgerald, F. Scott, 179
Floyd, Davis, 32
Foot, Samuel A., 171
"Friend to Alexander, A" (Thurber), 109-11
From Hero to Eternity (Jones), 177-78
Fryer, Judith, 174

Gallatin, Albert, 9, 13
Godey's Lady's Book, 175

"Golden Eagle Ordinary" (Polk), 113-15
Graham, John, 31
Granger, Gideon, 30
Grapes of Wrath, The (Steinbeck), 179
Gratidianus, 158, 159

Hallett, Charles A., 96-98, 176
Hamilton, Alexander, 9, 12, 20, 21, 22, 24, 38, 41, 42, 47, 51, 58, 59, 60, 61, 62, 63, 64, 65, 67, 77, 78, 79, 80, 81, 84, 89, 91, 94, 97, 99, 100, 101, 103, 104, 110, 129, 134, 136, 138, 141, 143, 148, 149, 150, 151, 152, 161, 165, 170, 176, 177, 181; actions in 1800 election, 12; duel correspondence, 15-18 passim; duel with Burr, 3-4, 15-22, 95, 97, 110, 141; events leading to duel, 15-18; final hours of, 23; intemperate statements provoke duel, 15; letters to wife, 19; opposes Burr in 1804 gubernatorial election, 14; possibility of rigged pistols of, 22; remarks on approaching duel, 18-19
Hamilton, Alexander (Madame Jumel's divorce lawyer), 43
Hamilton, Angelica (Hamilton's daughter), 80
Hamilton (Pavlo), 81-82
Hamilton (Smith), 79-80
Hamiltoniad (Hopkins), 63-64
Hancock, John, 6
Harris, Cyril, 130-32
Harrison, William Henry, 28
Hassan, Ihab, 177, 179
Hawthorne, Nathaniel, 174
Hay, George, 34, 36
Hayne, Robert Y., 171

Hearts Triumphant (Tupper), 134-35
Heller, Joseph, 178
Helmer, John, 180
Hemingway, Ernest, 177, 179
Henry VI, 165, 166, 167, 168, 170
History of the Administration of John Adams (Wood), 14, 49
Hogeland, Ronald W., 175
Holland Land Company, 12
Hopkins, Joseph R., 63-64
Hopkins, Lemuel, 49
Hosack, David, 23, 88
Hough, Emerson, 124-26

In Dubious Battle (Steinbeck), 179
Ingraham, Joseph Holt, 115-19, 171, 174
Invisible Man (Ellison), 178
Irving, Peter, 54, 65
Irving, Washington, 34, 137, 139, 145, 148

Jackson, Andrew, 26, 30, 31-32, 149, 152, 153, 172, 173
James, Henry, 174
Jay, John, 9, 10, 103
Jefferson, Thomas, 11, 12, 13, 29, 30, 31, 32, 33, 34, 49, 52, 54, 57, 67, 81, 83, 89, 90, 92, 94, 96, 97, 100, 101, 103, 125, 126, 127, 128, 131, 137, 138, 140, 141, 142, 143, 146, 151-52, 153, 170; aids prosecution of Burr, 34; as Burr persecutor, 93-94, 113-14, 129-30, 136, 148, 149-50, 152, 161, 169, 176, 177, 181; calls cabinet meetings to discuss Burr conspiracy, 30; convinced of Burr's conniving with Federalists, 14; courts Burr after duel, 24; issues proclamation condemning conspiracy, 32; reports to Congress on conspiracy, 32-33; tells Burr of Spanish concessions, 28
Jeffersoniad, The (Democraticus), 54-55
Johnny Got His Gun (Trumbo), 177
Jones, James, 177-78
Jumel, Eliza B. (second wife of Aaron Burr), 41-42, 43, 80, 100, 101, 102, 132, 134, 135, 140, 147, 148, 150, 152-53
Jumel, Stephen, 41, 80

Kafka, Franz, 179
Kendall, Amos, 172
Kent, James, 15
Kerouac, Jack, 179
Knox, General Henry, 6, 145

Ladd, William [pseud. Philanthropos], 61
Laeca, 159
Lansing, John, 14
Law, Marion Laird, 70, 176
Leggett, William, 150, 153
Lentulus, Publius, 159
Lerner, Gerda, 175
Letter to Aaron Burr, A (Ladd), 61-62
Lewis, Meriwether, 125, 126, 137-39
Lewis, Morgan, 5, 8, 14, 55, 58
Lewis and Clark Expedition, 125, 126
Lindsay, Merrill, 22
Little Burr: The Warwick of America (Pidgin), 142-45, 177
Livingston, Chancellor Robert R., 8
Livingston, Edward, 173
Longfellow, Henry Wadsworth, 172
Louis XI, 167, 168, 169

Lovejoy, Owen, 171
Lovelace, Robert, 161-65

McCrary, Ben, 98-100, 176
McDougall, General Alexander, 7
McManus, Jane, 41-42
MacRae, Gordon, 34, 37
Madison, Dolly Todd, 94, 95, 139, 140, 141, 142
Madison, James, 94, 95, 140, 141, 142, 146
Maggie (Crane), 177
Magnificent Adventure, The (Hough), 124-26
Mailer, Norman, 178
Malamud, Bernard, 179
Malcolm, Colonel William, 7
Man in the Gray Flannel Suit, The (Wilson), 178
Manlius, Gaius, 159, 160
March, Edward, Earl of. *See* Edward IV
Margaret of Anjou (Queen of Henry VI), 165, 166, 167, 168
Marquand, John P., 178
Marshall, John, 34, 36, 91, 93, 152
Martin, Luther: cared for by Burr, 38; defends Burr, 34; defends Chase, 25
Mason, John Mitchell, 62-63
Masters, Edgar Lee, 100-102, 176
Mead, Cowles, 32
Meigs, Jonathan, 130
Melville, Herman, 174
Merry, Anthony, 25-26, 28, 95, 124, 125, 146
Metellus, M., 159
Mexican Association, 27
Miller, Henry, 179
Minturn, William [pseud. Defenthy Wright], 83 86, 87, 98, 171, 174

Miranda, Francesco de, 28
Moncrieffe, Margaret, 6, 77, 100, 102, 119, 120, 121
Monmouth, Battle of, 7
Montagu, John Neville, Marquess of, 168
Montgomery, General Richard, 6, 47, 48, 76, 103, 115, 116, 120, 139, 142, 145
Moore, Bishop Benjamin, 23
Morgan, George, 30, 94
Mr. Jefferson's Burr (Raiden), 92-94, 176
Murena, L. Licinius, 159
My Theodosia (Seton), 135-39, 177

Nagel, Paul C., 173
Naked and the Dead, The (Mailer), 178
Narrative of the Suppression by Col. Burr, of the History of the Administration of John Adams (Cheetham), 49-50, 170
Native Son (Wright), 178
Neville, George, Archbishop of York, 167, 168, 169
Neville, John, Marquess of Montagu. *See* Montagu, John Neville, Marquess of
Neville, Richard, Earl of Salisbury. *See* Salisbury, Richard Neville, Earl of
Neville, Richard, Earl of Warwick. *See* Warwick, Richard Neville, Earl of
New York *American Citizen*, 14, 55, 56, 59, 66, 67
New York *Chronicle-Express*, 14
New York *Courier and Enquirer*, 68
New York *Evening Post*, 60, 68, 150

New York *Morning Chronicle*, 14, 54, 56, 58, 65
New York Star, 68
Nine Letters on the Subject of Aaron Burr's Political Defection (Cheetham), 14, 52-53, 170
Nirdlinger, Charles Frederic, 94-96, 98, 139-42
Nott, Eliphalet, 62

O'Connor, Flannery, 179
Ogden, Matthias, 5, 78, 103
Ogden, Peter V., 32
"On the Death of General Hamilton" (Anon.), 65
"On the Murder of Hamilton: A Scotch Ballad" (Anon.), 65
Oratio in Toga Candida (Cicero), 159
Oration, An (Mason), 62-63
Osterweis, Rollin G., 175

Paterson, William, 8
Patriot (ship), 37
Pavlo, Hattie May, 81-82, 94
Peggy (Burr's slave), 20
Pendleton, Nathaniel: amended version of duel statement, 21; as Hamilton's intermediary and second, 3, 17-22 passim; joint statement with Van Ness about duel, 21
Peppers, Nellie Whan, 128-30, 177
Perkins, Nicholas, 33
"Permanency of the American Union, The" (Anon.), 173
Philadelphia *Aurora General Advertiser*, 66, 67
Philadelphia *United States' Gazette*, 27, 67, 68
Philanthropos. *See* Ladd, William
Pidgin, Charles Felton, 79, 87-89, 92, 142-45, 156 n.21, 165, 169, 170, 176-77

Pierce, L. France, 89-92, 176
Pinckney, Thomas, 11
Piso, Calpurnius, 158
"Pistols Shed Light on Famed Duel" (Lindsay), 22
Pitcher, Molly, 144
"Plea, A" (Farrell), 70, 176
Plumer, William, 24
Poem on the Death of Genl. Alexander Hamilton, A (Anon.), 63
Point of No Return (Marquand), 178
Polk, William T., 113-15
"Portrait of Aaron Burr" (Anon.), 67
Prevost, Frederick (stepson of Aaron Burr), 20
Princeton, 4, 68
Private Journal of Aaron Burr, The (Burr), 39
Putnam, General Israel, 6, 118, 119

Raiden, Edward, 92-94, 176
Randolph, Edmund, 34
Randolph, John, 24, 25, 34
Reeve, Sarah Burr (sister), 4, 10, 39, 40
Reeve, Tapping (brother-in-law), 5, 8, 10
Richardson, Samuel, 161, 164, 165
Riesman, David, 180
Robin of Redesdale (Sir John Conyers), 168
Rodney, Caesar, 34, 93, 97
Rowson, Susanna, 176
Russell, Jonathan, 37
Rutland, Edmund, Earl of, 166

Salinger, J. D., 179
Salisbury, Richard Neville, Earl of, 165, 166
Sansay, Leonora, 20
Schuyler, Philip, 9, 11-12, 15
Scott, Sir Walter, 37

Seton, Anya, 135-39, 177
Silanus, D. Iunius, 159
"Skinners," 143
Smith, Chard Powers, 79-80, 81
Smith, John, 26, 122-23
Smith, Samuel, 13
Smith, Thomas, 8
Something Happened (Heller), 178
Sound and the Fury, The (Faulkner), 179
Stafford, Jean, 179
Stedman, Edmund Clarence, 48, 174
Steinbeck, John, 179
Stirrup Cup, The (Tyson), 132-34
Stoaks, Charles E., 86-87, 89, 171, 174
Street of Knives (Harris), 130-32
Sulla, Lucius Cornelius, 158, 159
Swartwout, John, 13, 148
Swartwout, Samuel, 32
Sweeney, Thomas B., 102-4

Tanner, Tony, 180-81
Taylor, James W., 171
Taylor, John, 15
Taylor, Peter, 34
Tender is the Night (Fitzgerald), 179
Three Soldiers (Dos Passos), 177
Thurber, James, 109-11
Todd, Dolly. *See* Madison, Dolly Todd
"To One Whom the World Reviled" (Webb), 69
Torquatus, L. Manlius, 158, 159
To the Federal Members of the House of Representatives of the United States (Woodward), 54
"To the Memory of Gen. Hamilton" (Patrioticus), 65
Trollope, Sir Andrew, 166
Trumbo, Dalton, 177
Truxtun, Thomas, 24, 29, 93

Tullus, L. Volcacius, 158
Tupper, Edith Sessions, 134-35
"Two Songs on the Brave General Montgomery" (Anon.), 71 n.2
Tyler, Comfort, 30, 32
Tyson, J. Aubrey, 132-34, 135

U.S.A. (Dos Passos), 179

Van Buren, Martin, 40, 150, 151
Vanderlyn, John, 88, 97, 98, 145-46, 147
Van der Voort, Carl, 80-81, 94
Van Ness, William Peter, 14, 60, 96; amended version of duel statement, 21-22; as author [pseud. Aristides], 53-54; as Burr's intermediary and second, 3, 15-22 passim; joint statement with Pendleton about duel, 21
Van Pelt, Reverend Dr. P. J., 42-43
Venable, William Henry, 121-24
Victim, The (Bellow), 179
Vidal, Gore, 145-53, 177, 179, 182
View of the Political Conduct of Colonel Aaron Burr, A (Cheetham), 14, 50-52, 170
Vindex (Burr defender), 65

Warwick, Richard Neville, Earl of, 143, 144, 165-70
Washington, George, 5-6, 78, 81, 96, 103, 117-18, 119, 133, 140, 143, 149, 151, 152, 177, 181
Washington *National Intelligencer & Washington Advertiser,* 67
Webb, Mrs. Joshua, 42, 69, 70
Webster, Daniel, 171-72, 172-73
Weehawken, N. J., 3, 9, 18, 21, 22, 43, 77, 80, 81, 99, 141
Weinberg, Helen, 179
Welty, Eudora, 111-13

Whyte, William H., Jr., 180
Wickham, John, 34
Wilkinson, James, 26, 29, 32, 33, 34, 35, 82, 85, 86, 87, 90, 91, 92, 97, 98, 103, 104, 122, 123, 129, 136, 149, 152, 174, 176, 177, 181; activities exposed, 36; activities in New Orleans, 32; appearance at Burr trial, 34-35; betrays Burr, 31; duplicity towards Burr, 27-28; early western plans of, 25; meets with Burr in 1805, 26-27; ordered to Sabine, 30; pensioner of Spain, 27; replaced as governor of Louisiana, 31
Wilson, Sloan, 178
Winant's Hotel, 42
Winesburg, Ohio (Anderson), 179
Wirt, William, 34, 35

Wood, John, 14, 49
Woodruff, Hezekiah N., 62
Woodville, Elizabeth (Queen of Edward IV), 167
Woodward, Augustus Brevoort [pseud. Epaminondas], 54, 55
Wright, Defenthy. See Minturn, William
Wright, Richard, 178

Yates, Robert, 8
York, Richard, Duke of, 165, 166, 170
Young, Philip, 179
Young Mrs. Blennerhassett, The (Peppers), 128-30, 177
Yrujo, Don Carlos Martinez de, 28, 124

PS169 B85 N6
+Aaron Burr and t+Nolan, Charles J

0 00 02 0197615 6
MIDDLEBURY COLLEGE